The Bank of Israel

Volume 2

Selected Topics in Israel's Monetary Policy

Edited by
Nissan Liviatan
Haim Barkai

OXFORD
UNIVERSITY PRESS

2007

OXFORD
UNIVERSITY PRESS

Oxford University Press, Inc., publishes works that further
Oxford University's objective of excellence
in research, scholarship, and education.

Oxford   New York
Auckland   Cape Town   Dar es Salaam   Hong Kong   Karachi
Kuala Lumpur   Madrid   Melbourne   Mexico City   Nairobi
New Delhi   Shanghai   Taipei   Toronto

With offices in
Argentina   Austria   Brazil   Chile   Czech Republic   France   Greece
Guatemala   Hungary   Italy   Japan   Poland   Portugal   Singapore
South Korea   Switzerland   Thailand   Turkey   Ukraine   Vietnam

Published by Oxford University Press, Inc.
198 Madison Avenue, New York, New York 10016

www.oup.com

Library of Congress Cataloging-in-Publication Data
Barkai, Haim [date]
    The Bank of Israel.
        p. cm.
    Includes bibliographical references and index.
    Contents: v. 1. The monetary history of Israel / Haim Barkai
        and Nissan Liviatan—v. 2. Selected topics in Israel's monetary
        policy / edited by Nissan Liviatan and Haim Barkai.
    ISBN-13 978-0-19-530072-7; ISBN 0-19-530072-6 (v. 1)
    ISBN-13 978-0-19-530073-4; ISBN 0-19-530073-4 (v. 2)
    1. Bank Yisra'el.   2. Banks and banking—Israel.
    3. Money—Israel—History.   4. Monetary policy—Israel.
    I. Liviatan, Nissan.   II. Title.
    HG3260.A7B40 2007
    332.4'95694—dc22 2006024501

9 8 7 6 5 4 3 2 1
Printed in the United States of America
on acid-free paper

Preface

This volume consists of six chapters that analyze in depth several topics addressed in volume 1. This preface explains the link between these articles and the historical review in volume 1.

Alex Cukierman's chapter discusses the independence of the Bank of Israel (BOI), mainly after the economic stabilization in 1985. The general process of disinflation around the globe, which began in the early 1980s, was entrusted to the central banks of the OECD countries. This signified a "regime change" in regard to the status of central banks, which stemmed global inflation by applying a tough monetary policy that made extensive use of key rates.

Cukierman attempts to *quantify* the increased independence of the BOI in the disinflation process. This topic has two aspects. The first is measuring the independence of the bank in both de jure and de facto terms. Although the BOI charter has not been amended since 1954, the year the bank was founded (except for the so-called "no-printing law," enacted in 1985), the BOI's actual independence has increased substantially. Gone are the days when the BOI could be considered as a branch of the Treasury, which dominated monetary decision making. In particular, in the BOI's early days the Treasury forced the central bank to finance fiscal deficits and impose financial repression on the financial sector so that it would provide the government with cheap finance. After 1985, a consensus between the BOI and the government gradually emerged, within the ambit of the inflation-target regime, representing the common interest of both governmental institutions in the maintenance of economic stability. Within the framework of this consensus, the BOI was given a big say in framing the nominal objectives of economic policy, which eventually led to price stability.

All of this, as stated, took place without a formal change in the 1954 BOI Charter. The basic difference of opinion between the BOI and the Treasury concerning the drafting of a new charter centered on the question of whether the charter should give priority to price stability over full employment, as recommended by the Levin Commission, which the government appointed to draft the new charter. Neither the government nor the Knesset (the Israeli parliament) approved this recommendation. Cukierman's quantitative analysis shows that even the Levin reforms would leave the BOI with less de jure independence than the central banks of many other countries enjoy.

The difficult challenge presented in this chapter is how to quantify the BOI's de jure and de facto independence. Such quantification is essential for any scientific analysis of central-bank independence, which is what Cukierman is trying to do. It is clear that subjective considerations cannot be avoided in weighting the diverse components of central-bank independence. The author, however, tries to minimize this shortcoming by applying the same criteria to central banks of different countries and to de facto and de jure independence.

Nathan Sussman's chapter subjects the BOI's application of interest-rate policy in the disinflation process to econometric analysis. This instrument, of course, plays a major role in the strategies of many countries' central banks. Most central banks conduct their monetary policies in accordance with the Taylor Rule, which states that a central bank should raise its rate when inflationary expectations exceed the inflation target and when actual output exceeds potential output (i.e., in the case of a boom in economic activity). Conversely, in the case of recession the rate should be lowered in order to stimulate the economy.

Sussman finds that although the BOI's policy seemed generally consistent with this rule, it deviated in two respects. First, his econometric research shows that the BOI has assigned less importance to unemployment in recent years than in earlier years. In this respect, the BOI toughened its monetary policy. Second, Sussman finds that the BOI applied the Taylor Rule mainly when inflation exceeded the upper bound of the inflation target. In these cases, it raised its rate in excess of the increase in inflation, thereby raising the real interest rate. In "normal" times, when inflation was within or below the target range (i.e., when the disinflation process was not threatened), the central bank's response was not significant. This means that the BOI implemented the tight monetary policy only in response to the menace of inflation going out of control.

Another important finding in this chapter is that one cannot reject the hypothesis that, in recent years, the BOI conducted its interest rate policies as if the true target were zero inflation instead of the positive announced rate. This still leaves unanswered the question of precisely what brought down inflation in the 1990s. Sussman believes that the main factor in the disinflation process was the increase in the real key interest rate, which dampened inflation via the output gap and the appreciation of the currency. His study, however, does not test this theory.

Michael Michaely's chapter describes the historic process of the liberalization of the external sector of the Israeli economy. Until 1977, the author explains, the liberalization process centered on the current account; after this year (marking the failed liberalization of Finance Minister Simcha Ehrlich) the effort focused on the capital account. The latter effort was culminated in 1998, when legislation reversed the practice in regard to foreign exchange transactions: instead of prohibiting any transaction unless specifically permitted, the new regime permitted everything unless specifically prohibited.

From a macroeconomic point of view, the liberalization of the balance-of-payments capital account was of paramount importance in imposing fiscal discipline on the government and, more generally, on the pace of Israel's integration into the global economy. It is hard to be an outlier in fiscal and monetary policies in the era of globalization, and the freedom of capital mobility forces policymakers to pay attention to this point. Specifically, an economy that strays from international norms is likely to be punished by foreign investors, who can easily move their capital out of the country and invest it elsewhere. This may bring about a financial crisis.

In fact, the imposition of fiscal discipline by "foreign markets" has been much more effective than by internal pressure in this direction (possibly because the former are considered "objective"). The BOI contributed to this process by moving ahead with liberalization and Israel's global economic integration.

Jacob Paroush's chapter on banking supervision touches upon the history of monetary policy at three junctions. First, there is a connection between the disinflation process and the transition from direct supervision of the banking system to a regulatory system. In an inflationary economy, there is an incentive to exploit the financial sector for the extraction of an inflation tax and to use it as leverage for the direction of investment activities. In a state of relative price stability, in contrast, the banking system can extricate itself from the Treasury's grip and cause supervision to rely more on regulatory measures such as capital requirements and single-borrower credit limits. In particular, the directed-credit system, which accounted for one-third of total credit during the inflationary period, was dismantled in the late 1980s.

The second point of contact between the development of monetary policy and banking supervision concerns international capital flows. Opening an economy to international capital flows forces the economy to adopt international norms of behavior, especially in the fiscal area. However, short-term capital flows tend to expose the economy to financial crises. Since the BOI pushed relentlessly on the issue of liberalization of capital flows, it also had to tighten its supervision of the banks in order to avoid financial crises.

The third nexus of monetary policy and banking supervision is the matter of interest rates. A disinflation process entails high real interest rates in order to attain price stability. High real interest rates, however, subject firms—the banks' customers—to financial stress. The ostensible result, at least in the short run, is a clash between price stability and financial stability.

The openness of the economy is also related to the degree of competition among the banks. As is well known, Israel's financial system is rather severely concentrated. This leads to another clash: between competitiveness and financial stability. The entrance of foreign banks may enhance competition but this process is constrained by tough supervision in the financial sector.

Oved Yosha (who unfortunately passed away during the course of this project), Sharon Blei, and Yishay Yafeh also discuss in their chapter the intervention of the BOI in the banking system. Historically, concentration in Israel has been rising, as the country's banking activity has not kept pace with economic growth. The question is whether this process is desirable. The authors show that enhancing stability at the expense of competitiveness is advantageous in a small economy, unlike in a large economy, where there are more opportunities to diversify risks.

Finally, although we believe in the supremacy of historical processes, we cannot deny the role of personalities. We consider it important to supplement the statistical series by citing the views of policymakers who were at the helm of the events. We wish to hear them explain their considerations and the constraints as they saw them. For this purpose, Nachum Gross conducted a series of interviews with top BOI officials during the history of the central bank and reported them in his interesting chapter. Of course, we have to take the policymakers' statements with a grain of salt. We believe that Nachum navigated his way through this "minefield" with the utmost care and consideration.

Contents

Tables and Figures

TABLES

FIGURES

Contributors

Nissan Liviatan, *The Hebrew University of Jerusalem, Economics Department*

Haim Barkai (Deceased), *The Hebrew University of Jerusalem, Economics Department*

Alex Cukierman, *Tel-Aviv University, The Eitan Berglas School of Economics*

Michael Michaely, *The Hebrew University of Jerusalem, Economics Department*

Nathan Sussman, *The Hebrew University of Jerusalem, Economics Department*

Nachum Gross, *The Hebrew University of Jerusalem, Economics Department*

Jacob Paroush, *Bar Ilan University, Economics Department*

Oved Yosha (Deceased), *Tel-Aviv University, The Eitan Berglas School of Economics*

Sharon Blei, *Humbolt University, Berlin*

Yishay Yafeh, *The Hebrew University of Jerusalem, Economics Department, CEPR and ECGI*

The Bank of Israel

1

De Jure, De Facto, and Desired Independence: The Bank of Israel as a Case Study

Alex Cukierman

This chapter recounts the evolution of the de jure independence of the Bank of Israel (BOI) since it was established in 1954, provides an international comparison, and assesses year-by-year changes in the bank's de facto independence since the economic stabilization in 1985. Although no attempt is made to evaluate the year-by-year evolution of de facto independence in the pre-1985 period, an estimate of its average level is provided as a benchmark for the latter period. Since the variability of de facto independence in the prestabilization era was substantially lower than following it, the average level of de facto independence before 1985 provides a reasonable summary statistic for this variable during the thirty years that culminated in the 1985 stabilization. Comparison of the average levels of de facto independence before and after 1985 reveals a quantum leap in this variable between these two broad periods.

The chapter also estimates the level of de jure independence embedded in the recommendations of the 1998 Levin Commission on reform of the Bank of Israel law. A section near the end of the chapter discusses factors related to the desired future level of independence. In particular, it evaluates the pros and cons of growth targets, the closely related use of the output-gap concept as an indicator for making interest-rate policy, and the Levin Commission's recommendation to vest the legal authority for the conduct of monetary policy with a monetary-policy committee.

It is important to stress at the outset that since the concept of independence used in this chapter did not evolve until the late 1980s and, in part, in the 1990s, the estimation of independence entails the retrospective application of modern concepts of central-bank independence (CBI) to the early years of Israeli statehood. During these years, the professional consensus about the roles of a central bank (CB) and its status within government were very different from those of the present. Furthermore, the structure of the Israeli economy was substantially different from the present structure, inducing different economic-policy priorities.[1]

The measurement of CBI has developed significantly during the past fifteen years. Such measurement makes it possible to study the impact of independence on the performance of the economy in areas such as inflation, growth, real rates, and investment. Studies of the effect of CBI on the performance of developed economies normally use de jure independence, derived from CB charters, as a proxy for the de facto independence of the central bank.[2] Obviously there are often differences between de facto and de jure independence and such differences may be wider in developing countries than in developed ones.[3]

De jure independence is only one factor, albeit a weighty one, in determining the de facto independence of a CB. Institutional changes that are not reflected in the CB's formal charter may often have profound effects on de facto independence. Due to substantial cross-country variety in institutional arrangements, existing measures of de jure independence often overlook changes in de facto independence that are not reflected in de jure independence. One way to incorporate these additional elements into formal measurements of CBI is to consider the entire institutional and economic structure within which the CB operates. Such an effort requires a closer look at additional features of the economies under consideration and, inevitably, involves judgmental elements. Nevertheless, it is a step toward the development of more comprehensive measures of de facto independence.

The BOI, which celebrated its fiftieth anniversary in 2004, is a case in point. Despite the relative immobility of the bank's charter during that half-century, substantial changes in the extent of fiscal dominance over monetary policy and the structure of the Israeli economy effected important changes in the modus operandi and the de facto independence of the bank, mostly after the 1985 stabilization.[4] At the methodological level, then, this chapter may be considered a case study that illustrates some of the factors that one should bear in mind when attempting to complement the information contained in standard measures of de jure CBI.

An important general lesson taught by this chapter is that de facto independence may change substantially without any perceptible changes in de jure independence. Three additional conclusions, specific to Israel, are: (1) Although the BOI has been more independent—de jure and de facto—since 1985 than before, the gain has been more dramatic at the latter level than at the former. (2) Until the mid-1990s, de facto independence was generally weaker than de jure independence. Since the mid-1990s, de facto independence has been stronger than de jure independence. (3) Although high by domestic historical standards, the BOI's de facto independence since the mid-1990s has not been as high as the current de jure independence of the central banks in the twenty-six countries that are either current or prospective members of the European Monetary Union (EMU).[5]

The chapter is organized as follows: after a brief description of standard measures of de jure independence, the next section presents data on the evolution of de jure independence of the BOI over the past fifty years and compares it with that in other developed and developing countries over the past two decades. It also examines the level of de jure independence that would have prevailed had the recommendations of the Levin Commission on reform of the BOI charter been accepted.[6] The following section sets forth a methodology for the measurement of de facto CBI and establishes comparability by using the same metric that is used to measure de jure independence. This section also discusses factors unrelated to law that have affected the BOI's de facto independence over time and the assumptions made in transforming these factors into numerical codes.

The next section presents and discusses the historical evolution of the BOI's de facto independence and evaluates the factors that have combined to enhance it. This is followed by a section that reflects on the desirable level of BOI independence in view of current empirical and theoretical knowledge about the effects of CBI and CB conservatism, and debates the pros and cons of growth and output-gap targeting. The final section offers concluding remarks.

EVOLUTION OF THE DE JURE INDEPENDENCE OF THE BANK OF ISRAEL

The Concept and Measurement of De Jure Central-Bank Independence

A layperson or an economist raised in the tradition of twenty or more years ago may question the need for central-bank independence in the first place. Why should a public policymaking institution be independent in its decisions from the democratically elected government?[7] The current consensual answer is that governments, since they try to attain several other objectives such as high employment and easy financing of their own expenditure, create a socially costly inflation bias. Thus, the delegation of authority to a relatively conservative institution that is more concerned than the government about price stability—that is, the central bank—is beneficial for society (Rogoff, 1985).

In keeping with this view, indices of de jure CBI focus on the extent to which the CB is directed by law to focus monetary policy on price stability as the only, or the main, purpose of such policy, even if this results in the de-emphasis of other goals such as growth and the financing of budget deficits. To be effective, this CB focus should be backed by sufficient independence in the choice of monetary instruments. Most importantly, the CB's decision-making auspices should not receive explicit or implicit instructions from government officials and should have enough personal and financial independence to be able to resist political pressures. Furthermore, there should be sufficiently effective constraints on government's ability to resort to inflationary finance. Thus, CBI does not mean carte blanche; instead, it means that the CB has a sufficiently clear mandate to focus mainly on price stability and has enough instrument independence to implement this mandate.

The recent literature contains several alternative indices of de jure CBI.[8] The index proposed here is based on a coding of sixteen different characteristics of CB charters that pertain to the distribution of authority over monetary policy, procedures for the resolution of conflicts between CB and government, the relative importance of price stability in CB objectives as stated in the law, the seriousness of limits on CB lending to government, and procedures for the appointment and dismissal of the CB governor. Cukierman, Webb, and Neyapti (1992) present a weighted index of these sixteen characteristics that they term LVAW. The scale of this aggregate index, as well as of individual de jure indices, ranges from 0 (the least possible independence) to 1 (maximum independence). The conventions used to code individual components of de jure independence and the aggregation procedure used to obtain the aggregate index are described in table A1.1 of the appendix. One advantage of the LVAW index is its availability for many countries during the second half of the twentieth century, thereby allowing us to compare the de jure independence of the BOI with that of other countries' CBs at different times.

De Jure Independence of the Bank of Israel over Time and in Comparison with Other Countries

Although the original Bank of Israel charter (1954) has been amended more than once during the past fifty years, only the 1985 amendment is relevant for our CBI index. This amendment, popularly nicknamed the "No-Printing Law," substantially limits government's legal ability to obtain advances from the BOI and stipulates that securitized borrowing from the central bank should be at market rates.[9] Table 1.1 describes the aggregate de jure independence of the BOI under the original 1954 law and under the law after the 1985 amendment against the background of the de jure independence of CBs in developed economies during the 1980s.[10] The table shows that under the original 1954 law the BOI had less de jure independence than the CBs of Germany, Switzerland, the United States, Canada, and the Netherlands, but more de jure independence than the CBs of Sweden, New Zealand, the United Kingdom, France, and Italy. Under the original statute, the de jure independence of the Bank of Israel ranked in the 41st percentile from the top. After the 1985 amendment, the BOI gained de jure independence, its LVAW index rising from 0.39 to 0.46. This elevated its ranking among the central banks of developed countries in the 1980s to the 27th percentile from the top. A similar qualitative picture emerges when the comparison

Table 1.1. De Jure Independence of the BOI before and after the "No-Printing" Amendment—Comparison with Developed Countries during the 1980s

Country	LVAW	Country	LVAW	Country	LVAW
Israel—1954	0.39	Ireland	0.44	New Zealand	0.24
Israel—1985	0.46	Netherlands	0.42	France	0.24
Israel—1998/99 (Levin Commission proposal)	0.61	Australia	0.36	Spain	0.23
W. Germany	0.69	Iceland	0.34	Japan	0.18
Switzerland	0.64	Luxembourg	0.33	Norway	0.17
Austria	0.61	Sweden	0.29	Belgium	0.17
Denmark	0.50	Finland	0.28		
United States	0.48	U.K.	0.27		
Canada	0.45	Italy	0.25		

Source: Table 2 in Cukierman, Webb, and Neyapti, 1992 and table A1.1 in appendix.

is made with the central banks of developing countries during the 1980s. Further details appear in table 2 of Cukierman, Webb, and Neyapti (1992).

The picture shown in table 1.1 changed quite a bit in the 1990s. During that decade, the de jure independence of many central banks—those of all countries that joined the euro zone in 1999; nearly all former socialist economies (FSEs), which established new central banks with very high levels of de jure independence; practically all Latin American economies; New Zealand; the United Kingdom; Sweden; and Japan—was substantially upgraded. The countries that joined the euro zone had to upgrade the de jure independence of their central banks to comply with the requirements of the Maastricht treaty. Partly for the same reason, prospective entrants to the European Monetary Union (EMU) in Central and Eastern Europe followed the same track. However, the flood of central-bank reforms in other FSEs, as well as in other parts of the world— always in the direction of more independence—reflects a growing professional consensus among policymakers and academics that high CBI is desirable.[11]

As a consequence of this global trend, the BOI has much less de jure independence, relative to other countries, at the beginning of the twenty-first century than it had after the 1985 "No-Printing Law" was passed. The discussion that follows documents some of the numerical dimensions of this process. As table 1.1 shows, the LVAW index of aggregate de jure independence for the BOI has been constant at 0.46 since 1985. In contrast, the average de jure independence embodied in the charters of twenty-six FSEs was 0.56 in the second half of the 1990s.[12] Even after the "No-Printing Law" passed, the Bank of Israel remained well below the median in this group of central banks. Only eight banks (those of Azerbaijan, Croatia, Kazakhstan, Macedonia, Romania, Tajikistan, Turkmenistan, and Ukraine) scored lower. Although the exact numerical value of the LVAW of the European Central Bank (ECB) as prescribed by the Maastricht treaty is not available, calculations by Sadeh (2003) suggest that a score of 0.76 would be overly restrictive as a lower bound.[13] Interestingly, the United Kingdom, Sweden, and Denmark, which chose not to join the EMU, also gave their CBs much more de jure independence during the 1990s. In the estimation of Sadeh (2003), the LVAW indices for these countries as of 2001 were 0.89, 0.92, and 0.70, respectively. In relative terms, then, the de jure independence of the BOI is substantially lower today than it was in the 1980s.

Estimating the Level of De Jure Independence Implicit in the Levin Commission Recommendations

In December 1997, Prime Minister Benjamin Netanyahu appointed a committee of experts to recommend an update of the BOI charter. The committee, headed by Supreme Court Justice (ret.) Dov Levin, was comprised of a former governor of the BOI, a former chair of the Knesset Finance Committee, two academic economists, one accountant, and one lawyer. In December 1998, after a year of deliberations, the committee presented the prime minister with its recommendations for reform of the Bank of Israel charter (Levin Commission, 1998). Although the legislature did not pursue the recommendations, it is interesting to examine the level of de jure independence that the committee envisaged.

A quick glance at the first column of table 1.1 suggests that the Levin Commission recommendations, if implemented, would raise the index of de jure independence of the BOI from 0.46 to 0.61. Three main factors would account for the increase: (1) Price stability takes precedence over other goals. (2) Instrument independence is asserted more strongly than in the existing law. (3) The set of circumstances under which a governor may be dismissed is narrowed. The adoption of the Levin Commission recommendations would boost the de jure independence of the BOI appreciably—to slightly above the median of the group of twenty-six FSEs, but still substantially below the indices of the Bank of England, the Bank of Sweden, and the ECB.[14]

The committee also recommended that authority over the conduct of monetary policy, currently vested solely with the governor of the Bank of Israel, be delegated to a five-member committee. The effect of this recommendation on independence is not immediately obvious and the LVAW index, as constructed, does not reflect it. A discussion of the likely effect of this recommendation on de facto independence under alternative scenarios appears later in a subsection on the "Internal Division of Powers over Monetary Policy at the BOI and the Levin Commission Recommendation" subsection.

EVALUATION OF THE DE FACTO INDEPENDENCE OF THE BANK OF ISRAEL—METHODOLOGICAL ISSUES AND ASSUMPTIONS

De facto independence need not coincide with de jure independence, of course. A disparity may occur for a variety of reasons: (1) Laws are strongly susceptible to lacunae, leaving implementation open to interpretation and interference by other institutions within general government. (2) Even when the law is clear and lacuna-free, imperfect compliance may cause slippage between the letter of the law and actual practice. (3) The economic and institutional structures within which the CB operates affect the CB's de facto independence even where de jure independence is strongly honored.

In the case of the Bank of Israel, such factors cannot be overemphasized. Until the 1985 stabilization, one of the BOI's main tasks was to channel and extend credit to various sectors of the economy. This was accomplished through an elaborate system of directed credit (DC). The BOI had relatively little influence on the size, composition, and terms of this credit. Furthermore, due to other institutional restrictions the bank did not have sufficient authority to operate effectively in the open market. In addition the capital market was highly segmented and dominated by noncompetitive elements. The combination of these factors seriously impeded the bank's practical ability to focus on the price-stability goal. Since the 1985 stabilization, however, this state of affairs has been changing gradually due to desegmentation, deregulation, and changes in the operating procedures of monetary policy. Some of these changes had profound effects on the de facto independence of the BOI even though, as shown in the previous section, the changes in de jure independence were relatively modest.

Here we describe the methods and assumptions that we used to measure the changes in the BOI's de facto independence before and after 1985 as well as within the post-1985 period. To make the findings as comparable as possible with de jure independence, we used the same codification system for both actual and de jure independence. In coding de facto independence, however, account was taken not only of the letter of the law but also of what happened in practice. Consequently, the effects of changes in institutional and related arrangements—such as the size of DC, the BOI's de facto freedom to conduct open-market operations, the magnitude of the budget deficit, the efficacy of limits on government's ability to borrow from the CB, the extent of deregulation of financial markets, the type of exchange-rate regime, and the existence or nonexistence of inflation targets—may be factored into the index. Although this methodology is inevitably judgmental in that it entails the evaluation and location of the effects of the aforementioned factors across the components of the index, it has two advantages. First, it imposes a minimum of discipline on the inevitably judgmental measurement of de facto CBI. Second, by committing itself to specific numerical values for the components of the index, it paves the way to a systematic and more precise future evaluation of the de facto independence of the bank.

Codification of De Facto Independence in the Pre-1985 Era

During much of the period before the 1985 stabilization, monetary policy was severely restricted by a combination of factors. The BOI was forced to act, to a large extent, like a development bank that grants cheap credit in volumes and under terms largely determined by outside players. Financial markets were strongly segmented and the bank had little practical latitude to conduct the open-market operations that were needed to absorb liquidity injections that government and the private sector created (Cukierman and Sokoler, 1993; Barkai and Liviatan, 2007a, d). Although the impact of those constraints on the ability and determination of the bank's management to keep inflation low varied somewhat, the variations were minor in comparison to the changes that followed the 1985 stabilization.

Therefore, as an initial approximation, we assume that the de facto independence of the BOI in the pre-1985 period was constant but allow for variations in the post-1985 period. To measure the actual values of the components of independence in the pre-1985 period, we use the codings of the corresponding de jure components in the 1954 law as a benchmark and adjust the codings, where necessary, to reflect the levels of de facto independence on these components. During this period, the existence of large-scale directed credit in magnitudes and under terms that were determined outside the CB, coupled with severe limitations on the bank's ability to conduct open-market operations, meant that despite its de jure authority the BOI's ability to control monetary policy was quite limited. In fact, the currently accepted goals of monetary policy were largely subjugated to the BOI's role as a development bank.[15] Under these conditions, the actual weight of price stability in the conduct of monetary policy and compliance with de jure lending restrictions were substantially lower than their legally mandated counterparts.[16]

Codification of De Facto Independence in the Post-1985 Era

The post-1985 period is characterized by sustained gradual processes of institutional change that, in many cases, have had appreciable consequences for the de facto independence of the BOI. The most important of them are the reduction of DC (mostly through attrition), periodic increases in ceilings on the total stock of short-term Treasury bills (MAKAM) culminating in their total abolition at the end of 2001, desegmentation of credit markets, deregulation of capital flows, and flexibilization of the exchange rate. The introduction of inflation targets in December 1991 falls into this category as well. Additionally, a substantial increase in the short-term key rate, starting in the mid-1990s, points to an increase in the relative emphasis on price stability.[17]

Despite the 1985 "no-printing" amendment, the law leaves some latitude for the monetization of budget deficits, for several reasons. First, the government is free to convert its substantial foreign exchange receipts at the BOI without passing them through the foreign-exchange market and spending the proceeds domestically. Second, although the BOI may mop up the consequent increase in liquidity by issuing short-term Treasury bills, the amount of liquidity that the bank could absorb by means of this instrument was capped until the end of 2001.[18] The ceiling was often effective, forcing the bank to rely on auctioned deposits to mop up liquidity. For reasons elaborated in the next subsection, these auctioned or time deposits (PAZAK) may not allow the bank to absorb liquidity as effectively as it could by issuing Treasury bills (MAKAM). Third, even in the absence of institutional constraints, the maintenance of low inflation in the face of large deficits entails unpopularly high interest rates and makes it more difficult for the BOI to focus on the objective of price stability, thereby limiting its de facto independence. The introduction of inflation targets in 1991 marked the beginning of a process in which these targets replaced the exchange rate as a nominal anchor. Initially, the target was treated like a prediction rather than a commitment to deliver a certain rate of inflation. However, the stringency and effectiveness of inflation targets gradually increased during the 1990s as both government and the BOI increasingly construed the target as a commitment and also gradually lowered it (figure 1.1). Table A1.3 in the appendix builds a judgmental coding of these and other effects into the index. The third part of the appendix lists the conventions followed to code the components of de facto independence using the same classification as that used to code de jure independence. The groups of variables affected are those related to the authority over monetary policy, lending restrictions, and CB goals. The general conventions for the coding of the last-mentioned variable between 1986 and 1994 are straightforward and are relegated to the appendix. Since the considerations involved in coding this variable from 1995 onward rely on broader economic considerations, they are treated in the discussion that follows.

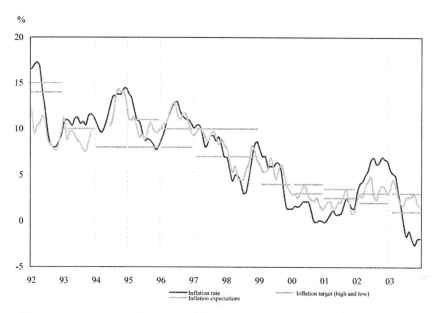

Figure 1.1. Inflation Target, Actual Inflation, and Inflation Expectations.
Source: BOI.

Sometime in the early to mid-1990s, the short-term interest rate became an important and highly visible instrument of monetary policy. After resting at rather low levels until 1994, the real short-term rate (as measured by the real rate on short-term Treasury bills) rose markedly in 1995, leveled off at 4%–5% until 1997, climbed to 6% in 1998, remained at or above this level until 2000, and fell back to 4% or less from 2001 and on.[19] Thus, real short-term real rates were uncharacteristically high during the six years from 1995 to 2000. From the eve of this high-interest era (1994) to its termination (2000), actual annual inflation plummeted from over 12% to slightly over 1%.

The onset of this high-interest period may be thought of as the beginning of a process of reduction in the BOI's implicit output target. Until then, the bank probably had, at least implicitly, an output target that exceeded the potential level of output. Under such circumstances, as has been well known since the early 1980s, discretionary monetary policy is susceptible to an inefficient inflation bias (Kydland and Prescott, 1997; Barro and Gordon, 1983). Some time during the early 1990s, central bankers and international institutions such as the IMF internalized this fact, leading to a worldwide uptrend in CB independence and an accompanying decrease in CB implicit output targets. The high-interest period in 1995 may well have been set in motion by the adoption of a similar point of view by decision makers at the BOI.

Since this point of view was novel at the time, the public may not have noticed it for a while. Consequently, inflation expectations did not fully internalize this change for some time. Measurements of inflation expectations as derived from the capital market support this statement by showing that, during the first three years of the high-interest era, average annual inflation expectations ranged from 9% to 11% (Liviatan, 2007, table 17.3).[20]

A relatively simple way to conceptualize the change in BOI policy and the initial lack of public response to it is to posit that, at the outset, the bank had an implicit output target that was above the potential. Then, at some point during the mid-1990s, the implicit output target declined and became equal to potential output. For several years following the change in policy, however, the public continued to believe that the CB had an above-potential output target. Under such circumstances, it may be shown that the real interest rate is higher, on average, than its natural level as long as the lower output target is not fully credible. The fourth part of the appendix demonstrates this within a New Keynesian framework formulated by Clarida, Gali, and Gertler (1999). Importantly, initially imperfect credibility of the lower output target is necessary for the attainment of above-natural-average real rates. Had the public become aware of the lower output target immediately, real rates would have remained at their natural level on average (see appendix).

Liviatan (2007) shows that monetary expansion was slower during the high-interest era than in the early 1990s, confirming that monetary policy became more restrictive in terms of both interest rates and growth rates of money supply. Liviatan argues that, since prices and wages are stickier than the nominal exchange rate, this led to an incipient appreciation of the real exchange rate that was followed later on by a partial reversal of this tendency.[21]

Importantly, the mechanism outlined here and the one stressed by Liviatan are complements rather than substitutes. In fact, both are needed for a full understanding of the reason for the change in BOI policy in the mid-1990s and of its economic consequences. Be that as it may, there is little doubt that the era of high real rates is associated with the de-emphasis of output objectives by the BOI. To reflect these considerations, we raised the actual value of the "objectives" code from 0.4 in 1994 to 0.6 for the 1995–97 period.

During the next three years, the importance attributed to price stability appears to have increased again, for several reasons: (1) After an upturn in inflation in 1998, the inflation target was reduced in 1999 to its lowest level ever (to that time) and the real rate was raised further. (2) Regressions of actual inflation on lagged values of the inflation target show that, while the target had no significant impact on inflation in the first half of the 1990s, it had a sizable and significant impact on inflation from 1996 on.[22] (3) Taylor rules and exchange-rate-based interest-rate-reaction functions estimated for the July 1993–December 2001 period generally underestimate the interest rate set by the BOI from 1997–98 on (Melnick, 2002). To reflect these factors, the code was raised from 0.6 in 1997 to 0.9 in 1998 and was held at this level until 2001.[23]

Following a "deal" between the BOI and the Ministry of Finance in late 2001, the key rate was lowered by 200 basis points in December of that year. The resulting substantial reduction in the real rate was reversed during the second half of 2002 and in 2003. To reflect the dip, we reduced the code to 0.8 for 2002 and returned it to 0.9 for 2003.

Treasury Bills, Time Deposits, Swaps, Government Foreign-Exchange Transactions, and Instrument Independence

Until it was abolished at the end of 2001, the ceiling on the value of short-term Treasury bills that the BOI could issue on behalf of the government prompted the bank to apply a restrictive monetary policy by accepting time deposits (PAZAK) or offering swaps to the banking system. This tendency was particularly evident in the second half of the 1990s. Since they are offered only to the banking system, the two last-mentioned instruments have a more limited scope than Treasury bills, which are offered to the public and are also more liquid because they are traded on the secondary market. Accordingly, the bank can mop up a given amount of liquidity at lower cost by means of Treasury bills than by means of time-deposit accounts or swaps negotiated through the banking system.

Thus, the source of authority over the size of Treasury bill balances has implications for the efficiency of the monetary-policy instruments available to the bank. Hence, the lifting of the ceiling on Treasury bill balances in the mid-1990s and the elimination of the ceiling in 2001 enhanced the bank's de facto instrument independence, as explained in the appendix. The bank did not wait long to exercise its control over the superior instrument. Indeed, from the end of 2001 to the end of 2002 the Treasury bill balance increased by about 25% (from NIS 35 billion to slightly under NIS 44 billion) whereas the balance in time-deposit accounts decreased by more than NIS10 billion.[24]

In its capacity as the government's banker, however, the BOI converts any amount of foreign exchange that the government desires into domestic currency and vice versa.[25] An important implication of this arrangement is that, by converting its dollar balances into NIS to finance current expenditure, the government may circumvent the spirit of the 1985 "No-Printing" Law. As long as legal ceilings on the issuance of Treasury bills existed, the BOI did not have enough instrument independence to sterilize the effect of such conversions on the money supply. Since the ceilings were removed in December 2001, the bank has been able to utilize its ability to issue Treasury bills to absorb the impact of such transactions on the monetary base, thereby maintaining the spirit of the No-Printing Law. But government's ability to use its considerable foreign-exchange balances to finance excesses of expenditures over tax revenues may induce a bias toward excessive use of this source of finance.

The loan guarantees extended to the government of Israel by the United States following the second Gulf War may have a similar effect. The government may invoke the guarantees to borrow abroad without necessarily spending the proceeds at the time. Such an action normally bolsters foreign exchange reserves in the first phase and expands the money supply when the government decides to spend all or some of these additional reserves domestically. Such events underscore the need to equip the BOI with enough instrument independence to mop up the excess liquidity that is created in the second phase.

EVOLUTION AND ROOTS OF THE DE FACTO INDEPENDENCE
OF THE BANK OF ISRAEL

Table 1.2 shows the aggregate de facto independence level of the BOI as characterized by the weights of the LVAW index. For comparison purposes, the aggregate de jure value of the same index is presented as well. The detailed codings underlying the de facto aggregate index appear in table A1.3 of the appendix; the detailed conventions used to generate those codes are set forth in the second and third parts of the Appendix. The aggregate level of de facto independence, based on these weights and codes, is denoted by AVAW.

Table 1.2 supports several general conclusions: (1) the BOI has had much more de facto independence, on average, in the post-1985 period than before. (2) Its average de jure independence has also increased since 1985, but by a substantially lower factor than its de facto independence. (3) Whereas de facto independence was substantially lower than de jure independence in the pre-1985 period, it was slightly higher than de jure independence, on average, in the post-1985 period.[26] (4) Despite constant de jure independence, de facto independence in the post-1985 era has varied considerably (see table 1.2).

For all these reasons, the 1985 stabilization marks a watershed in the periodization of CBI in Israel. Although this statement applies to both de jure and de facto CBI, it is much more dramatic in regard to the latter type. Taking a look at the progression of de facto independence after stabilization, we see that an initial dramatic jump in 1986 was followed by a decline that resulted in a local trough in 1989, succeeded by a return to approximately the 1986 level in 1994.[27] The period immediately following (1995–98) was characterized by additional and considerable increases in de facto CBI.

Since the mid-1990s, generally speaking, de facto independence has been uniformly higher than in previous years and also substantially higher than de jure independence. In fact, the de facto independence of the BOI since the mid-1990s has been in the upper range of de jure independence of developed

Table 1.2. Evolution of the De Facto Independence of the Bank of Israel

Year	AVAW (de facto)	Memo: LVAW (de jure)	Year	AVAW (de facto)	Memo: LVAW (de jure)
Pre-1985	0.13	0.46	1994	0.51	0.46
Post-1985 (avg.)	0.53	0.46	1995	0.55	0.46
1986	0.50	0.46	1996	0.52	0.46
1987	0.44	0.46	1997	0.57	0.46
1988	0.39	0.46	1998	0.64	0.46
1989	0.32	0.46	1999	0.64	0.46
1990	0.39	0.46	2000	0.69	0.46
1991	0.44	0.46	2001	0.66	0.46
1992	0.43	0.46	2002	0.66	0.46
1993	0.46	0.46	2003	0.64	0.46

countries' CBs in the 1980s, with only Germany, Switzerland, and, sometimes, Austria having higher scores (table 1.1). It also is in the same range as the average de jure independence of transition economies in the 1990s. This level, however, is much lower than the current levels of de jure independence of the ECB, the Bank of England, and the Bank of Sweden. These findings suggest that various nonlegislative changes that modify the CB's institutional framework may affect de facto independence quite dramatically even without any changes in the law or in law abidance.[28] A more general lesson from the case of the BOI is that legal indices of CBI should be supplemented by additional institutional evidence.

Sensitivity Analysis

Eijffinger and Schaling (1993) and Eijffinger and van Keulen (1995) claim that, at least for developed economies, the importance of de jure characteristics related to the assignment of authority over monetary policy, the procedures for conflict resolution, and the relative importance prescribed by law to price stability far outweigh the importance of other parameters. In some versions of their study, they go as far as to assign positive weights *only* to these three de jure variables. In contrast, the total weight that the LVAW index assigns to these three variables is merely 0.3.

To examine the sensitivity of the qualitative results of our study to these weighting assumptions, two alternative versions of the aggregate indices were calculated. One, whose de jure value is labeled LVES, assigns respective weights of 0.4, 0.4, and 0.2 to the allocation of authority for monetary policy, the procedures for resolution of conflicts between government and the CB, and the extent of focus on price stability as prescribed by law. All other variables are assigned zero weights. This weighting scheme, however, appears extreme in that it totally ignores the seriousness of the restrictions on lending to government. To account for this factor while continuing to focus strongly on the variables stressed by Eijffinger and Schaling, a second index, whose de jure value is labeled LVESX, was calculated. LVESX is a weighted average of the narrow LVES index and the subaggregate of all restrictions on CB lending to government,[29] which were weighted at 0.6 and 0.4, respectively. Essentially, this index assigns total weights of 0.48 to the "policy formulations" group, 0.12 to "objectives," and 0.4 to the "lending restrictions" group, and neglects the "CEO" group.

The evolution of the de facto (denoted AVESX) and the de jure (LVESX) values of the aggregate index, based on this weighting scheme, is shown in the second column of table A1.3 in the appendix. The data suggest that practically all the qualitative results attained by use of the wider LVAW index carry over to the narrower index. A similar conclusion is obtained when the calculations are performed again with the even narrower LVES index (not shown).

Interestingly, the post-1985 value of the LVESX index, 0.38, is substantially lower than the average value of the same index for the central banks of transition economies in the 1990s. The average de facto value of this index (AVESX) in the post-1985 period, however, falls into the same range as the average value of the de jure index (LVESX) in transition economies.[30]

Domestic and Global Factors behind the Changing Independence of the Bank of Israel

The developments reviewed above raise an interesting question about the growing independence of the BOI: what factors triggered and sustained the process? This subsection discusses possible factors and attempts to evaluate their relative importance. There is little doubt that the most important trigger for the increase in the independence of the BOI was the bitter experience with triple-digit inflation in 1977–85, particularly several failed stabilization attempts and the substantial amount of energy that the senior political leadership of the country had to invest in order to make the 1985 stabilization a success.[31]

Following the success of the 1985 stabilization, a public and political consensus lined up behind the need for strong measures to prevent the recurrence of episodes such as those that had made the stabilization necessary. Since until 1985 monetary policy had effectively been conducted by politicians through the Ministry of Finance, the blame for the high inflation was laid squarely on the political establishment. Given this view, it was natural to seek policymaking institutional reform in ways that would limit the influence of the political establishment on monetary policy. The 1985 "No-Printing" amendment to the BOI charter was one consequence of this trend. Another was the appointment, in 1986, of a politically unaffiliated academic, Michael Bruno, as governor of the BOI. Bruno, who was rather independent personally as well as politically, was allowed to start and sustain a long-term process of structural reforms of the financial sector that probably would not have been tolerated before the hyperinflation period. More generally, following the debacle of the high-inflation period, the political establishment became more receptive to professional advice. At the time these processes unfolded, the idea that CBI was a desired feature was still a novelty among professional economists. Therefore, it makes sense to trace the increases in BOI independence during the second part of the 1980s mainly to domestic forces.

During the 1990s, additional domestic and global developments reinforced the trend. First, financial stability became more important due to a gradual increase in the importance of the Israeli financial markets. Since financial stability and price stability correlate positively in the long run, this led to further support for an independent BOI. Second, the globalization of financial markets, in which Israel took part by phasing out its restrictions on capital and currency flows, made an independent CB more necessary. In a world of unrestricted capital mobility, the benefits of stable monetary policies in terms of access to international financial markets and capital inflows are greater than in a world with capital-account restrictions. By the same token, the cost of unstable monetary policies in terms of capital flight and related disruptions is substantially higher in a world of unrestricted capital mobility. Both factors add to the desirability of CBI. This trend was reinforced by the fact that, by the beginning of the 1990s, most developed economies had slashed their inflation rates to levels far below 5% while Israeli inflation still chugged ahead in double digits. This systematic inflation differential established a premium for domestic-currency-denominated financial assets and complicated the management of monetary policy, making it desirable to try to eliminate the premium by aligning Israeli inflation with the OECD levels for good.

Finally, during the 1990s an international professional consensus formed around the belief that CBI is a "free lunch" because it reduces inflation without hurting growth.[32] This consensus, as it evolved, permeated international institutions such as the IMF and led to a broad-based global process of upgrading de jure CBI.[33] In Israel, it may well have contributed to the introduction of inflation targets at the beginning of the 1990s and facilitated the buildup of the public consensus needed to implement the conservative policies that the BOI applied in the second half of the 1990s.

HOW INDEPENDENT SHOULD THE BANK OF ISRAEL BE?
A VIEW FROM ACADEMIA

During the past two decades, theory and evidence have converged to create a consensus that CBs should have a high level of effective conservatism, that is, independence. Empirical work has demonstrated that CBI reduces long-term inflation without affecting average output in developed economies and that it reduces long-term inflation and *raises* average long-term growth in developing economies.[34] At the theoretical level, the case for CBI is supported by the argument that due to various motives like employment, seignorage, and balance-of-payments considerations, political authorities are susceptible to an inefficient inflation bias that may be alleviated by the delegation of authority over monetary policy to a sufficiently conservative CB.[35] However, as Rogoff (1985) points out, this does not necessarily imply that the CB should be a strict inflation targeter if society *also* puts some positive weight on the stabilization of output,[36] since a strict inflation targeter (or an ultraconservative CB) underemphasizes output stabilization relative to price stability. Rogoff's work in particular suggests that a CB should have instrument independence and should be more conservative than society but should not be ultraconservative.

This leaves quite a bit of latitude for the choice of CB conservatism (CBC). Woodford (2003) demonstrates that in the presence of price and wage stickiness, maximization of the welfare of the representative individual implies that the CB should base its policy on a variant of the well-known Taylor (1993) rule, an interest-rate rule that assigns positive weights to deviations of inflation from target and to the output gap. The weights should depend on the structure of the economy. The basic intuition underlying the response of the interest rate to inflation is that, in the presence of price and wage stickiness, inflation distorts relative prices and leads to inefficient production and consumption decisions. Hence, a policy that stabilizes inflation around a low target and reduces unexpected inflation contributes to welfare by reducing these distortions. Depending on the structure of the economy, this may imply that the interest rate should respond positively to the output gap as well. Woodford's concept of the output gap refers to the difference between the level of output in the presence of sticky prices and the level of output in their absence.[37] The behavior of Woodford's output gap, however, may be quite volatile, making the correspondence between his concept and the smooth measures of the output gap utilized by central banks in practice rather tenuous.

A more recent argument in favor of CBI is related to its impact on capital flows. The globalization of financial markets and the associated increase in the sensitivity of capital flows to unstable domestic policies amplifies the importance of CBI as a credible guardian, and a signal of, nominal stability. This need, however, is partly attenuated by the fact that open capital markets also exert more discipline on the ministry of finance and, through it, on the political establishment.

Should the Bank of Israel Have a Growth Target?

One way to make sure that a relatively independent CB also pays attention to the stabilization of output is to establish de jure growth targets. Arguments in favor of growth targets for the BOI are often made in Israel, particularly during recessions. Indeed, the Levin Commission report on reform of the BOI Law recommends that the bank be required to take growth into consideration in its policymaking criteria.

What does this imply for the desired level of conservatism of the BOI? An important insight is that the optimal level of conservatism, or effective independence, should depend on the structure of the economy. In particular, if a decrease in the short-term interest rate has a strong and sufficiently sustained effect on economic activity and a relatively small and distant effect on inflation, a relatively low level of conservatism in the conduct of monetary policy is indicated. If the converse is true, a high level of conservatism in targeting inflation—perhaps even strict inflation targeting—is warranted. These considerations have a direct bearing on whether the BOI should or should not be assigned growth targets. In particular, if due to Israel's inflationary history a rate cut would have a powerful and rapid effect on inflation, the introduction of legally mandated growth targets may not be a good idea. In other words, if the tradeoff between the impact of monetary policy on economic activity and its impact on inflation is small, it may be best, even for a relatively liberal society, to refrain from instructing the CB to attain growth targets.[38]

However, even if econometric methods demonstrate that the recent Israeli tradeoff coefficient is large, several additional considerations should be kept in mind. First, requiring the BOI, through legislation or in other institutional ways, to attain growth targets may open the door for political pressure on the bank to conduct a policy of permanently low real interest rates. Given Israel's inflationary history and its legacy of formal and informal indexation arrangements, such a policy may have a swift upward effect on inflation expectations, the speed of their adjustment, and in turn, actual inflation.

Finally, there is a widespread consensus within the economic profession and the community of policymakers that monetary policy cannot affect potential output and, therefore, should not be used to try to influence its path. By implication, reasonable "growth targeting" should be directed at offsetting cyclical fluctuations in output rather than trying to change the path of potential output, over which it has no influence. In other words, growth targets should be applied to the cyclical components of output rather than to total output. To apply this principle in practice, the growth rate of actual output must be separated into two components: "potential output" and "cyclical output." The following subsection discusses the monetary-policy perils associated with such a separation.

The Perils of Output-Gap Stabilization

Nobody knows the time path of potential output for sure. Although hindsight clears up some of the uncertainty, normally there is much uncertainty about the level of this variable (current and expected in the near future) at the time monetary policy choices have to be made. Since the output gap is defined as the difference between actual and potential output, this uncertainty also infiltrates the output gap. A major implication of this observation for the choice of monetary-policy measures is that, due to poor real-time knowledge about the output gap, flexible inflation (or growth) targeters condition their policies on a variable that is measured with a substantial amount of error.

In an important article, Orphanides (2001) shows that during the second half of the 1970s and in some of the 1980s, the Fed systematically overestimated potential output, leading to substantial overestimation of the magnitude of the recession during those years. Since the Fed behaved as a flexible inflation targeter, these forecasting errors induced a monetary-policy stance that was eventually considered, with the benefit of hindsight, excessively expansionary—thus contributing to the U.S. inflationary bulge of the second half of the 1970s. The fact that output slumped badly during the second half of the 1970s is well known and undisputed. At issue here is how much of the decrease traces to cyclical elements over which monetary policy has some temporary impact, as against how much was due to changes in potential output, over which monetary policy has little impact, if any.

Since forecasting errors are positive sometimes, negative at other times, and normally not persistent, one may think at first blush that policy errors induced by poor measurement of the output gap should not inject persistent errors into the choice of monetary policy. Unfortunately, this is not the case with the output gap. Cukierman and Lippi (2005) show that errors in forecasting potential output and the output gap are generally serially correlated and that the average magnitude of the serial correlation depends on the fundamentals of the economy. The intuitive reason is that, unlike forecasts of many variables in which the true values become known at a one-period lag, the true values of potential output and the output gap are not revealed with certainty even after the fact. Consequently, monetary-policy errors that are made by flexible inflation (or growth) targeters become serially correlated as well. At times when potential output approximates the trend, the measured persistence in policy is small and may not constitute a serious problem for growth targeting. At times when potential output deviates severely from the trend, however, policy errors may prove quite persistent over time. Thus, when growth targeting is applied, the inherent unobservability of the output gap is particularly dangerous for nominal stability around and after turning points in the path of potential output.[39]

Since inflation depends on the output gap, this problem may arise under strict inflation targeting as well. However, since in this targeting method the poorly measured output-gap variable does not enter into the objective function of the CB, the policy errors are likely to be smaller. This intuition is backed by the discussion in section 5.1 of Cukierman and Lippi (2005), who show, using a retrospective New Keynesian model of the economy, that the more conservative the CB is, the smaller the difference between the interest rates chosen in the presence and in the absence of uncertainty about potential output and the output gap.

Internal Division of Powers over Monetary Policy at the BOI and the Levin Commission Recommendation

From the de jure standpoint, the final authority over monetary policy within the BOI is vested with the governor of the bank. This legal status strongly resembles that of the governor of the Reserve Bank of New Zealand since the 1989 reform. However, it differs from most other central banks—for example, the Bank of England, the Fed, and the ECB—in which the ultimate internal authority over monetary policy resides with a monetary policy committee (MPC). One of the main recommendations of the Levin Commission on reform of the BOI law was to vest authority for monetary policy with a five-person MPC: the governor, two deputy governors, and two outside independent experts who do not hold positions in other branches of government, industry, or the private banking system. To date, the committee's recommendations have not been implemented.

Since the issue concerns the redistribution of authority *within* the bank (counting the independent outside experts as part of the bank), ostensibly the proposed reshuffling would not affect the independence of the bank vis-à-vis the government and various interest groups. Whether this would be the case in practice depends on two factors: (1) the degree of internal cohesion in the MPC and its members' ability to implement a policy that a majority of members approves despite the existence of prior dissenting views, and (2) the extent to which the outside members of the committee are truly independent of both the executive and legislative branches of government and of various economic interest groups. If these two conditions—inner cohesion and outer independence—are met, the formation of an MPC may actually enhance the BOI's de facto independence by strengthening its ability to resist outside pressures. The experience of the Bundesbank and the more recent experience of the ECB suggest that, when these conditions are satisfied, the MPC can withstand outside pressures more easily due to its collective responsibility. If one or more of the conditions is not satisfied, however, the switch to a MPC may lessen de facto independence.

The BOI Governor as the Economic Advisor to the Government

The original 1954 charter ordains the governor of the Bank of Israel as the government's official economic advisor. In this capacity, BOI governors are expected to attend and address meetings of the ministerial committee for economic affairs and of the Knesset (parliament) and may express their views and recommendations on economic policy issues that lie outside the BOI's purview, such as fiscal policy and the size of the budget deficit. Although governors cannot vote on these matters, the informal influence of this additional role of theirs has been important in some cases. Despite doubts expressed by some former governors about the desirability of this unique feature of the governorship, the function has managed to survive to the present day.

The governor's economic-advisor function is a two-edged sword. On the one hand, it establishes a legal basis for attempts by the governor to shape the economic environment in which monetary policy operates. It also facilitates the sharing of professional economic information between the bank and the government. During the early years of Israeli statehood, the latter characteristic was particularly important. On the other hand, it has been argued that the economic-advisor function prevents the governor from publicly criticizing the government's economic policies when the bank, in its professional opinion, considers them misguided.[40]

How does the governor's role as economic advisor to the government affect the independence of the BOI? There are two opposing effects, both related to the foregoing discussion. In his/her advisory capacity, the governor may acquire some influence on other areas of public policy that determine the constraints with which monetary policy has to cope; fiscal policy is a prominent example. However, the advisory function may make it more difficult for the bank to focus on the price-stability objective.

CONCLUDING REMARKS

The case of the Bank of Israel suggests that, due to various institutional developments unrelated to laws, such as the introduction of inflation targets; the discontinuation of directed credit; and changes in the degree of integration of capital markets, in the type of exchange-rate regime, and in fiscal discipline, de facto independence may change quite dramatically even under an unchanged CB charter.

The stabilization of inflation in 1985 was a watershed for the independence of the BOI in both the de jure and the de facto senses. Since the stabilization, de jure independence has increased moderately and de facto independence has gained dramatically. Before the stabilization, de facto independence was substantially lower than de jure independence. Since the stabilization, average de facto independence has been somewhat stronger than de jure independence, even though the "no-printing" amendment raised the level of de jure independence. Before the amendment, in the early 1980s, the 1970s, and before, the de jure independence of the BOI rested at the 40th percentile or so among developed countries. Despite the amendment, the BOI's relative de jure independence was substantially lower in 2001 than in the 1980s, since the de jure independence of many central banks was strongly upgraded during the 1990s.

The arguments in this chapter are based on a modern notion of CBI that considers a central bank more independent the more intensively it focuses on price stability, the more tightly it controls the instruments of monetary policy, the more effective the limitations on lending to government are, and the more emphatic the personal independence of the CB governor is. The advantage of this index is that, in addition to covering a wide range of issues, it is available for many countries in different periods of time, thereby allowing us to compare the de jure independence of the BOI with that of other countries' CBs in different periods.

However, the index excludes a feature that may have had some impact on the independence of the bank, particularly during the early statehood years: the quality of the BOI Research Department in comparison with that of other economic-research entities in Israel. The first Governor of the BOI, David Horowitz, gave the first director of the Research Department, David Kochav, and his successors carte blanche to recruit individuals solely on the basis of professional considerations. This strategy paid off in that, to this day, the Bank of Israel Research Department is the country's finest macroeconomic research entity, adding the weight of "professionalism" to the bank's policy positions.

This characteristic probably places the de facto independence of the Bank on a higher level than that captured by the indices in this chapter. This factor may have mattered during the BOI's first thirty years, when the general conception was that the bank and the Finance Ministry should formulate macroeconomic policy by consensus. Due to the powerful position of the ministry and of government at large, however, one doubts whether the inclusion of this additional factor would substantially affect the broad conclusions expressed here. To reinforce this view, we note that during the bank's first three decades, one of the main policy goals was to encourage investment in order to stimulate real growth. This was done by largely subjugating currently conventional CB objectives to the role of the BOI as a development bank through the mechanism of directed credit. David Horowitz publicly endorsed this policy. In an exchange with Don Patinkin in the early 1970s about the BOI's role in controlling the money supply, Horowitz argued that the bank should adapt its policies to those of government. During these three decades, the BOI was effectively characterized by a multiplicity of goals, of which price stability ranked low in priority. This was very much in the spirit of the Keynesian consensus that dominated professional economic thinking at the time.

In view of the narrowness of Israel's capital markets during those decades, this general approach might have made some sense at the time. It is much less likely to do so today, as current Israeli policymakers confront a totally different level of development of the economy and of domestic and international capital markets. Even if there were some merit to the low level of independence and the related multiplicity of goals imposed on the Bank of Israel during its first three decades, this is no longer the case. Although the de facto independence of the BOI is much higher today than it was in those distant years, government's ability to induce large increases in the monetary base by converting foreign exchange in order to finance potential deficits may handicap the bank's ability to deliver long-term price stability. But, since it fully controls the issue of Treasury bills today, the BOI is better equipped than in the past to deal with this problem, if it arises.

This raises an important and difficult question: what level of conservatism (independence) would be appropriate for the BOI in the future? The preceding section reviews some of the considerations involved in designing a socially optimal framework of operation for a CB. In particular, it takes up the thorny question of whether a CB should also be assigned a growth target. Instead of rehashing the arguments in that section, I will conclude with several observations that reflect a broad current intellectual consensus: (1) Since monetary policy cannot affect real variables in the long run, it has a comparative advantage in assuring price stability in the long term. (2) Insofar as real objectives such as "growth" are assigned to a CB, they should be limited to short-term counter-cyclical policies and administered in doses of magnitudes that should preferably be left to the CB. (3) Casual evidence suggests that, in the long run, a higher level of CB conservatism is associated with lower real rates.

A notable conclusion of this chapter is that the BOI's de facto independence has been consistently higher than its de jure independence since the mid-1990s.[41] This discrepancy invites various political pressures on the CB. Thus, during the second half of the 1990s, the head of the Manufacturers Association of Israel asked the attorney general to declare particular monetary-policy measures taken by the bank to be in violation of the BOI Law and several Members of Knesset proposed bills that would restrict the bank in various ways to make it more dependent on the Knesset Finance Committee. In 2002, then-Finance Minister Silvan Shalom proposed the delegation of authority over monetary policy to a seven-member committee that, apart from three members affiliated with the BOI, would be recruited from other branches of government and of the economy. Thus, the external members could outvote those from the bank. These episodes suggest that the current relatively high level of de facto independence may not endure for long without some upgrading of de jure independence.

Finally, the structure of the economy and the response of inflation and inflation expectations depend on the monetary-policy rule. This is the so-called "Lucas critique." After a change in the monetary-policy rule, the public gradually adjusts its expectation-formation process. In Israel, it made such an adjustment to the new policy regime that followed the 1985 stabilization. A similar if less dramatic shift, reinforcing the trend toward price stability, probably occurred after the BOI moved toward a more conservative policy in the mid-1990s. One of the considerations often neglected by scholars in the choice of central-bank conservatism is that a policy-rule change associated with a decrease in conservatism leads to changes in the expectation-formation process, which makes price stability costlier to maintain.[42] In view of the rather grim inflation memories of the Israeli public, the public's expectation-formation process may take a sudden change for the worse. The exchange-rate bulge and the inflation spike that occurred after the BOI abruptly cut the key interest rate in late 2001 supports the view that this risk should not be taken lightly.

APPENDIX

Coding and Aggregation of Legal Variables

Table A1.1 of the appendix translates CB charters into numerical codes on the basis of the sixteen basic underlying variables of the LVAW aggregate index. Each variable is coded on a scale of 0–1, where 0 stands for the minimal level of independence and 1 for the maximal level. The LVAW index is obtained by a two-round judgmental aggregation procedure. In the first round, sixteen features of de jure independence are aggregated into eight subgroups. These eight subgroups are then further aggregated to obtain the LVAW index.[43] The weights used in the second and last round of aggregation are appointment and dismissal procedures and term of governorship—0.20; source of authority over monetary policy, CB targets, and severity of limitations on advances to government—0.15 each; limitations on securitized lending, source of decision about CB lending, and other miscellaneous features of lending limitations—0.10 each; and the width of the circle of potential borrowers from the CB—0.05.[44] The implementation of those principles to calculate aggregate legal independence is summarized in Table A1.2.

Conventions for Coding of Individual Components of De Facto Independence in the Pre-1985 Era

To reflect the features discussed in the "Codification of De Facto Independence in the Pre-1985 Era" section and in accordance with the definitions in table A1.1, the components of "who formulates" and "final authority" are adjusted downward from de jure codings of 0.67 and 0.2 to de facto codings of 0.2 and 0, respectively. This is summarized in the row labeled "De facto CBI—before 1985" in table A1.3. The same conjunction of institutional factors also means that the de facto weight given to price stability was even lower than the modest de jure code for this variable. In reflection of this judgment, the 0.4 code for the "objectives" variable in the 1954 charter is replaced with a value of 0.1. Additionally, the de facto value of the variable "Who appoints the CEO?" (i.e., the governor) is scaled down from the de facto code of 0.5 to 0.25 to reflect the fact that, although CEOs are formally appointed by the president of Israel, they are actually appointed by a decision of the prime minister and the minister of finance that is ratified by the government.

Last but not least, since at the time the CB was obligated, either directly or indirectly, to lend to the government and to governmental and private companies designated by the government, at terms that were also designated by various governmental agencies, most codings of the lending limitation (LL) variables have been scaled downward. (Details appear in the last eight figures in the first row of table A1.3.) To fully appreciate the meaning of the coding decisions made in this subsection and the next, the reader is advised to use table A1.1 as a reference.

Table A1.1. De Jure Variables and Their Codings

Group	Definition of Variable	Variable	Levels of Independence and Their Meanings	Numerical Codings
Governor	Governor's term of office (years)	*too*	1. *too* ≥8	1
			2. 8 > *too* ≥ 6	0.75
			3. *too* = 5	0.50
			4. *too* = 4	0.25
			5. *too* < 4	0
	Who appoints the Governor?	*app*	1. Governor appointed by CB board	1
			2. Governor appointed by council composed of members from executive and legislative branches as well as from CB board	0.75
			3. Governor appointed by legislative branch (Congress, king)	0.50
			4. Governor appointed by executive branch (council of ministers)	0.25
			5. Governor appointed by decision of one or two members of executive branch (e.g., prime minister or minister of finance)	0
	Provisions for dismissal of Governor	*diss*	1. No provision for dismissal	1
			2. Dismissal possible only for nonpolicy reasons (e.g., incapability or violation of law)	0.83
			3. Dismissal possible and at discretion of CB board	0.67
			4. Dismissal for policy reasons at legislative branch's discretion	0.50
			5. Unconditional dismissal possible at legislative branch's discretion	0.33
			6. Dismissal for policy reasons at executive branch's discretion	0.17
			7. Unconditional dismissal possible at executive branch's discretion	0
	Is Governor	*off*	1. Governor prohibited by law from holding any other office in government	1

Continued

Table A1.1. Continued

Group	Definition of Variable	Variable	Levels of Independence and Their Meanings	Numerical Codings
	allowed to hold another office?		2. Governor not allowed to hold any other office in government unless authorized by executive branch	0.5
			3. Law does not prohibit Governor from holding another office	0
Policymaking	Who formulates monetary policy?	*monpol*	1. CB alone has authority to formulate monetary policy	1
			2. CB participates in formulation of monetary policy together with government	0.66
			3. CB participates in formulation of monetary policy in an advisory capacity	0.33
			4. Government alone formulates monetary policy	0
	Government directives and resolution of conflicts	*conf*	1. CB given final authority over issues clearly defined in the law as CB objectives	1
			2. Government has final authority only over policy issues not clearly defined as CB goals or in case of conflict within CB	0.8
			3. In case of conflict, final decision made by a council whose members are from CB, legislative branch, and executive branch	0.6
			4. Legislative branch has final authority on policy issues	0.4
			5. Executive branch has final authority on policy issues, but subject to due process and possible protest by CB	0.2
			6. Executive branch has unconditional authority over policy	0
	Is CB given an active role in formulating the government budget?	*adv*	1. Yes	1
			2. No	0
CB goals		*obj*	1. Price stability mentioned as the only or major goal, and in case of conflict with government CB has final authority to pursue policies aimed at achieving this goal	1

		2. Price stability mentioned as the only goal	0.8
		3. Price stability mentioned along with other objectives that do not seem to conflict with price stability (e.g., stable banking)	0.6
		4. Price stability mentioned with a number of potentially conflicting goals (e.g., full employment)	0.4
		5. CB charter does not set any objectives for CB	0.2
		6. Some goals appear in the charter but price stability is not one of them	0
Lending limitations	Limitations on advances	*lla*	
		1. Advances to government prohibited	1
		2. Advances permitted but subject to limits in terms of absolute cash amounts or to other types of relatively strict limits (e.g., up to 15% of government revenues)	0.66
		3. Advances subject to relatively accommodative limits (e.g., advances may exceed 15% of government revenues or are specified as fractions of government expenditure)	0.33
		4. No legal limits on advances; their quantity is subject to periodic negotiations between government and CB	0
	Limitations on securitized lending	*lls*	
		Specification of levels identical to those for advances	
	Who decides on control of terms of lending?[a]	*ldec*	
		1. CB controls terms and conditions of government borrowing from it	1
		2. Terms of CB lending specified in the law, or CB given legal authority to set these terms	0.66
		3. The law leaves decisions about the terms of CB lending to government to negotiations between CB and executive branch	0.33
		4. Executive branch alone decides the terms of CB lending to government and imposes them on CB	0
	How wide is the circle of potential borrowers from CB?	*lwidth*	
		1. Only central government may borrow from CB	1
		2. Central and state governments as well as all political subdivisions may borrow from CB	0.66
		3. In addition to the institutions mentioned under 2, public enterprises may borrow from CB	0.33
		4. CB can lend to all of the above as well as to the private sector	0

Continued

Table A1.1. Continued

Group	Definition of Variable	Variable	Levels of Independence and Their Meanings	Numerical Codings
	Type of limit, where such a limit exists	*ltype*	1. Limit specified as an absolute cash amount	1
			2. Limit specified as a percentage of CB capital or other liabilities	0.66
			3. Limit specified as a percentage of government revenues	0.33
			4. Limit specified as a percentage of government expenditures	0
	Maturity of loans	*Lmat*	1. Maturity of CB loans limited to a maximum of 6 months	1
			2. Maturity of CB loans limited to a maximum of one year	0.66
			3. Maturity of CB loans limited to a maximum of more than one year	0.33
			4. No de jure upper bounds on the maturity of CB loans	0
	Restrictions on interest rates[b]	*lint*	1. Interest rate on CB loans must be at market rate	1
			2. Interest rate on CB loans to government cannot be lower than a certain floor	0.75
			3. Interest rate on CB loans cannot exceed a certain ceiling	0.50
			4. No explicit legal provisions regarding the interest rate on CB loans	0.25
			5. Law stipulates no interest-rate charge on government's borrowing from the CB	0
	Prohibition on lending in primary market	*lprm*	1. CB prohibited from buying government securities in primary market	1
			2. CB not prohibited from buying government securities in primary market	0

Source: Cukierman, 1992, table 19.1.

[a] Terms of lending concern maturity, interest, and amount of loans, subject to the relevant legal limits.

[b] The rationale for the classification of this variable is that minimum rates are likely to have been devised in order to discourage borrowing from the CB while maximum rates are probably meant to facilitate borrowing from the CB. However, the requirement of a minimum rate is classified below "market rates" because minimum rates, when they exist, are usually lower than market rates.

Table A1.2. Individual and Aggregate Codings of De Jure Independence of the Bank of Israel—1954 Law, 1985 Amendment, and Levin Commission Proposal

	Year of Enactment or Revision of Bank of Israel Law	LVAW	CEO				Policy Formulation				Advances	Limitations on Lending							Sum of Weights
			Term of Office	Who Appoints	Dis-missal	Other Offices	Who Formu-lates	Final Authority	Role in Budget	Objectives		Securitized Lending	Terms of Lending	Potential Borrowers	Type of Limit	Maturity of Loans	Interest Rates	Primary Market	
Original law	1954	0.39	0.50	0.50	0.50	0.50	0.67	0.20	0.00	0.40	0.33	0.00	0.66	1.00	0.00	0.66	0.25	0.00	
After "no printing" amendment	1985	0.46	0.50	0.50	0.50	0.50	0.67	0.20	0.00	0.40	0.66	0.00	0.66	1.00	0.00	0.66	1.00	0.00	
Levin Comm. proposal	1998/9	0.61	0.50	0.50	0.83	1.00	1.00	0.60	0.00	1.00	0.66	0.00	0.66	1.00	0.00	0.66	1.00	0.00	
Weights-LVAW			0.0500	0.0500	0.0500	0.0500	0.0375	0.0750	0.0375	0.1500	0.1500	0.1000	0.1000	0.0500	0.0250	0.0250	0.0250	0.0250	1.0000

Table A1.3. Individual and Aggregate Codings of the Components of de Facto Independence of

Year	Actual Aggregate Independence AVAW	AVESX	Memo Item Legal LVAW	Average CEO	Term of Office	Who Appoints	Dis-missal	Other Offices	Average Monpol + conf	Who Formu-lates	Final Authority
Prior to 1985	0.13	0.05	0.42	0.44	0.50	0.25	0.50	0.50	0.0500	0.20	0.00
1986	0.50	0.36	0.48	0.44	0.50	0.25	0.50	0.50	0.1000		
1987	0.44	0.33	0.48	0.44	0.50	0.25	0.50	0.50	0.1250		
1988	0.39	0.30	0.48	0.44	0.50	0.25	0.50	0.50	0.1500		
1989	0.32	0.28	0.48	0.44	0.50	0.25	0.50	0.50	0.1750		
1990	0.39	0.31	0.48	0.44	0.50	0.25	0.50	0.50	0.2000		
1991	0.44	0.35	0.48	0.44	0.50	0.25	0.50	0.50	0.2000		
1992	0.43	0.35	0.48	0.44	0.50	0.25	0.50	0.50	0.2000		
1993	0.46	0.37	0.48	0.44	0.50	0.25	0.50	0.50	0.2000		
1994	0.51	0.45	0.48	0.44	0.50	0.25	0.50	0.50	0.3000		
1995	0.55	0.50	0.48	0.44	0.50	0.25	0.50	0.50	0.3714		
1996	0.52	0.51	0.48	0.44	0.50	0.25	0.50	0.50	0.4428		
1997	0.57	0.57	0.48	0.44	0.50	0.25	0.50	0.50	0.5142		
1998	0.64	0.65	0.48	0.44	0.50	0.25	0.50	0.50	0.5856		
1999	0.64	0.68	0.48	0.44	0.50	0.25	0.50	0.50	0.6570		
2000	0.69	0.75	0.48	0.44	0.50	0.25	0.50	0.50	0.7284		
2001	0.66	0.75	0.48	0.44	0.50	0.25	0.50	0.50	0.7998		
2002	0.66	0.78	0.48	0.44	0.50	0.25	0.50	0.50	0.8998		
2003	0.64	0.76	0.48	0.44	0.50	0.25	0.50	0.50	0.8998		
Mean: 86-03	0.52	0.50	0.48								
Memo items		Legal LVESX									
De jure-1954		0.33		0.50	0.50	0.50	0.50	0.50	0.2675	0.67	0.20
De jure-1985		0.38		0.50	0.50	0.50	0.50	0.50	0.2675	0.67	0.20
Weights-LVAW			0.2000	0.0500	0.0500	0.0500	0.0500		0.1500	0.0375	0.0750
Weights-LVESX									0.4800		

the Bank of Israel

Role in Budget	Objectives	Average-LL	Time after 1985 Amendment-1	Overall Budget Surplus	Advances	Securitized Lending	Terms of Lending	Potential Borrowers	Type of Limit	Maturity of Loans	Interest Rates	Primary Market
						Limitations on Lending						
0.00	0.10	0.03			0.00	0.00	0.15	0.00·	0.00	0.00	0.00	0.00
0.00	0.40	0.67	0	3.9								
0.00	0.40	0.55	1	0.1								
0.00	0.30	0.48	2	−2.4								
0.00	0.30	0.39	3	−5.4								
0.00	0.30	0.45	4	−4.8								
0.00	0.30	0.55	5	−3.1								
0.00	0.40	0.51	6	−4.9								
0.00	0.40	0.56	7	−4.5								
0.00	0.40	0.64	8	−3.3								
0.00	0.60	0.63	9	−4.3								
0.00	0.60	0.57	9	−5.8								
0.00	0.60	0.62	9	−4.4								
0.00	0.90	0.65	9	−3.7								
0.00	0.90	0.63	9	−4.2								
0.00	0.90	0.72	9	−2.0								
0.00	0.90	0.64	9	−4.0								
0.00	0.80	0.63	9	−4.4								
0.00	0.90	0.56	9	−6.0								
0.00	0.40	0.38			0.33	0.00	0.66	1.00	0.00	0.66	0.25	0.00
0.00	0.40	0.51			0.66	0.00	0.66	1.00	0.00	0.66	1.00	0.00
0.0375	0.1500	0.5000			0.1500	0.1000	0.1000	0.0500	0.0250	0.0250	0.0250	0.0250
	0.1200	0.4000										

Conventions for Coding of Individual Components of De Facto Independence in the Post-1985 Era

Authority over monetary policy (total weight: 0.15). The original Bank of Israel Law (1954) vested the BOI with considerable de jure instrument independence. In the pre-1985 era, however, as explained above, much of this power remained on the books only. After the 1985 stabilization, the legal provisions that empowered the BOI to conduct monetary policy gradually became operational and more meaningful with the phaseout of DC and the flexibilization of the exchange rate. The flexibilization of the Treasury bill ceiling in August 1994 and the indexation of this ceiling to the CPI from then on enhanced the bank's instrument independence somewhat. The authority-over-policy factor gained further importance in December 2001 when the Treasury bill ceiling was abolished altogether.[45] The desegmentation process, the deregulation of capital movements, and further flexibilization of the exchange rate gave the bank additional operational freedom. (Figure 1.2 shows the progression of the exchange-rate band.)

The combination of these elements is reflected in a combined coding of the "who formulates" and "final authority" variables (total weight: 0.113). Before 1985, the de facto value of the code for this combination of variables was 0.05. Presumably it increased by a factor of 4 but did so only gradually, after the phaseout of DC became sufficiently important and the exchange-rate band sufficiently flexible. More specifically, the code was doubled to 0.1 in 1986 and then raised linearly to 0.2 between 1987 and 1990. To reflect the flexibilization of the Treasury bill ceiling and its indexation in 1994, the code from that year and on was increased by 0.1, bringing its value to 0.3.

To reflect the additional gradual increase in independence due to the combined effect of desegmentation, the further widening of the exchange-rate band, and the influence of the global professional revolution associated with the introduction of inflation targets in many countries, it is assumed that this process elevated the index to 80% of its maximal value (0.8) in 2001. To reflect the graduality of its progression, it is assumed that the process began in 1994 and proceeded linearly until 2001. The code was raised again by 0.1 from 2002 on to reflect the total elimination of ceilings on balances of Treasury bills at the end of 2001.

Lending limitations (total weight: 0.5). The value of this group of variables is based on a judgmental coding of the sum of the lending-limitation variables. The post-1985 coding of the de jure value of this total is 0.513 (table A1.3). It is assumed that, starting in 1986, this figure also reflects the de facto value of the total, provided that the total government budget deficit is zero but that each percentage point increase in the deficit/GDP ratio, as conventionally measured, lowers the code by 0.04. The de facto level of stringency of limitations on lending to government is determined as a negative function of the budget deficit for two reasons. First, as discussed above, government can raise the level of liquidity despite the 1985 "no-printing" amendment by selling its foreign reserves to the BOI. The larger the budget deficits, the more likely government is to do this. Second, higher deficits raise real interest rates and increase public pressure on the BOI to "ease" the burden of high rates by injecting liquidity.

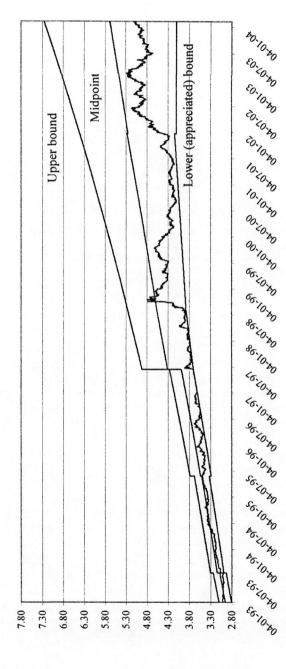

Figure 1.2. NIS Exchange Rate against Currency Basket.
Source: BOI.

Finally, to reflect the gradual impact of reductions in various types of DC (as well as the gradual increase of interest rates on such credit) on the effectiveness of the lending limitations, it was assumed that this process was implemented gradually between 1986 and 1995 and that it raised the index to 80% of its maximal possible value (0.8) by the latter year. During this period, the contribution of this factor to the index is assumed to rise linearly.

Targets or objectives (weight: 0.15). It is assumed that after the trauma of hyperinflation and the political efforts expended to stabilize it, the focus on price stability as the main policy goal became much stronger in 1986 than it had been before. To reflect this, the value of this variable was raised fourfold, from 0.1 to 0.4, and held at this level through 1987. It was then reduced to 0.3 in 1988 to reflect the relaxation of the exchange-rate anchor and kept at this value until 1991. To reflect the initial introduction of inflation targets in late 1991, the code was returned to 0.4 in 1992 and held there until 1994.

Negative Correlation between the Real Rate and the Central Bank's Output Target under Conditions of Imperfect Credibility

One result of an increase in the CB's emphasis on price stability is recognition of the fact that it does not pay to systematically aim at a level of output that surpasses potential output. When the output target goes down and becomes equal to potential output for the first time, the public does not sense the change for a while, creating a situation in which the bank's true (normally implicit) output target is equal to potential output but the public still believes that it exceeds the potential. The early stages of stabilization of low inflation may conform to such a pattern. Using a New Keynesian framework surveyed by Clarida, Gali, and Gertler (1999) (CGG), this appendix shows that, under such circumstances, the bank will set a real rate that exceeds the Wicksellian natural rate of interest.

The behavior of the economy is described by:

$$x_t = -\varphi(i_t - E_t\pi_{t+1}) + E_t x_{t+1} + g_t \tag{1}$$

$$\pi_t = \lambda x_t + \beta E_t \pi_{t+1} + u_t \tag{2}$$

where x_t and π_t are the output gap and inflation, $E_t x_{t+1}$ and $E_t\pi_{t+1}$ are the expected values of these variables conditioned on the information available to the public in period t, i_t is the short-term nominal interest rate, g_t is a demand shock, u_t is a cost shock, and φ, λ and β are positive coefficients. The stochastic behavior of the two shocks is stationary but persistent and is formulated as

$$g_t = \mu g_{t-1} + \hat{g}_t \quad 0 < \mu < 1 \tag{3}$$

$$u_t = \rho u_{t-1} + \hat{u}_t \quad 0 < \rho < 1$$

Here $\hat{g}_t$ and $\hat{u}_t$ are innovations to the cyclical components of demand and costs, respectively, and μ and ρ characterize the persistence of these shocks. The first equation in (3) states that the output gap is negatively related to the ex ante real rate of interest and positively related to the expected future output gap. The latter appears in the output-gap equation in order to reflect the notion that, since individuals smooth their consumption, expectations of higher consumption in the period to come (associated with higher expected output) lead them to demand more current consumption, which raises current output. Within this construct, the CB influences the output gap and inflation by its choice of the short-term nominal interest rate—which, given inflation expectations, determines the real short-term rate. Note that the CB affects inflation through the mediation of the output gap.

Here, as in the stylized models of sticky staggered prices pioneered by Calvo (1983), current inflation depends on inflation expectations. In this type of model, only a fraction of firms have the opportunity to adjust their price each period and, due to the costs of price adjustment, each firm exercises this opportunity at discrete intervals. Hence, when a firm is given an opportunity to adjust its price, the higher the inflation expectations, the larger the adjustment it will make. The positive dependence of inflation on the output gap is based on the view that this gap is a measure of excess demand and is shared by both forward looking, as well as backward looking, models of an economy in which output is determined by demand.

One dimension of an increase in the effective conservatism or independence of the CB is that the initially positive discrepancy between desired and potential output dwindles to zero. It is convenient to model this by considering two types of central bankers, one who incurs losses whenever the output gap swerves from a target that is $k\%$ above potential and another whose output target is equal to potential output. Until it internalized the inefficiency associated with output targets that are above potential, the BOI belonged to the first type. After it internalized the inefficiency, it became a CB of the second type. Below I refer to the first type as a relatively "level conservative" CB, to distinguish it from Rogoff's (1985) conception of conservatism, which refers to the relative importance that the CB attributes to the stabilization of inflation and output. Whenever the term "conservatism" appears here, it should be construed as referring to the first type of conservatism.

Both types of CBs dislike deviations of inflation and of output from their respective targets and disagree only about their output targets. The goal of either type is to minimize

$$\frac{1}{2}E_0 \sum_{t=0}^{\infty} \delta^t [\alpha(x_t - k)^2 + \pi_t^2] \tag{4}$$

where δ is a discount factor and α is the relative importance attributed by both types of CBs to the stabilization of output. Here $k > 0$ for the more liberal (more dependent) CB and $k = 0$ for the more conservative (more independent) CB. I shall proceed by solving this problem for any k and then compare the levels of the real rate chosen by each type of CB.

Under conditions of discretion, a "type k" CB chooses in each period the nominal interest rate, i_t, and a contingent path for future interest rates in order to minimize the expression in equation (4), subject to the structure of the economy in equations (1), (2) and (3) and taking expectations as given. The Euler equations necessary for an internal minimum of this problem are given by

$$x_t - k = -\frac{\lambda}{\alpha}\pi_t, \quad t = 0, 1, 2, \ldots. \tag{5}$$

This condition states that, in each period, the marginal cost of deviating from the output target is equal to the marginal cost of deviating from the inflation target (i.e., zero). Note that this condition depends on the effective level of CB independence (or conservatism), as characterized by the size of k. In particular, a positive k implies that the CB is willing to tolerate a positive deviation of inflation from its target even when output is at its potential level.

Consistent modeling of imperfect credibility requires some adjustment of the informational assumptions made in CGG. In particular, if the public has full current information about all economic variables and shocks (as CGG assume), it can immediately work out the current value of k from the interest rate, thereby eliminating imperfect credibility. To focus on imperfect-credibility situations, I assume that, except for the interest rate, the public observes all variables and shocks at a one-period lag while the CB observes them contemporaneously. This represents a minimal deviation from the original framework and prevents the public from immediately inferring the CB's output target by observing the current interest rate. It also makes the CGG framework more realistic. Suppose now that, after a sustained period during which it had an output target above potential ($k > 0$), the CB lowers its target to the level of potential output ($k = 0$) but the public's perception of the target, k^e, remains positive. Since the actual value of k is 0, the CB behaves in a way that will satisfy condition (5) above at $k = 0$.

$$x_t = -\frac{\lambda}{\alpha}\pi_t, \quad t = 0, 1, 2, \ldots \tag{6}$$

The public, however, believes that the CB is behaving in a way that will satisfy the condition

$$x_t^e - k^e = \frac{\lambda}{\alpha}\pi_t^e, \quad t = 0, 1, 2, \ldots \tag{7}$$

where $k^e > 0$ is the discrepancy between desired and actual output as perceived by the public, and x_t^e and π_t^e denote the corresponding perceptions of the output gap and inflation. Cukierman (2004) shows that, under these circumstances, the actual values of inflation, the output gap, and the real interest rate are expressed respectively by

$$\pi_t = \alpha q \rho u_{t-1} + \frac{\alpha}{\alpha + \lambda^2}\hat{u}_t + \frac{\alpha^2 \beta}{\lambda(\alpha + \lambda^2)}k^e \tag{8}$$

$$x_t = -\lambda q \rho u_{t-1} - \frac{\lambda}{\alpha + \lambda^2}\hat{u}_t - \frac{\alpha \beta}{\alpha + \lambda^2}k^e \tag{9}$$

$$r_t = \frac{1}{\varphi}\left[\lambda q \rho(1 - \rho)u_{t-1} + \frac{\lambda}{\alpha + \lambda^2}\hat{u}_t + g_t + \frac{\alpha \beta}{\alpha + \lambda^2}k^e\right] \tag{10}$$

Equation (10) implies that the expected value of the real interest rate is given by

$$Er_t = \frac{\alpha\beta}{\varphi(\alpha+\lambda^2)}k^e \qquad\qquad (11)$$

which is positive as long as k^e is positive. Thus, as long as the public believes that the CB is targeting an above-potential output level, a CB that has recently begun to target potential output is led to choose an interest rate that exceeds the Wicksellian natural rate (in this version of the model the Wicksellian natural rate is zero). Note, in view of equations (8) and (9), that imperfect credibility also leads to a positive average rate of inflation and to a below-potential average level of output. Indeed, such has been the case during stabilizations of inflation in OECD countries.

Cukierman (2004) also shows that where perfect credibility is present (i.e., $k^e = 0$) the average real rate rests at its natural level, average inflation is zero, and output is equal to its potential level on average. Thus, a *fully credible* reduction of the CB output target to the potential level neither causes the real rate to deviate systematically from its natural level nor induces inflation and output to swerve systematically from their targets.

The difference between this case and a state of imperfect credibility ($k^e > 0$) may be understood intuitively as follows: a positive value of k^e under imperfect credibility leads to systematically positive inflation expectations, which via equation (2) raise actual inflation. To spread the costs of the output and inflation gaps efficiently, the CB raises the real rate beyond its natural level, thereby depressing average output to a below-potential level. Under perfect credibility, in contrast, average inflation expectations are zero. Thus, the CB does not need to *systematically* hold the real rate above its natural level in order to spread the costs of the output and inflation gaps efficiently.

One may argue that the public may use the contemporaneous observation of the interest rate in equation (10) to sharpen its perception of the value of k. One way to extend the model in order to account for such a possibility is to reformulate k as a stochastic variable and to recognize that, from equation (10), an observation of the interest rate amounts to an observation of a linear combination of k and of the innovations $\hat{u}_t$ and $\hat{g}_t$ to costs and aggregate demand. Within such an extended framework, k^e will be equal to the expected value of k, assuming that the combination of k and of these innovations is linear. Cukierman (2004) argues that although such an extension changes some of the details of the model, it does not alter the basic conclusion, i.e., a decrease in k from a positive value to zero will be followed by a period during which average real interest rates surpass the natural rate.

Table A1.4. The Behavior of the Ex Ante Real Rate of the Bank of Israel since Mid-1989

Date	Bank of Israel Nominal Rate of Interest	Inflation Expectations (for the next 12 months)	Bank of Israel Real Rate of Interest
06/1989	10.92	12.14	-1.09
07/1989	11.2	13.86	-2.34
08/1989	10.29	14.31	-3.52
09/1989	13.3	13.82	-0.46
10/1989	16.85	17.43	-0.49
11/1989	15.86	15.45	0.36
12/1989	16.51	18.23	-1.45
01/1990	18.2	21.62	-2.81
02/1990	18.98	20.92	-1.60
03/1990	18.16	17.39	0.66
04/1990	15.87	13.13	2.42
05/1990	14.5	15.10	-0.52
06/1990	14.38	17.99	-3.06
07/1990	15.19	17.42	-1.90
08/1990	15.02	20.10	-4.23
09/1990	16.54	21.97	-4.45
10/1990	15.89	20.45	-3.79
11/1990	15.11	19.24	-3.46
12/1990	14.41	17.51	-2.64
01/1991	15.2	17.37	-1.85
02/1991	14.85	15.15	-0.26
03/1991	14	15.72	-1.49
04/1991	13.19	13.88	-0.61
05/1991	13.65	14.63	-0.85
06/1991	13.73	14.69	-0.84
07/1991	13.88	15.95	-1.79

Date	Bank of Israel Nominal Rate of Interest	Inflation Expectations (for the Next 12 Months)	Bank of Israel Real Rate of Interest
06/1993	12.76	8.68	3.75
07/1993	11.85	8.47	3.12
08/1993	10.16	7.75	2.24
09/1993	9.45	7.59	1.73
10/1993	9.48	8.63	0.78
11/1993	9.75	9.70	0.05
12/1993	10.24	–	
01/1994	11.04	–	
02/1994	11.1	–	
03/1994	11.1	–	
04/1994	11.1	–	
05/1994	11.54	–	
06/1994	12.19	10.23	1.78
07/1994	12.81	11.14	1.50
08/1994	13.32	13.32	0.00
09/1994	15.07	14.39	0.59
10/1994	16.73	13.96	2.43
11/1994	16.78	14.15	2.30
12/1994	18.47	12.99	4.85
01/1995	18.51	11.17	6.60
02/1995	18.31	10.95	6.63
03/1995	17.23	11.39	5.24
04/1995	15.82	10.10	5.19
05/1995	15.02	9.11	5.42
06/1995	14.49	9.40	4.65
07/1995	14.44	8.81	5.18

Date	Bank of Israel Nominal Rate of Interest	Inflation Expectations (to 12 Months Ahead)	Bank of Israel Real Rate of Interest
06/1997	14.47	8.62	5.39
07/1997	13.66	9.23	4.06
08/1997	13.78	9.70	3.72
09/1997	14.49	9.15	4.89
10/1997	14.55	8.34	5.73
11/1997	14.57	8.86	5.24
12/1997	14.61	8.29	5.84
01/1998	14.56	7.82	6.25
02/1998	13.89	6.52	6.92
03/1998	13.43	5.35	7.67
04/1998	13.07	5.96	6.71
05/1998	12.71	4.68	7.67
06/1998	12.34	4.46	7.54
07/1998	12.05	4.55	7.17
08/1998	10.50	5.60	4.64
09/1998	10.07	6.36	3.49
10/1998	10.28	8.15	1.97
11/1998	13.51	7.72	5.38
12/1998	14.56	6.63	7.43
01/1999	14.56	6.18	7.90
02/1999	14.48	5.44	8.58
03/1999	13.99	5.35	8.20
04/1999	13.41	5.60	7.40
05/1999	12.86	6.86	5.61
06/1999	12.86	5.79	6.68
07/1999	12.81	4.50	7.95

Date	Bank of Israel Nominal Rate of Interest	Inflation Expectations (to 12 months ahead)	Bank of Israel Real Rate of Interest
06/2001	7.25	2.08	5.07
07/2001	6.78	2.08	4.61
08/2001	6.61	2.86	3.65
09/2001	6.61	3.52	2.98
10/2001	6.61	1.97	4.55
11/2001	6.38	0.87	5.46
12/2001	5.63	0.93	4.65
01/2002	3.98	2.33	1.62
02/2002	4.04	2.86	1.15
03/2002	4.60	2.64	1.91
04/2002	4.65	3.74	0.88
05/2002	4.89	4.32	0.55
06/2002	7.26	4.82	2.32
07/2002	9.66	2.78	6.69
08/2002	9.65	2.32	7.17
09/2002	9.64	3.30	6.14
10/2002	9.69	3.82	5.65
11/2002	9.64	3.57	5.86
12/2002	9.61	2.94	6.48
01/2003	9.43	3.48	5.75
02/2003	9.43	4.23	4.99
03/2003	9.39	3.31	5.88
04/2003	9.21	1.99	7.08
05/2003	8.87	1.37	7.40

08/1991	14.53	16.20	−1.44	08/1995	14.21	9.76	4.05	08/1999	12.31	5.55	6.40
09/1991	15.08	16.85	−1.51	09/1995	14.18	10.67	3.17	09/1999	12.30	6.10	5.84
10/1991	21.55	16.23	4.58	10/1995	14.80	10.03	4.33	10/1999	12.30	5.07	6.88
11/1991	24.15	16.76	6.33	11/1995	15.26	9.59	5.18	11/1999	12.23	3.80	8.12
12/1991	19.43	15.10	3.76	12/1995	15.19	9.75	4.96	12/1999	11.93	3.31	8.34
01/1992	15.85	12.14	3.31	01/1996	14.70	10.13	4.15	01/2000	11.39	2.86	8.29
02/1992	13.75	9.54	3.84	02/1996	15.04	10.58	4.03	02/2000	10.87	2.98	7.67
03/1992	11.74	10.31	1.30	03/1996	15.05	10.75	3.88	03/2000	10.50	2.52	7.79
04/1992	11.79	10.59	1.09	04/1996	15.24	11.78	3.10	04/2000	10.14	3.00	6.93
05/1992	11.76	11.40	0.32	05/1996	16.01	12.62	3.01	05/2000	9.85	3.76	5.87
06/1992	11.5	10.73	0.70	06/1996	17.01	12.84	3.69	06/2000	9.86	3.65	5.99
07/1992	11.69	8.73	2.72	07/1996	18.58	11.55	6.30	07/2000	9.82	2.68	6.95
08/1992	11.73	8.34	3.13	08/1996	17.69	11.06	5.97	08/2000	9.64	2.31	7.17
09/1992	11.63	7.89	3.47	09/1996	17.11	11.66	4.88	09/2000	9.39	2.19	7.05
10/1992	11.7	7.69	3.72	10/1996	16.81	11.62	4.65	10/2000	9.06	2.53	6.37
11/1992	10.94	8.40	2.34	11/1996	16.44	10.70	5.18	11/2000	8.87	1.82	6.93
12/1992	10.84	9.76	0.98	12/1996	16.36	9.58	6.19	12/2000	8.63	1.25	7.29
01/1993	11.51	11.20	0.28	01/1997	15.82	9.30	5.97	01/2001	8.45	1.60	6.75
02/1993	12.79	8.85	3.62	02/1997	15.22	9.69	5.05	02/2001	8.12	2.03	5.97
03/1993	12.69	9.66	2.76	03/1997	14.96	10.06	4.46	03/2001	7.87	2.15	5.60
04/1993	12.69	9.68	2.74	04/1997	14.96	9.72	4.77	04/2001	7.57	1.26	6.23
05/1993	12.99	9.35	3.33	05/1997	14.99	9.20	5.30	05/2001	7.56	1.43	6.04

Source: Bank of Israel.

Notes

In writing this chapter, I benefited from very useful discussions with Nissan Liviatan and remarks by Yossi Gibre, Nachum Gross, David Kochav, Akiva Offenbacher, Efraim Sadka, Meir Sokoler, Avia Spivak, Zvi Urbach, and Moshe Sanbar. Evgenia Dechter and Asaf Nagar provided research assistance.

1. The use of modern metrics to evaluate BOI independence may appear out of context to policymakers who operated during the early statehood years. The concluding section offers additional remarks about this tension.
2. Early contributions to the literature on this matter include Grilli, Masciandaro, and Tabellini (1991), Cukierman, Webb, and Neyapti (1992), Alesina and Summers (1993), Cukierman, Kalaitzidakis, Summers, and Webb (1993), and Eijffinger and Schaling (1993). A survey appears in Cukierman (1998). In all these studies, including the present one, CBI is taken to represent the mandate and the ability of the CB to focus mainly or mostly on achieving price stability even at the relative neglect of other goals such as stabilization of output and financing of budget deficits. Thus, the concept of CBI as used here may also be thought of as the degree of effective conservatism of the CB.
3. For details, see chap. 19 of Cukierman (1992).
4. For extensive surveys of Israel's monetary history before the 1985 stabilization, including the pre-statehood and pre-BOI eras, see Barkai and Liviatan (2007a) and Barkai and Liviatan (2007b, c). The period immediately preceding the stabilization is surveyed in Barkai and Liviatan (2007d) and the post-1985 period in Liviatan (2007). A colorful account of the dominance of fiscal policy over monetary policy in the pre-1985 era appears in Barkai (2002).
5. Since all are bound by the Maastricht treaty, these countries are ultimately expected to establish a level of de jure independence equal to that of the European Central Bank. Thus, except for a few countries (e.g., the United Kingdom, Sweden, Denmark, and Switzerland), monetary policy in the post-enlargement euro zone will be managed by a highly independent CB.
6. The Levin Commission, established in December 1997 by then Prime Minister Benjamin Netanyahu, submitted a report with recommendations for reform of the Bank of Israel charter in December 1998 (Levin Commission, 1998). The legislature, however, did not pursue the recommendation.
7. Such questions are occasionally raised by academic economists as well (Stiglitz, 1998).
8. For the most comprehensive of them, see Cukierman, Webb, and Neyapti (1992) and chap. 19 of Cukierman (1992).
9. The amendment replaced Section 45 of the original 1954 BOI Law and is classified as Amendment 15.
10. Table A1.2 in the appendix presents the individual codings that underlie the aggregate CBI indices for the original (1954) and the amended (1985) laws.
11. This global trend is described in Cukierman (1998). Detailed documentation of central-bank reforms in FSE and their effect on inflation in FSE appears in Cukierman, Miller, and Neyapti (2002).
12. Calculated from table 1 in Cukierman, Miller, and Neyapti (2002), on the basis of the most recent charters available.
13. This number is the average of the LVAW index for twenty-three current and prospective members of EMU in 2001. The treaty of Maastricht requires all the national central banks to eventually upgrade their national charters to the level prescribed by the treaty. Since not all current and prospective members have

completed this process in 2001 the figure in the text constitutes a lower bound for the de jure independence of the European System of Central Banks.

14. The United Kingdom was absolved from having to align the Bank of England charter with the independence levels required by the Maastricht treaty but chose to make most of the adjustments anyway.

15. Until 1970, this subjugation was amplified by the existence of a 9% de jure ceiling on nominal interest rates. Since inflation was frequently higher than 9% during this period, the ceiling often prevented the BOI from maintaining positive real short-term interest rates.

16. A description of the precise mapping of these facts into numerical codings for the individual components of de facto independence appears in the second part of the appendix.

17. This subsection discusses the issues broadly. The specific coding details are presented in the third part of the appendix.

18. The BOI, unlike the Fed, does not keep a stock of seasoned government securities on hand. To absorb liquidity, it relies partly on the issue of short-term Treasury bills, which are formally considered a government liability. Up to the ceiling, the quantity of Treasury bills is determined largely by the BOI.

19. A similar qualitative picture emerges from table A1.4 of the appendix, which provides data on the real rate that the BOI paid private banks for funds deposited with it.

20. The widespread availability of both indexed and nonindexed government bonds in the Israeli financial markets makes it possible to estimate expected inflation by calculating the difference between nominal and real rates of interest on instruments of similar maturity and financial quality.

21. Liviatan produces evidence supporting this view. This pattern is consistent with Dornbusch's overshooting hypothesis (Dornbusch, 1976). See also Liviatan (1984).

22. A monthly regression of annual moving averages of inflation rates on a lagged value of the inflation target, measured conformably, did not yield a significant coefficient between 93 and 95 (twelve observations). A similar regression for the 1996 to mid-2003 period produced a significant positive coefficient in the vicinity of 1 (thirty observations) and a substantially higher adjusted R-squared. Although the first sample is rather small, these regressions are consistent with the view that the target has been more strongly construed as a commitment since 1996.

23. Melnick's estimated reaction functions imply that the BOI behaved as a strict inflation targeter during this period (Melnick, 2002).

24. Bank of Israel, *Annual Report,* 2002, appendix table to the balance sheet, 1985–2002.

25. Amounting to full sterilization of the impact of the government's foreign-exchange transactions on the market exchange rate.

26. The extremely low level of de facto independence obtained for the pre-1985 period is consistent with Barkai's account of matters in the 1960s and the 1970s (Barkai and Liviatan, 2007a, c).

27. During the post-1985 period, only in the years around 1989 did the BOI have less de facto independence than de jure independence.

28. Cukierman, Miller, and Neyapti (2002) found that de jure independence in transition economies has a negative impact on inflation only after the liberalization process has gone far enough. To explain this, they argue that law abidance and the degree of liberalization may be positively related, making the latter a proxy for the former. See also Eijffinger and Stadhouser (2003). However, I am not aware of any evidence of perceptible changes in law abidance in Israel. The assumption that law abidance in Israel has been constant over time, at least since the 1960s, appears to be reasonable.

29. Culled from Cukierman, Webb, and Neyapti (1992).
30. For details about this index in transition economies, see table 1 of Cukierman, Miller, and Neyapti (2002).
31. For a comprehensive description of the high-inflation era and the periods shortly preceding and following stabilization, see Bruno (1993).
32. Grilli, Masciandaro, and Tabellini (1991) applied the expression to this context after having found, for developed economies, that de jure CBI has a negative impact on inflation and no impact on growth. For developing countries, Cukierman et al. (1993) found that proxies for de facto CBI have a similar negative impact on inflation and a positive impact on growth.
33. For details, see Cukierman (1998).
34. A nonexhaustive list of references includes Grilli, Masciandaro, and Tabellini (1991), Cukierman, Webb, and Neyapti (1992), chap. 20 of Cukierman (1992), Alesina and Summers (1993), and Cukierman et al. (1993).
35. For summaries of these arguments, see Cukierman and Liviatan (1990) and part I of Cukierman (1992).
36. A strict inflation targeter is a CB that cares only about inflation and its stabilization. The term traces to Svensson (1997).
37. Woodford's argument relies on a quadratic approximation of the utility of the representative consumer. For New Keynesian models and parameter values that are considered reasonable for the U.S. economy, Woodford concludes that the inflation deviation should be assigned a greater weight than the output gap.
38. For a more detailed discussion of the pros and cons of growth targets for the BOI, see Cukierman (2003).
39. This statement is consistent with recent empirical findings in Orphanides and Williams (2005), who used real-time data about policymakers' perceptions of potential output during the 1970s and compared these perceptions with current estimates (as of October 1999) of the historical data. Using the "current" version of potential-output estimates as a proxy for the actual values of potential output during the 1970s, they found highly persistent deviations between the current and the real-time estimates of the output gap. (See their figure 3 in particular.)
40. Former governor Moshe Sanbar argued (1977) that the advisory function impairs the bank's ability to act as the "compass and the conscience" of the economy (in the words of David Horowitz, the first governor of the BOI). Interestingly, the newspaper article in which Sanbar expressed this opinion was written after Prime Minister Menachem Begin reprimanded BOI Governor Arnon Gafny for publicly criticizing a budget proposal that the minister of finance had submitted to the Knesset. Begin claimed that since the governor can air his views within the government in his capacity as the government's economic advisor, he should refrain from publicly criticizing the government's economic policies.
41. Although this conclusion is partly based on judgment, an alternative way of codifying independence shows it to be robust. Further experimentation with additional codification systems is always desirable. In view of the added widening of the discrepency between de facto and de jure independence since 1998, however, it is very likely that the conclusion in the text reflects reality, at least from that time on.
42. An empirical documentation of such a process in the United States appears in Orphanides and Williams (2005). Woodford (2003) suggests that an appropriately chosen commitment enhances the CB's ability to stabilize the real economy while attaining the inflation target on average.

43. Cukierman (1992) presents an unweighted version of the same characteristics (LVAU). Other indices, such as those used by Bade and Parkin (1988), Alesina (1988, 1989), Grilli, Masciandaro, and Tabellini (1991), and Eijffinger and Schaling (1993), may for the most part be approximated by subsets of the components of the LVAW (or of the LVAU) index.
44. For further details, see section 19.3 of Cukierman (1992).
45. The broader meaning of Treasury bills as a monetary-policy instrument and its flexibilization are discussed in the subsection of the text entitled "Treasury Bills, Time Deposits, Swaps, Government Foreign-Exchange."

References

Alesina, A. "Macroeconomics and Politics." *NBER Macroeconomics Annual 3* (1988): 13–52.

———. "Politics and Business Cycles in the Industrial Democracies." *Economic Policy* 8 (1989): 57–98.

Alesina, A., and L. Summers. "Central Bank Independence and Macroeconomic Performance: Some Comparative Evidence." *Journal of Money, Credit and Banking* 25 (1993): 151–62.

Bade, R., and M. Parkin. "Central Bank Laws and Monetary Policy." Manuscript. University of Western Ontario, October 1988.

Barkai, H. "A Central Bank in Chains." In *Five Decades of Israeli Economy: A Festschrift for M. Sanbar's 75th Anniversary,* ed. H. Barkai. Rishon Lezion: College of Management, 2002 (Hebrew).

Barkai, H., and N. Liviatan. "The Establishment of the Bank of Israel: the Legal and Institutional Framework of Israel's Central Bank." Pages 58–69 in H. Barkai and N. Liviatan, *The Bank of Israel, Vol. 1: The Monetary History of Israel.* New York: Oxford University Press, 2007a.

———. "Emergence of the Monetary Texture and Macroeconomic Developments, 1948–1954." Pages 30–57 in H. Barkai and N. Liviatan, *The Bank of Israel, Vol. 1: The Monetary History of Israel.* New York: Oxford University Press, 2007b.

———. "The Monetary Legacy of the British Mandate." Pages 25–30 in H. Barkai and N. Liviatan, *The Bank of Israel, Vol. 1: The Monetary History of Israel.* New York: Oxford University Press, 2007c.

———. "Israel's Great Inflation." Pages 139–193 in H. Barkai and N. Liviatan, *The Bank of Israel, Vol. 1: The Monetary History of Israel.* New York: Oxford University Press, 2007d.

Barro R. J., and Gordon R. "A Positive Theory of Monetary Policy in a Natural Rate Model." *Journal of Political Economy* 91 (1983): 589–610.

Bruno M. *Crisis, Stabilization and Economic Reform: Therapy by Consensus.* Oxford: Oxford University Press, 1993.

Calvo G. "Staggered Prices in a Utility Maximizing Framework." *Journal of Monetary Economics* 12, no. 3 (1983): 383–98.

Clarida R., J. Gali, and M. Gertler. "The Science of Monetary Policy: A New Keynesian Perspective." *Journal of Economic Literature* 37 (December 1999): 1661–707.

Cukierman, A. *Central Bank Strategy, Credibility and Independence: Theory and Evidence.* Cambridge, MA: MIT Press, 1992.

————. "The Economics of Central Banking." In *Contemporary Economic Issues—Macroeconomics and Finance,* ed. Wolf Holger, 37–82. New York: Macmillan Press, 1998.

————. "Should the Bank of Israel Have a Growth Target?—What Are the Issues?" School of Economics, Tel-Aviv University, August 2003. http://www.tau.ac.il/~alexcuk/pdf/growth-target.pdf.

————. "A Note on the Relation between the Real Rate and the Central Bank's Output Target Under Perfect and Imperfect Information." October 2004. http://www.tau.ac.il/~alexcuk/pdf/real-rate-credibility.pdf.

Cukierman, A., P. Kalaitzidakis, L. H. Summers, and S. B. Webb. "Central Bank Independence, Growth, Investment and Real Rates." *Carnegie-Rochester Conference Series on Public Policy* 39 (Autumn 1993): 95–145.

Cukierman, A., and F. Lippi. "Endogenous Monetary Policy with Unobserved Potential Output." *Journal of Economics Dynamics and Control,* V. 29, issue 11 (November 2005) 1951–1983.

Cukierman, A., and N. Liviatan. "Rules, Discretion, Credibility and Reputation." *Bank of Israel Economic Review* 65 (July 1990): 3–25 (Hebrew).

Cukierman, A., G. P. Miller, and B. Neyapti. "Central Bank Reform, Liberalization and Inflation in Transition Economies—An International Perspective." *Journal of Monetary Economics* 49 (March 2002): 237–64.

Cukierman, A., and M. Sokoler. "Monetary Policy and Institutions in Israel—Past, Present and Future." *Bank of Israel Economic Review* 65 (March 1993): 67–123.

Cukierman, A., S. Webb, and B. Neyapti. "The Measurement of Central Bank Independence and its Effect on Policy Outcomes." *World Bank Economic Review* 6 (September 1992): 439–58.

Dornbusch, R. "Expectations and Exchange Rate Dynamics." *Journal of Political Economy* 84 (1976): 1161–76.

Eijffinger S., and M. van Keulen. "Central Bank Independence in Another Eleven Countries." *Banca Nazionale del Lavoro Quarterly Review* 192 (1995): 39–83.

Eijffinger, S., and E. Schaling. "Central Bank Independence in Twelve Industrial Countries." *Banca Nazionale del Lavoro Quarterly Review* 184 (March 1993): 64–68.

Eijffinger, S., and P. Stadhouder. "Monetary Policy and the Rule of Law." CEPR Discussion Paper 3698, 2003.

Elkayam, D. "The Inflation Target and Monetary Policy—A Model for Analysis and Prediction." Manuscript. Bank of Israel, 2000 (Hebrew).

Grilli, V., D. Masciandaro, and G. Tabellini. "Political and Monetary Institutions and Public Financial Policies in the Industrial Countries." *Economic Policy* 13 (1991): 341–92.

Kydland, F. E., and E. C. Prescott. "Rules Rather Than Discretion: The Inconsistency of Optimal Plans." *Journal of Political Economy* 85 (1977): 473–92.

Levin Commission. Final Report—Discussion, Conclusions and Recommendations. December 1998 (Hebrew).

Liviatan, N. "Tight Money and Inflation." *Journal of Monetary Economics* 13 (1984): 5–15.

————. "The Emergence of an Independent Monetary Policy and Macroeconomic Developments after the 1985 Stabilization." Pages 195–272 in H. Barkai and N. Liviatan, *The Bank of Israel, Vol. 1: The Monetary History of Israel.* New York: Oxford University Press, 2007.

Melnick, R. "A Peek into the Governor's Chamber: The Israeli Case." Interdisciplinary Center, Herzliyya, 2002.

Orphanides, A. "Monetary Policy Rules based on Real-Time Data." *American Economic Review* 91, no. 4 (2001): 964–85.

Orphanides, A., and J. Williams. "The Decline of Activist Stabilization Policy: Natural Rate Misperceptions, Learning, and Expectations." *Journal of Economics Dynamics and Control,* V. 29, issue 11 (November 2005): 1927–50.

Rogoff, K. "The Optimal Degree of Commitment to a Monetary Target." *Quarterly Journal of Economics* 100 (1985): 1169–90.

Sadeh, T. "A Sustainable EU-27 Single Currency? Political Criteria for Optimal Currency Areas." Manuscript. Department of Political Science, Tel-Aviv University, June 2003.

Sanbar, M. "On the Independence of the Bank of Israel." *Yedioth Ahronoth,* December 11, 1977 (Hebrew).

Stiglitz, J. "Central Banking in a Democratic Society." *De Economist* 146 (1998): 199–226.

Svensson, L. E. O. "Inflation Forecast Targeting: Implementing and Monitoring Inflation Targets." *European Economic Review* 41 (June 1997): 1111–46.

Taylor, J. "Discretion versus Policy Rules in Practice." *Carnegie-Rochester Conference Series on Public Policy* 39 (1993): 195–214.

Woodford, M. *Interest and Prices—Foundations of a Theory of Monetary Policy.* Princeton: Princeton University Press, 2003.

2

Monetary Policy in Israel, 1986–2000: Estimating the Central Bank's Reaction Function

Nathan Sussman

The evolution of monetary policy conducted by central banks has recently reached an important juncture. Starting in the nineteenth century, central banks' monetary policy was aimed at pegging the price of gold, the price of silver, and the level of currency exchange rates. As such, it was mainly used to achieve price stability. The deep global recession in the 1930s and the development of alternative macroeconomic models and policies affected the classical role of monetary policy. No longer responsible only for exchange rate (price) stability, central banks were also assigned with countercyclical policy duties. The inflation of the 1970s and early 1980s, occasioned partly by monetary expansion during the recession that followed the oil price hikes, caused central bank policy to revert to its more traditional role, the maintenance of price stability or the attainment of inflation targets. The slide into what became a prolonged global recession at the beginning of the twenty-first century has again raised the issue of the appropriate framework for the monetary-policy mix.

The formulation of monetary-policy rules for the future cannot be undertaken without first assessing the performance of monetary policy in the past. While monetary-policy goals are often announced by central-bank or government officials, and although actions taken by central banks are in many respects observable, the intent with which actions are taken is opaque. In particular, the absence of a simple monetary-policy reaction function that assigns predetermined and specific actions to various realizations of the policy targets makes it difficult to infer what type of central banker is at issue by simply observing his/her actions. Furthermore, one cannot necessarily infer the type of central banker by relying on the self-proclaimed type (Barro and Gordon, 1983).

Recently, two approaches have been used to estimate the weight that central banks assign to the pursuance of a low inflation target, on the one hand, and countercyclical policy, on the other. The first, formulated by Clarida, Gali, and Gertler (CGG [2000]), constructs a forward-looking central-bank reaction function and estimates it for the United States and some other major economies. Bar-Efrat and Bufman (2002) estimated a similar model for the Israeli economy in the 1997–2001 period. Dudu Elkayam (2001) estimated a variant of the CGG model that includes a time-varying inflation target and obtained similar results to those of CGG. Another variant of CGG (Melnick, 2002) assumes a small open economy and includes an interest-parity condition. An additional popular approach, based on a model by Taylor (1993), includes a central-bank reaction function that is part of a small macroeconomic model. Recently, Segherri (2002) estimated Taylor equations for the advanced economies. The major findings, varying only by degree, are that central banks, in all countries surveyed, switched from a more balanced reaction function, which suggested that they attempted to reduce inflation and pursue a counter-cyclical monetary policy, to a policy aimed mainly at aggressive disinflation.

This chapter analyzes the policies pursued by the Bank of Israel (BOI) in the late 1980s and the 1990s. In contrast to most of the literature, which estimates the CCG and Taylor models in predetermined samples of the different policies used, we use a break test to determine policy changes. Our analysis shows that the switch to a tougher disinflationary policy from a more accommodating one was achieved mainly by setting the short-term *real interest rate* at a persistently high level. This is quite different from the reaction-function changes reported in international studies, according to which central banks cracked down on inflation by dealing aggressively with *short-term* deviations of the inflation rate from its target while the Bank of Israel responded aggressively only to large deviations. Taken together, our results suggest that the BOI followed a type of band (Ss) rule, in which it conducted a persistent disinflationary policy that was significantly affected neither by minor deviations of inflation from the target nor by the output gap but responded aggressively whenever the upper bound of the band was threatened.

In Israel, it is the government that sets the inflation target. These targets were not always welcomed by the BOI and were subject to much debate. In a policy game (Svensson, 1997), the central bank may override the fiscal authority's target. Our results do not allow us to reject the hypothesis that since 1995–96 the BOI, like its European counterparts, has pursued an implicit zero-inflation target rather than the time-varying inflation target set by the government. Finally, our econometric method also allows us to analyze some interesting aspects of the central bank's short-term behavior. In particular, we show that the BOI's short-term policy is not always consistent with its long-term objectives. We suggest that these deviations may be interpreted as policy errors.

MONETARY POLICY AND THE DISINFLATION PROCESS IN ISRAEL, 1985–2000

In 1985, the Government of Israel implemented a package of measures aimed at halting inflation, which verged on hyperinflation and threatened the economy with financial collapse. However, as figure 2.1 shows, the disinflation process was rather slow in comparison with disinflations in advanced economies. A partial explanation of the dynamics of the gradual disinflation process may be found in the conduct of monetary policy. Monetary policy during that period

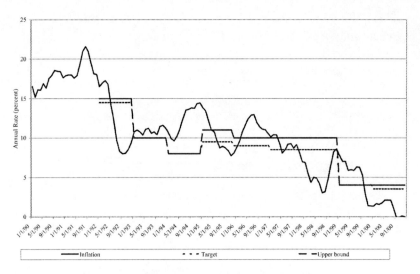

Figure 2.1. Inflation and Inflation Targets: Israel, 1990–2000.

evolved in two distinct yet related dimensions. The first relates to the increasing importance attached to the disinflation process and the role of monetary policy in implementing it. The second refers to the choice of monetary targets and instruments employed to reduce inflation.

With respect to the emphasis on disinflation, one may argue that the importance and pace of further disinflation after the steep decrease in 1985 was subject to debate. This was definitely the case in the mid-1990s when inflation fell to around 10% and even more so when it slipped to the low single-digit range. There was no consensus among economists about the payoff of reducing inflation within the single-digit range (for example, from 8% to 4%) while the costs were thought to be considerable. This led to a series of overt disagreements between the BOI, which favored a more aggressive disinflationary stance, and the Ministry of Finance. Only after 1999 did the central bank free itself of the political constraints that had affected its disinflation policy earlier in the period.

Consequently, until the late 1990s the BOI was constrained in implementing persistent tough monetary policies. Until then, whenever tough policies encountered difficulties in the form of recession or currency appreciation, the central bank preferred to ease the monetary stringency. After the 1985 stabilization, the government implemented a full peg to the U.S. dollar and, later, to a five-currency "basket." The ensuing recession in 1988, however, coupled with currency appreciation, led to the adoption of a more flexible exchange-rate regime that included an adjustable exchange-rate band that, in 1991, became an upward-sliding one. Thus, the existence of fairly high core inflation was formally acknowledged.

Since 1991, when the inflation-target regime was first instituted, the approach toward setting the target was very gradual with the exception of

Figure 2.2. Inflation, Inflation Expectations, and the Bank of Israel Key
　　　　　Rate, 1990–2000.

the target set in 1998 (figure 2.1). During this period, monetary policy was quite
aggressive in dealing with upward deviations from the target or from inflation
expectations (figure 2.2). Afterward, however, it tended to compromise.
Another view of this policy stance is shown in figure 2.3, which shows how the
real monetary lending rate was raised in two steps. The first step was taken after
1991, when real short-term interest rates became persistently positive. The
second step, taken in late 1994 and early 1996 in response to inflation spikes, set
the real interest rate at relative high levels. After inflation responded favorably

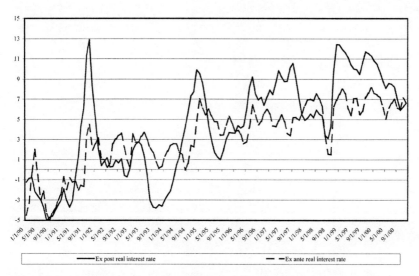

Figure 2.3. Real Interest Rate: Israel, 1990–2000. Quarterly Data in Annual Terms
　　　　　(percent).

in 1998, however, the tight interest-rate policy was eased somewhat. Only in 1999 and 2000 did the BOI maintain high real interest rates even as inflation declined, resulting in very high real short-term interest amid very low inflation.

In sum, the 1990s may be divided into several subperiods in the conduct of monetary policy. From 1987 to 1992, the policy seemed to accommodate inflation. The 1992–94 years were an in-between subperiod, in which the real interest became positive. Since late 1994, the BOI has kept real interest rates high most of the time. Even so, there were times when monetary policy seemed to signal something other than an uncompromising stance with respect to disinflation. In the following sections, we ask whether ostensible lapses in the bank's anti-inflationary persistence are what they seem to be or whether they are part of a consistent policy reaction function.

METHODOLOGY

We use two methods to estimate the BOI's reaction function. Our goal is to estimate a model in the spirit of CGG (2000) that is also consistent with the Taylor model (1993) and estimates reported by Segherri (2002). The estimates of all the scholars mentioned above, however, were formulated in view of a sample selection based on observing the behavior of the actual real interest rate. In this chapter, we test for stochastic properties and introduce a break test to obtain endogenously the timing of the break in the reaction function. The break test also reveals significant deviations from the reaction function due to what we define as policy errors or inconsistencies.

We begin this section by outlining the CGG approach and describing the break test.

The CGG Approach

We follow the methodology presented in CGG (1998), which is essentially a two-stage GMM procedure for the estimation of a simple forward-looking policy rule with partial adjustment.

The central-bank behavior function is:

$$r_t^* = \alpha + \beta E[\pi_{t+n}|\Omega_t] + \gamma E[x_t|\Omega_t] \tag{1}$$

where r^* is the target for the short-term nominal interest rate, π_{t+n} is inflation expectations, and x is the current output gap. Ω denotes the information set at time t. This specification assumes a fixed real rate of return (real interest rate) in the economy.

Assuming partial adjustment at rate ρ of the actual nominal interest rate, r, to the target rate, r^*:

$$r_t = (1-\rho)r_t^* + \rho r_{t-1} + \nu_t \tag{2}$$

The baseline equation estimated by CGG is:

$$r_t = (1-\rho)\alpha + (1-\rho)\beta\pi_{t+n} + (1-\rho)\gamma x_t + \rho r_{t-1} + \varepsilon_t \tag{3}$$

One may add to the baseline function any number z of variables that may affect the central bank's decision to attain the target.

$$r_t = (1-\rho)\alpha + (1-\rho)\beta\pi_{t+n} + (1-\rho)\gamma x_t + \rho r_{t-1} + \xi z_t + \varepsilon_t \qquad (4)$$

The test of interest to us is whether β is greater or smaller than 1. $\beta > 1$ implies an aggressive anti-inflationary stance; $0 < \beta < 1$ implies an accommodating response.

One may accommodate the basic model to include the existence of the explicit announced inflation target in Israel.[1] Denoting π_t^T as the inflation target at time t, we may write equation (4) as:

$$\begin{aligned}
r_t = {} & (1-\rho)\alpha + (1-\rho)\beta\pi_{t+n} + (1-\rho)\gamma x_t + \rho r_{t-1} + \xi z_t \\
& + (1-\rho)(1-\beta)\pi_t^T + \varepsilon_t
\end{aligned} \qquad (4^*)$$

Break Tests

The sample used to estimate the reaction function was chosen on the basis of observation of the actual real interest rates in the countries for which the estimates were obtained. Typically, the behavior of real interest rates allowed us to identify change in the policy regime. The identifying assumption was that higher ex post real interest rates signal a move from an accommodating anti-inflationary stance to a more aggressive anti-inflationary policy. While much can be inferred from these observations, they cannot establish the exact timing of the regime change. Furthermore, such a change in the real interest rate may originate not in a policy change but, among other things, in fortunate economic developments that the central bank has exploited. Moreover, a non-recurrent change in the real interest rate does not necessarily signal a change in the parameters of the reaction function. The break test allows us to distinguish among the hypotheses that seek to explain monetary-policy changes.

In this section, we follow the Perron break-test methodology, also employed in Liviatan and Sussman (2002), to estimate the following break test:

$$\Delta r_t = \alpha + \beta_1 r_{t-1} + \beta_2 \Delta r_{t-1} + \beta_2 \pi r_t^e + \beta_4 x_t + \gamma D_P + \delta D_L + \varepsilon_t \qquad (5)$$

The break test involves the dynamic estimation of the reaction function (4) that allows, assuming that the dependent variable is stationary, for long- and short-term breaks that are captured by the dummy variables D_L and D_P, respectively:

$$D_L = \begin{cases} 0 & t < t_L \\ 1 & t >= t_L \end{cases}$$

$$D_p = \begin{cases} 0 & t \neq t_p \\ 1 & t = t_p \end{cases}$$

If the dependent variable has unit root properties, the break dummies may be interpreted as long-term breaks (D_P) and changes in trend (D_L). Since in a unit root series, shocks have a permanent effect on the dependent variable, a single-period break, captured by the D_P dummy, has an effect equivalent to that of a permanent increase in interest rates by the coefficient β_1. The break test is used to answer the following question: given the values of the economic fundamentals that determine the central bank's policy, are there any significant long-term breaks, that is, long-term policy shifts, or short-term breaks, that is, deviations from the long-term policy? If we find a significant long-term break (or breaks), we may infer that a policy shift has occurred. Finding a short-term break (or breaks) may help us to study deviations from the policy. The deviations may be interpreted as responses to specific short-term events (shocks) or as policy inconsistencies or errors.

We estimate the reaction function recursively for the entire sample, moving the dummy variables forward one observation at a time. The most significant break in terms of the t-statistic is selected as the most significant policy shift. We then split the sample in two and reestimate the equation for the two subsamples in order to find additional breaks. The same procedure is followed for the short-term breaks.

Estimation of Structural Breaks in the CGG Model

The estimation procedure that we follow in this chapter combines the CGG reaction-function estimation with the break test. We first use the break test to identify breaks in the data. Once we obtain the significant breaks, we estimate the full CGG model, taking account of the breaks that we found by introducing dummies for them. This allows us to take advantage of a larger sample than previously used (Bar-Effrat and Bufman, 2002) and to obtain a consistent quantitative measure of the policy shift.

As we show below, this methodology allows us to distinguish among various hypotheses about the nature of the policy shift. The shift to a tougher stance on inflation may be the reflection of four, not necessarily mutually exclusive, policy measures: (1) a stronger reaction to inflation expectations (higher β in terms of equation [5]); (2) weakening of the emphasis on countercyclicality (lower γ in terms of equation [5]); (3) greater persistence in dealing with inflation (reflected in a larger change in ρ, the effect of lagged policy on current policy); and (4) a change in the real interest rate or the (unannounced) inflation target of the central bank, as shown in equation (5).

The methodology also allows us to take account of short-term policy deviations that we obtained form the break tests in the estimation of the structural model. Thus, we may consistently account for outliers that may otherwise, given the relatively small sample, affect the estimators for the policy-response variables.

RESULTS

The Data

We use the following variables in the empirical section of this chapter (all are monthly unless indicted otherwise):

r—the nominal lending rate of the Bank of Israel, announced monthly by the governor.

π^e—inflation expectations as derived from the capital market, i.e., as the difference between CPI-indexed bonds and nonindexed bonds of identical maturity.

π^T_t—the inflation target as announced by the government, taken as the average of the lower and upper bands of the target.

X—the GDP gap, measured as the difference between actual GDP and potential GDP (GDP trend).

M2—the M2 aggregate at month's end.

π—the inflation rate, calculated monthly as the change in the CPI during the past year.

πq—the inflation rate, calculated monthly as the change in the CPI during the past quarter.

e—the monthly US$–NIS exchange rate.

er—the monthly real US$–NIS exchange rate.

U—the unemployment rate (quarterly data)

Mesh—the "S-index," the BOI's composite state-of-the-economy index.

Stochastic Properties

Before attempting to estimate any of the regressions, we should investigate the stochastic properties of the main variables. Observing the first column in table 2.1, we find, interestingly, that the central bank's interest rate and inflation expectations have different stochastic properties. The nominal interest rate was quite volatile throughout the period; inflation expectations seemed to decline monotonically. Therefore, the statistical properties of the data suggest that there is no unique relationship between the interest rate and inflation expectations. Instead, there were (at least) two different behavioral rules during the 1990s. Furthermore, it is inappropriate to use the unemployment rate in a policy-reaction function because this rate has unit root properties and cannot be statistically cointegrated with the nominal interest rate. The variable that serves as the output gap has stochastic properties that are consistent with the stochastic process that governs the central bank's interest rate.

Table 2.1. Unit Root Test Results

Sample	1:1990–12:2000		1:1990–12:1993		1:1995–12:2000	
r_t	−3.157	Stationary	−4.111	Trend stationary	−2.073	Stationary
	(−2.883)*		(−3.504)*		(−1.944)*	
π^e_t	−3.864	Trend stationary	−3.870	Trend stationary	−1.951	Stationary
	(−3.444)*		(−3.504)*		(−1.944)*	
X_t	−4.321	Stationary	−3.453	Stationary	−3.574	Stationary
	(−3.481)**		(−2.992)*		(−3.522)**	
Ut	−1.569	Unit root	−2.029	Unit root	−4.932	Trend stationary
	(−2.883)*		(−2.992)*		(−4.089)**	

* 5% critical value
** 10% critical value

Table 2.2. Perron Break Test Results

	Long-Term Break		One-Period Break	
	August 1994	October 1991	August 1998	November 1998
Sample	1:1990–12:2000	1989:6–12:1993	1:1995–12:2000	1:1995–12:2000
Dependent variable	$\Delta(r_t)$	$\Delta(r_t)$	$\Delta(r_t)$	$\Delta(r_t)$
C	0.017 (0.020)	0.039 (0.027)	0.051 (0.023)	0.023 (0.019)
r_{t-1}	−0.282 (0.008)	−0.373 (0.054)	−0.269 (0.049)	−0.168 (0.040)
$\Delta(r_{t-1})$	0.406 (0.072)	0.386 (0.083)	0.475 (0.089)	0.390 (0.078)
π_t^e	0.169 (0.027)	0.180 (0.061)	0.189 (0.037)	0.149 (0.037)
X_t	−0.002 (0.020)	−0.016 (0.032)	−0.028 (0.020)	−0.013 (0.017)
D_P	−0.009 (0.008)	0.052 (0.008)	−0.016 (0.005)	0.027 (0.004)
D_L	0.009 (0.002)	0.003 (0.005)	−0.001 (0.002)	0.001 (0.002)
N	132	48	72	72
R^2adj	0.37	0.73	0.46	0.61
D.W.	1.97	2.66	2.39	2.04

Standard errors are in parentheses.

Break Tests

We estimated equation (5) on the basis of monthly data for the 1990–2000 period. Although this period cannot be viewed as a "long term," we nevertheless attempted to find breaks and policy deviations in the data. We tried several specifications of equation (5)—the entire specified model and versions omitting variables that turned out to be insignificant. All versions point to a break in the middle of 1994 (table 2.2). This corresponds quite nicely with figure 2.3, which shows the increase in the real monetary lending interest rate, and with anecdotal evidence about a policy-regime change that occurred around that time. Using the estimated coefficient, we calculate a permanent change of about 1 percentage point in the real interest rate.

We then divide the sample to two subsamples—1990–93 and 1995–2000—and reestimate equation (5). Again, before we interpret the results it is useful to test for the stochastic properties of the variables. Table 2.1 shows that during the first subperiod the main variables are trend-stationary, that is, stationary around a declining trend. Therefore, a finding of a significant single-period dummy (DP) means that there was a "long-term" change in interest rates. During the second subperiod, all the variables are stationary; therefore, a significant DP at this time may be interpreted as a nonrecurrent (short-term) deviation from the rule.

During the first subperiod, we find one significant long-term break in October 1991. Consulting table 2.2, we learn that the real interest rate rose by about 5 percentage points. This change echoes the switch from the exchange-rate peg policy that was pursued in 1985–91 (from the beginning of the stabilization program) to an inflation-target policy. It also corresponds to the shift to a sliding exchange-rate band. Arguably, this break signaled the onset of a new monetary policy that was based on a CGG-type reaction function. The switch to a Taylor-type rule is usually associated with an increase in the real interest rate. The BOI shifted its policy gradually: in 1992 it started to pursue an inflation target, but only in 1994 do we see a relatively permanent increase in the real interest rate. The econometric tests also suggest that the change in 1994 was qualitatively more significant than the one in 1991.

Turning to the second subsample, following the policy shift in 1994, we encounter two significant single-period dummies: August 1998 and November 1998. These dummies may be interpreted as deviations from the rule pursued in the late 1990s. While the rate hike of November 1998 followed a global financial crisis that erupted a month earlier, the rate cut in August 1998 may be viewed as a policy deviation. According to the break tests reported in table 2.2, the magnitude of this deviation was 1.6 percentage points. One interpretation is that if the central bank had adhered to its policy reaction function, the rate cut in August 1998 would not have been as steep. Alternatively, one may speculate that had the financial crisis in October 1998 not occurred, the decline in August might have signaled a regime change toward a lower real interest rate.

Table 2.3 summarizes the results of the break tests. It may be readily seen that once the breaks are accounted for by their respective dummies, the reaction function is quite robust with respect to the point of departure. Furthermore, the output-gap variable is insignificant and even carries the wrong sign. This analysis suggests that the main changes during the 1990s are related to the desired level of the central bank's short-term real interest-rate target, which may be interpreted as the central bank's commitment to disinflation. This view is quite different than the one reported by CGG (2000), in which changes in the parameters of the reaction function are identified. In particular, the response to changes in inflation expectations is more aggressive and interest-rate changes are more persistent. In the following section, we use the results of the break tests to estimate CGG (2000)–type equations.

Table 2.3. Estimates Based on Break-Test Results

Sample	1:1990–12:2000	1:1992–12:2000	1:1995–12:2000
Dependent variable	$\Delta(r_t)$	$\Delta(r_t)$	$\Delta(r_t)$
C	0.025 (0.015)	0.021 (0.014)	0.025 (0.016)
r_{t-1}	−0.259 (0.029)	−0.204 (0.029)	−0.185 (0.035)
$\Delta(r_{t-1})$	0.377 (0.053)	0.393 (0.050)	0.402 (0.065)
π_t^e	0.149 (0.019)	0.163 (0.023)	0.144 (0.028)
X_t	−0.011 (0.015)	−0.013 (0.014)	−0.012 (0.014)
D1994	0.009 (0.002)	0.006 (0.001)	
D1991:10	0.052 (0.006)		
D1998:8	−0.017 (0.006)	−0.016 (0.004)	−0.016 (0.004)
D1998:11	0.023 (0.006)	0.026 (0.004)	0.026 (0.004)
N	132	108	72
R^2adj	0.66	0.67	0.69
D.W.	2.20	2.35	2.15

Standard errors are in parentheses.

Estimation of the CGG Model

In this section, we employ the CGG estimation method to estimate the reaction function of the Bank of Israel. Due to the possibility of simultaneity, CGG employ a generalized method-of-moments estimation, which uses as instruments various macroeconomic variables that may implicitly enter the policymakers' reaction function or that may correlate with determinants of the reaction function: deviation of inflation expectations from target and the output gap.

We start with a simple estimation of the CGG model for the entire sample period. Table 2.4 reports the results of the estimation of equation 3. We used three measures of real activity—output gap, changes in unemployment, and changes in the S-index. Although the estimated equations yield similar results, the one that uses the output gap provides the most sensible results. The output-gap measure is very small but significant, suggesting that policymakers assigned some, but very little, weight to countercyclical policy in the 1990s.

Table 2.4. GMM Estimations of Simple Reaction Function

Sample	1:1990– 12:2000	1:1990– 12:2000	1:1990– 12:2000	1:1990– 12:2000	7:1992– 12:2000
Equation	(1)	(2)	(3)	(4)	(5)
Dependent variable	(r_t)	(r_t)	(r_t)	(r_t)	(r_t)
C	0.004	0.008	0.005	0.008	0.00006
	(0.001)	(0.002)	(0.001)	(0.001)	(0.002)
r_{t-1}	0.907	0.858	0.910	1.294	0.795
	(0.013)	(0.016)	(0.011)	(0.014)	(0.012)
π_t^e	0.081	0.106	0.057	0.072	0.206
	(0.006)	(0.023)	(0.008)	(0.005)	(0.012)
X_t	0.013	−0.001	0.0008	0.026	0.022
	(0.006)	(0.001)	(0.0005)	(0.004)	(0.004)
r_{t-2}				−0.415	
				(0.012)	
π_t^T					−0.003
					(0.0005)
β Aggressiveness	0.87	0.75	0.63	0.60	1
γ	0.13	0.007	0.008	0.21	0.11
ρ	0.91	0.86	0.91	0.88	0.80
N	130	130	130	130	102
R^2adj	0.87	0.87	0.87	0.90	0.94
D.W.	1.27	1.22	1.26	1.99	1.35

Standard errors are in parentheses.
Equation (1) is in natural logs.
X_t: (1) GDP gap. (2) ΔU (3) ΔMesh (4) GDP gap (5) GDP gap
Instruments include the following variables at lags of $t_{-1} - t_{-12}$: $r, y, \Delta e, \Delta er, \Delta m2, \pi q$
Aggressiveness (see CGG, 2000) is defined as the coefficient of inflation expectations divided by the coefficient of $1 - r_{t-1}$.

Although little attention was paid to countercyclical policy, the central bank's stance with respect to changes in inflation expectations was rather mild. The estimated degree of aggressiveness ranges from 0.63 to 0.87, that is, less than 1.[2] This implies that throughout sample period the central bank was accommodating rather than aggressive toward changes in inflation expectations. This aggressiveness factor is much lower than that reported by CGG (1998) for the main Western economies: 1.3 for Germany, 2 for Japan, and 1.8 for the United States. The countercyclical policy parameter in equation (1), γ, resembles that found by CGG (1998), as does the parameter of policy persistence, ρ, which falls into the range of 0.9.

Interpretation of the results in table 2.4 suggests that during the 1990s, the Bank of Israel's conduct of monetary policy, as reflected in its reaction function, was similar in most respects to that of the major Western central banks. The only noticeable difference was a weaker stance on changes in inflation expectations.

One possible explanation of our results is that we omitted the inflation target from the estimated specification. The basic specification assumes that the BOI had a zero-inflation target. The announced target, however, was always greater than zero although it declined over time. Over the years, deviations from the target were not ostracized and central bankers "paid" for missing the target only by absorbing criticism from the daily press. Since these deviations were quite significant, we cannot rule out the possibility that the central bankers had a "real" inflation target that was different from the one announced by the government. Moreover, since at least 1995, the BOI has had a stronger stance on disinflation than the government (which sets the target). Therefore, it is not clear that a specification including the government-specified inflation target does not contain biases of its own.

The result of including the inflation target is reported in table 2.4, equation (5). Notably, this specification raises the aggressiveness factor to 1 and entails a small reduction in persistence from 0.9 to 0.8. The similarity between both specifications suggests that our basic result, high persistence and accommodating behavior, remains valid.

A problem that emerges from our estimation is that all reported regressions suffer from a low Durbin-Watson coefficient. Note that all of the estimations were made using the Hanson pre-whitening procedure, which should already account for serial correlation in the error term. This suggests that the regressions suffer from an omitted-variable problem. We tried to estimate the equations with several additional variables suggested by CGG (1998): lagged inflation, changes in money supply, the Fed and Bundesbank rates, and the real NIS–US$ exchange rate. Like CGG (1998), we found that these variables are either insignificant or contribute very little to the estimation. In particular, they do not resolve the problem of a low Durbin-Watson value.

Therefore, we estimated equation (1) of table 2.4 using the second lag of the interest rate. Equation (4) shows that by adding an additional lag we can eliminate the serial correlation in the errors. This estimation, however, results in the reweighting of the central bank's reaction function in favor of countercyclical

Table 2.5. GMM Estimations of Reaction Function with Structural Break in 1994

Sample	1:1990–12:2000	1:1990–12:2000	1:1990–12:2000	1:1990–12:2000
Equation	(1)	(2)	(3)	(4)
Dependent variable	r_t	r_t	r_t	r_t
C	0.007 (0.001)	0.005 (0.001)	0.007 (0.002)	−0.004 (0.009)
r_{t-1}	0.873 (0.016)	1.760 (0.032)	0.872 (0.016)	0.664 (0.011)
π_t^e	0.102 (0.007)	0.069 (0.008)	0.100 (0.008)	0.194 (0.016)
X_t	0.051 (0.014)	0.166 (0.016)	−0.001 (0.001)	0.019 (0.009)
X_t*D1994	−0.051 (0.020)	−0.166 (0.019)	0.001 (0.001)	
r_{t-1}*D1994				0.100 (0.009)
r_{t-2}		−0.842 (0.023)		
D1994				
β, Aggressiveness	0.80	0.84	0.77	0.58/.82
γ	0.4/0	2.02/0	0.008/0	0.056/0.088
ρ	0.87	0.92	0.87	0.66/0.76
N	130	130	130	130
R²adj	0.88	0.83	0.87	0.88
D.W.	1.23	1.98	1.22	2.15

Standard errors are in parentheses.

Equation (1) and (2) are in natural logs.

X_t: (1) GDP gap. (3) ΔU

Instruments include the following variables at lags of $t_{-1}-t_{-12}$: $r, y, \Delta e, \Delta er, \Delta m2, \pi q$

Aggressiveness (see CGG, 2000) is defined as the coefficient of inflation expectations divided by the coefficient of $1-r_{t-1}$.

policy and away from inflation expectations. Alternatively, the existence of strong serial correlation may be interpreted as high persistence, which fits nicely with the view that we provided earlier, stressing persistence as seen in the consistent maintenance of a high real interest rate.

After having found a break in the data around August 1994, we proceeded to estimate equation (3) with a structural-break dummy, that is, a break dummy in the coefficients. We estimated a variety of regressions with a variety of break dummies. Table 2.5 reports our significant findings. Before analyzing them, we should report the hypotheses that the data refuted. We could not find a break in the policy-aggressiveness coefficient, β. Neither could we find evidence for compound changes, for example, a change in persistence and a change in aggressiveness.

The most significant break seems to be the decline in the role of countercyclical policy. Equations (1), (2), and (3) seem to show that after the break in August 1994 the BOI assigned no weight to countercyclical policy in its reaction function. Although the attempt to control for serial correlation (equation [2]) generates an implausibly high measure of countercyclical policy, the basic outcome remains the same.

In equation (4), we tested for a change in policy persistence and found a minor increase. The overall result, however, was such that both parameters, persistence and aggressiveness, are lower in this specification than in the benchmark specifications of table 2.4.

Finally, we estimated the model for the post-break period (1995–2000). Table 2.6 reports our results. Equation (1) seems to indicate that the aggressiveness factor rose from 0.8 to 1.1 during this period. The countercyclical-policy reaction parameter is also quite high (0.5), at odds with earlier findings. However, once we introduce another lag to the interest rate (equation [2]), similar results to those obtained throughout were obtained again, that is, the reaction of the central bank to inflation expectations and its persistence did not change in the second half of the 1990s. We can also find support for the declining role of countercyclical policy during that period. In equation (3), which includes the inflation target, we discover again that the target contributes very little to the outcomes of the relevant coefficients. If anything, the outcomes are somewhat lower than the benchmark specification (equation [1]), suggesting that Elkayam's (2002) finding may be due largely to the behavior of the BOI before 1995, after which the bank actually pursued a zero-inflation target.

Table 2.6. GMM Estimations of Reaction Function with Dummies

| Sample | 1:1995–12:2000 | 1:1995–12:2000 | 1:1995–12:2000 |
Equation	(1)	(2)	(3)
Dependent variable	r_t	r_t	r_t
C	0.003 (0.001)	0.006 (0.001)	0.013 (0.003)
r_{t-1}	0.904 (0.011)	1.283 (0.010)	0.854 (0.022)
r_{t-2}		−0.380 (0.008)	
π_t^e	0.107 (0.007)	0.080 (0.040)	0.134 (0.014)
X_t	0.046 (0.004)	−0.002 (0.002)	0.0185 (0.005)
D1998:8	−0.016 (0.001)	−0.013 (0.000)	−0.016 (0.001)
D1998:11	0.044 (0.003)	0.026 (0.001)	0.0256 (0.001)
π_t^T			0.002 (0.0005)
Aggressiveness	1.11	0.83	0.92
γ	0.48	0	0.11
ρ	0.90	0.90	0.85
N	72	72	72
R^2adj	0.96	0.98	0.97
D.W.	1.60	2.02	1.20

Standard errors are in parentheses.

The equation is in natural logs.

X_t: the GDP gap.

Instruments include the following variables at lags of t_{-1}–t_{-12}: r, y, Δe, Δer, $\Delta m2$, πq

Aggressiveness (see CGG, 2000) is defined as the coefficient of inflation expectations divided by the coefficient of $1-r_{t-1}$.

Expansions of the Bank of Israel Reaction Function

The CGG estimates reported above indicate that the Bank of Israel did not behave as major central banks did. However, figure 2.3 shows that the BOI raised real interest rates quite aggressively in some instances. In this subsection, we attempt to account for this behavior by expanding the basic CGG model to include a variable that measures positive deviations of actual inflation from the inflation target:

$$dev_t = \begin{cases} 0 & \pi_t <= \bar{\bar{\pi}}_t \\ \pi_t - \bar{\bar{\pi}}_t & \pi_t > \bar{\bar{\pi}}_t \end{cases}$$

where $\bar{\bar{\pi}}_t$ is the upper limit of the inflation target band (see figure 2.1).

The results of the estimation, reported in table 2.7, support the hypothesis that the BOI acted aggressively only when *actual* inflation deviated from the target. This form of aggressiveness, which an observer might regard as panic, also seems to have declined somewhat after 1994. In the later years, the central bank reacted aggressively but less intensively to these deviations, perhaps indicating that it was more confident than it had been about its ability to attain the target.

Table 2.7. GMM Estimations of Reaction Function with Deviations from Inflation Target

Sample	1:1992–12:2000	1:1992–12:2000
Equation	(1)	(2)
Dependent variable	r_t	r_t
C	0.009 (0.001)	0.005 (0.001)
r_{t-1}	0.896 (0.006)	0.907 (0.009)
π_t^e	0.006 (0.004)	0.057 (0.006)
X_t	0.079 (0.009)	0.094 (0.013)
X_t^*D1994	−0.092 (0.011)	−0.106 (0.013)
Deviation	0.010 (0.001)	0.016 (0.003)
Deviation*D1994		−0.006 (0.003)
β, Aggressiveness	0.6	0.6
γ	0.8/0	1/0
ρ	0.90	0.90
N	108	108
R²adj	0.93	0.93
D.W.	1.17	1.18

Standard errors are in parentheses.
Equations (1) and (2) are in natural logs.
X_t: (1) GDP gap.
Instruments include the following variables at lags of $t_{-1} - t_{-12}$: $r, y, \Delta e, \Delta er, \Delta m2, \pi q$
Aggressiveness (see CGG, 2000) is defined as the coefficient of inflation
expectations divided by the coefficient of $1 - r_{t-1}$.

EVALUATION OF BOI POLICY

Above, we outlined the policy-reaction function of the Bank of Israel. In particular, we showed that the BOI did not behave in the same manner as the central banks surveyed by CGG. How should we evaluate this outcome? One straightforward measure for the success of the policy may be gleaned by observing the difference between the inflation target and actual inflation. Another measure that we propose is the difference between actual inflation and inflation expectations. The first measure gauges how well the central bank used its policy instrument to attain its target. Missing the target may lower the credibility of the central bank. The second measure provides a proxy for the cost of a potential failure of monetary policy. Deviations of actual inflation from inflation expectations have real costs (Sussman, 2000) since they may cause real changes in key macroeconomic variables such as real wages (unemployment) and real interest rates (investment).

Figure 2.4 plots these two measures. Both are quite volatile, making it seem as though the central bank had difficulties in achieving its inflation target. Moreover, this failure apparently resulted in substantial and obviously unforeseen differences between expected and actual inflation. It is useful to calculate the mean deviation and coefficient of variation (volatility) of the two measures. The results of these calculations, reported in table 2.8, allow us to draw several conclusions.

1. There seems to be a tradeoff between accuracy and volatility in terms of controlling inflation. May this finding be generalized to other countries? See Woodford (2001) for discussion of some of these issues.

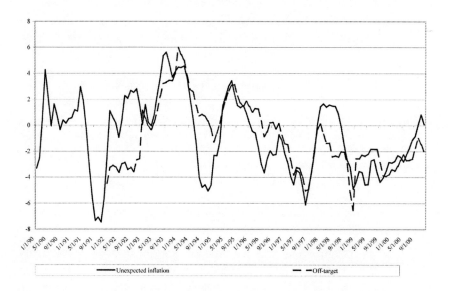

Figure 2.4. Deviations from Inflation Target and Inflation Expectations: Israel, 1990–2000 (percent).

Table 2.8. Deviation of Actual Inflation from Target and from
            Expected Inflation

	1990–2000		1990–94		1995–2000	
	π-target	π-π^e	π-target	π-π^e	π-target	π-π^e
Mean	−0.8%	−0.8%	0.3%	0.4%	−1.6%	−1.4%
Std. deviation	2.9	2.6	3.3	3.0	2.3	2.1
Coefficient of variation	3.9	3.0	12.9	8.5	1.4	1.4

2. The public tended to believe the announced inflation target. The deviations reported in the table for both measures are similar, indicating that, on average, inflation expectations tend to follow the announced target.

3. The BOI's reaction function generated relatively volatile deviations from the target and from inflation expectations. The standard deviations and the coefficients of variation are high. This suggests that the economy was exposed to significant risks related to instability in real variables.

4. The central bank's reaction function and its effect on the economy changed in the second half of the 1990s. During the early 1990s, the BOI tended, on average, to err slightly on the upper side of the target and expectations and volatility were quite high. In the second half of the 1990s, the bank tended to undershoot the target and inflation expectations. The error was much larger than in the early 1990s but volatility was smaller. Did the BOI become better at controlling inflation? Did it become more conservative? May the emphasis on the inflation target at the expense of conducting countercyclical policy account for this change? Was the economy exposed to fewer shocks during the latter period? Either way, given the observed enhanced ability to control the inflation rate as reflected by lower volatility, it is unlikely that the Bank of Israel consistently erred. A more likely interpretation the findings suggests that the BOI pursued a tougher disinflationary policy than the one agreed to with the government. By so doing, it also misled the public. The findings in table 2.6 (compare equation [1] with equation [3], which includes the government-set inflation target) provide some econometric evidence for this claim.

CONCLUSIONS

The variety of approaches that we used to estimate the reaction function, and the policy evaluation flowing from this analysis, tend to support the claim that the Bank of Israel's reaction function in the 1990s differed from those of the central banks studied by CGG and Segherri (2002). We found little evidence that the central bank had become more resolute in fighting off deviations of actual inflation from inflation expectations (or the inflation target). Although the aggressiveness coefficient in our regressions increased slightly in the late 1990s, it remained low by Western standards. We found evidence supporting the hypothesis that the Bank of Israel had abandoned countercyclical policy measures in the late 1990s. The phenomenon of countercyclical policy measures was characteristic of most central banks surveyed at the time.

The BOI implemented its policy in the 1990s mainly by raising the ex post real interest rate and keeping it high. Thus, disinflation was achieved primarily through real currency appreciation and economic slowdown. It seems that while the Bank of Israel was persistent in its policy, it did not respond more aggressively to changes in inflation expectations in the late 1990s than it did in the early 1990s. However, it did respond to deviations of inflation from the upper bound of the inflation target band. Therefore, one may argue that the BOI adopted an Ss-type rule, that is, refraining from an immediate and aggressive response to changes in inflation expectations until actual inflation deviated from target in a significant way. Moreover, it seems that after 1995, the actual inflation target pursued by the Bank of Israel was zero—much lower than the government's official target.

Our findings may explain the similar and high volatility of the deviations from the inflation target, or from inflation expectations, reported in table 2.8. This high volatility may be inefficient and inflict considerable costs for the economy (Woodford, 2001). Finally, our method allowed us to identify two short-term policy inconsistencies. The first is related to the rate cut in August 1998. Our estimations show that this was a departure from the rule observed before and after that point. Its political reasons have not escaped observers of the Israeli economy. The second deviation relates to the BOI's response to the October 1998 financial crisis. The finding that it was a nonrecurrent deviation suggests that the response was efficient this time, since it did not permanently alter the behavior of policy in the wake of an exogenous shock to the economy.

APPENDIX: THE EFFECT OF MONETARY POLICY ON UNEMPLOYMENT

As this chapter showed, the Bank of Israel's reaction function since the second half of the 1990s was focused only on fighting inflation. Even before 1995, the weight of countercyclical policy in the reaction function was low. Critics of BOI monetary policy have suggested that the policy adversely affected unemployment. Indeed, Liviatan and Sussman (2002), Lavi and Sussman (1999), and Sussman (2000) showed that the tough stance on inflation contributed directly to unemployment through the effect of real interest rates on aggregate demand and indirectly via the effect of surprise disinflation on labor demand. Here we provide new estimates of the effect of the monetary-policy rule on unemployment in Israel.

We assume, like Taylor (1993), that interest rates affect actual output in two ways—through investment and through consumption. We assume that the effect on consumption is temporary and the effect on investment is more lasting due to its effect on the accumulation of the capital stock. The accumulation of capital stock affects future hiring decisions and, in turn, feeds into higher unemployment in a more permanent way.

We define unemployment as the sum of the natural unemployment rate U^N and the temporary one U^T:

$$U_t = U_t^N + U_t^T \tag{I.1}$$

The Longer-Term Effect

Assuming a CES production function, we can estimate a labor-demand curve and then estimate the effect of real interest rates on capital accumulation (investment) and calculate the effect of real interest rates on labor demand:

$$L_t^D = L(\alpha, K_t, w_t) \tag{I.2}$$

$$\frac{dK_t}{dt} = f(r_t, \bullet) \tag{I.3}$$

We estimated labor demand as a function of real wages, capital stock, and TFP in a two-stage least-squares approach, controlling for labor-supply effects such as participation rates, the share of labor with eleven to sixteen years of schooling, immigration, and unemployment benefits. Table A2.1 reports the results.

Table A2.1. Estimates of the Effect of the Bank of Israel Monetary Reaction Function on Unemployment

Sample: Equation	1973–2002 (1)	1990–2002 (2)	1990–2002 (3)
Dependent variable	L	Δk	ΔU_t
C	4.29 (0.55)	0.004 (0.001)	−0.003 (0.001)
TFP_t	0.64 (0.07)		
K_t	0.68 (0.02)		
W_t	−0.38 (0.04)		
r_t		−0.055 (0.018)	0.124 (0.055)
Δk_{t-1}		0.316 (0.113)	
Δk_{t-2}		0.536 (0.107)	
N	120	52	52
R^2adj	0.98	0.85	0.07
D.W.	0.50	2.13	1.74

Standard errors are in parentheses.
All variables are in logarithms.
Equation (1): two-stage least-squares estimation using labor-force participation rates, immigration, average unemployment benefit rate, and share of labor with 11–16 years of schooling as a proxy for labor supply.
Equation (2): quarterly market real interest rate on overdraft, at 3-period lag.
Equation (3): quarterly market real interest rate on overdraft, at 1-period lag.

We then estimated the effect of the real interest rate on investment. We found that investment, as measured by the change in capital stock, is sensitive to the real interest rate. The results are reported in table 2.1. Given the coefficients reported, a 1 percentage-point change in the quarterly real interest rate reduces capital stock by 0.2% a year. If the real short-term interest rate in developed economies is 1%–2%, this implies that by raising real interest rates to 4%–5%, the Bank of Israel caused the capital stock to fall short of its otherwise desired level by 0.4%–0.6%.

Using the estimated labor-demand function, the effect of persistent high real interest at levels above 4% per year would translate into a loss of 0.3%–0.5% of jobs per year, quite a significant fraction given that this effect is cumulative. The persistence of the reaction function as shown above suggests that a permanent real interest rate that is *1 percentage point higher* than necessary to achieve the inflation target could have caused a cumulative job loss of 1.5% of the labor force during the 1995–2004 period.

Short-Term Effects

To estimate the effect of the Bank of Israel's reaction function on short-term unemployment, we assume that quarterly changes in the unemployment rate are due to changes in short-term employment:

$$U_t^T = \frac{dU_t}{dt} \tag{I.4}$$

We then estimate the following equation to obtain the short-term effect of real interest rates on unemployment:[3]

$$\Delta U_t = \alpha + r_t + \varepsilon_t \tag{I.5}$$

The results, reported in table 2.1, suggest that a 1 percentage point increase in the quarterly real interest rate raises short-term unemployment by about 0.1%. Although the effect is small—since we defined transitory unemployment as the change in the unemployment rate—these small effects may accumulate due to hysteresis. At the maximum, assuming full hysteresis, the cumulative effect on unemployment of a 1 percentage-point increase in the quarterly real interest rate could render up to 3.5% of the labor force jobless. Taken together, the long-term and short-term effects may account for anywhere from 1.5 to 5 percentage points of the reported unemployment rate. Thus, assuming a natural unemployment rate of 5%–6%, much of today's unemployment rate, nearly 10%, can be traced to tight monetary policy.

Notes

The "Monetary Policy and the Disinflation Process in Israel, 1985–2000" section (pp. 47–50) is based on Liviatan and Sussman (2002).

1. I thank Dudu Elkayam for this suggestion.
2. The upper bound of the confidence interval of the estimated parameters yields an aggressiveness factor of 1.39.

3. This specification omits other possible variables that may affect transitory unemployment. We assume, however, that other labor-supply or demand shocks do not correlate with real interest rates and are part of the error term.

References

Bar-Efrat, O., and G. Bufman. "The Bank of Israel's Reaction Function: Can Interest-Rate Changes be Predicted?" *Economic Quarterly* (March 2002): 46–60 (Hebrew).

Barro, R. J., and D. B. Gordon. "Rules, Discretion and Reputation in a Model of Monetary Policy." *Journal of Monetary Economics* 12 (July 1983): 101–21.

Clarida, R., J. Gali, and M. Gertler. "Monetary Rules in Practice: Some International Evidence." *European Economic Review* 42 (1998): 1033–67.

———. "Monetary Policy Rules and Macroeconomic Stability: Evidence and Some Theory." *Quarterly Journal of Economics* 115, no. 1 (February 2000): 147–80.

Elkayam, D. "Inflation Target and Monetary Policy—a Forecasting Model." Discussion Paper 2001.1. Bank of Israel Monetary Department, 2001 (Hebrew).

Lavi, Y., and N. Sussman. "The Phillips Curve in Israel and its Induced Policy Shifts." In *Inflation and Disinflation in Israel*. Bank of Israel Conference Proceedings, Jerusalem, 1999.

Liviatan, N., and N. Sussman "Disinflation Process in Israel in the Past Decade." In *The Israeli Economy, 1985–1998: From Government Intervention to Market Economics*, ed. A. Ben-Bassat, 129–56. Cambridge, MA: MIT Press, 2002.

Melnick, R. "A Peek into the Governor's Chamber: The Israeli Case." Interdisciplinary Center, Herzliyya, 2002.

Segherri, S. "A Stylized Model of Monetary Policy." *World Economic Outlook* (April 2002): 95–98.

Sussman, N. "The Effect of Surprises on Real Wages and Unemployment in a Disinflationary Process." *Economic Quarterly* (September 2000): 441–48 (Hebrew).

Svensson, L. E. O. "Optimal Inflation Targets, 'Conservative' Central Banks, and Linear Inflation Targets." *American Economic Review* 87 (1997): 98–114.

Taylor, J. B. "Discretion versus Policy Rules in Practice." *Carnegie-Rochester Series on Public Policy* 39 (1993): 195–214.

Woodford, M. "The Taylor Rule and Optimal Monetary Policy." *American Economic Review* (2001): 232–37.

3

The Liberalization of Israel's Foreign-Exchange Market, 1950–2002

Michael Michaely

THE LEGAL FRAMEWORK

In interwar Palestine, foreign-exchange transactions were completely unrestricted under the British Mandate as they were in Britain itself. When World War II began, however, controls were imposed. The basic legal framework for their existence and implementation was the Defense (Finance) Regulation of 1941. In 1948, when the State of Israel was established, the government adopted this statute (like a variety of other Mandatory laws and regulations) and, by amending it periodically, used it to control foreign-exchange transactions and restrict the foreign-exchange market for the next thirty years.

In March 1978, the existing law was replaced by the Foreign Exchange Control Law, 5738-1978. This change followed the important step of liberalization in the market, which we discuss in some detail below. The lifespan of the new law, although somewhat shorter than that of its predecessor, was also substantial: it governed foreign-exchange activity until May 1998, when it was replaced by a third law.

The laws of 1948 (i.e., the 1941 Regulation) and 1978 shared one essential element: both proscribed any foreign-exchange transaction that the controlling authority did not specifically permit. Thus, they were accompanied by regulations that allowed specific transactions. Such permits could be general or comprehensive (e.g., allowing anyone to import a given product), class-specific (e.g., allowing charitable institutions to import a given product), or personal (allowing Mr. Y. to import a given quantity of a given product during a given period.) The list of permits was periodically changed and provided, in essence, the guidelines for the application of foreign-exchange controls.

The third major legal change, introduced in May 1998, marked a radical conceptual departure from its two predecessors by moving from a "positive list" to a "negative list."[1] Whereas the two earlier laws prohibited everything unless specifically permitted, the new law declared every transaction permissible unless specifically prohibited. Thus, the new statute was accompanied by changing lists of prohibitions rather than by lists of permissions.

Finally, right at the start of 2003, foreign-exchange controls were abolished altogether (still within the framework of the 1998 law). Since then, all foreign-exchange transactions have been completely unrestricted with only one exception: regulation of activities by financial sectors in order to reduce risks. The most important example of this type concerns foreign-exchange transactions by the banking system, which are regulated by the supervisor of banks. Similarly, transactions of pension funds and insurance companies are regulated by the relevant authorities.

The 1948 (1941) law assigned responsibility for the mechanism of foreign-exchange control to the controller of foreign exchange at the Ministry of Finance and the Foreign Exchange Division, which he headed. Thus, the controller determined, issued, and managed the list of permits. This official was responsible, at a critical period in the operation of the control system, for the foreign-exchange budget (the nature of which is discussed below) and for monitoring and enforcing the law. The 1978 law abolished the division and transferred its functions to a newly established Department of Foreign-Exchange Control at the Bank of Israel (the director of which became the controller of foreign exchange). Thus, the handling of foreign-exchange controls moved from the Ministry of Finance to the Bank of Israel. Two years before the total deregulation of foreign exchange in January 2003, this department (and the function of controller) ceased to exist as such and was renamed the Foreign Exchange Activity Department. Its functions became, primarily, those of monitoring, collecting data on foreign-exchange transactions (which transactors must still provide), and research.

The life-spans of the two laws that prevailed during most of this time—those of 1941 (1948–77) and 1978 (1978–99)—correspond roughly to two subperiods into which we may divide the period analyzed here (1950–2002). In the first subperiod, from the early 1950s to 1977, significant liberalization of foreign-exchange control took place mainly in current-account transactions, that is, imports and exports of goods and services, and, to some extent, unilateral transfers. From late 1977 on, the liberalization process focused largely on capital-account transactions. It is this distinction that marks the analysis of the subperiods.

LIBERALIZATION OF CURRENT-ACCOUNT TRANSACTIONS, 1950–77

Foreign-Exchange Allocation: The 1950s

As we recall, the law adopted by the government of Israel upon the establishment of the state—the Mandate-era Defense (Finance) Regulation—prohibited all foreign-exchange transactions except those specifically permitted. Indeed, hardly any "general" permits existed at first; each transaction required a specific permit. On the foreign-exchange receipts side, all proceeds had to be submitted to the government and sold to it at the official exchange rate (or, for a short while, at one of several rates).[2] To pay for external transactions, one required a specific permit and a specific foreign-exchange allocation.

For imports of goods and services (the main component of external transactions), the issue of permits was governed mostly by a two-stage mechanism. First, foreign exchange had to be allocated; this was done by the Foreign Exchange Department of the Finance Ministry, headed by the controller of foreign exchange. Then an import permit was issued by one government ministry or another, depending on the nature of the imports. For instance, the Ministry of Industry and Trade handled imports of industrial raw materials, the Ministry of Agriculture dealt with agricultural materials, and the Ministry of Health concerned itself with medical supplies. It was the issue of the import permit that ensured that the foreign-exchange allocation for payment would be made.

At first, this mechanism worked haphazardly. By 1952, however, a first attempt had been made to set the allocations within a "foreign-exchange budget" that was drawn up for fiscal year 1952–53. Starting with the 1953–54 budget, an annual foreign-exchange budget was drawn up by a newly established office at the Ministry of Finance, the Bureau of the Budget.[3] The point of departure for the foreign-exchange budget was the revenue side. Revenues included all receipts of foreign exchange save short-term capital movements (external borrowing or use of the foreign reserves). Naturally, this budget was an estimate rather than a commitment. The expenditure side, however—which theoretically equaled total revenues—was a commitment of an absolute rather than conditional nature, although the allocation of foreign exchange for the purposes specified in the budget was not entirely automatic. The budget determined the magnitude of imports by categories. Depending on the nature of the category, the relevant ministries were given an allowance made up of the total value of the import permits that they were entitled to issue. Any issue of an import permit by a ministry (like any expenditure) had to be validated by a representative of the Finance Ministry. Only thus was the attendant allocation of foreign exchange assured.[4]

This mechanism of foreign-exchange allocation and import permits lasted throughout the 1950s. In the early 1960s, following a gradual liberalization process that will be surveyed shortly, it lost much of its practical significance. By 1964, the foreign-exchange budget was discontinued altogether.

Severe Foreign-Exchange Shortage and Its Alleviation: The First Half of the 1950s

In the late 1940s and early 1950s, an overwhelming "shortage" of foreign exchange (i.e., excess demand at the official price) developed. If Israel had had a free market for foreign exchange, a substantial real devaluation would have taken place as a consequence of two developments: on the one hand, a marked increase in demand for imports and, consequently, for foreign exchange, which must have taken place with the dramatic increase in population and in production during Israel's first few years, and, on the other hand, stability—if not decline—in "autonomous" sources of foreign exchange (unilateral transfers and long and medium-term external borrowing).

Israel's economic policy, however, led to substantial appreciation, rather than devaluation, of the real rate of exchange. Large fiscal deficits and monetary expansion resulted in strong inflationary pressures, even though a massive system of price controls and rationing repressed expression in the form of higher domestic prices. Concurrently, the nominal exchange rate remained unchanged between September 1949 (when it was raised by just 7%) and February 1952. Even in terms of the controlled and repressed official prices, substantial real appreciation was evident. Thus, from the end of 1949 to early 1952 the (official) cost-of-living index rose by roughly 50%, whereas the dollar prices of Israel's imports climbed by 20%—a 25% excess of the former over the latter. Again, this happened at a time when a free market for foreign exchange would have engendered a large real depreciation.

One indication (although not a measurement) of the extent of disequilibrium in a foreign-exchange market—or the intensity of a "shortage" of foreign exchange—is the gap between black-market and official exchange rates.[5] Table 3.1 shows where Israel stood in this regard.

The process of nominal devaluation that began in February 1952 drastically attenuated the disequilibrium in the foreign-exchange market. A system of multiple exchange rates was introduced, in which two rates—.714 and 1.000 Israel pounds (IL) per dollar—were added to the existing rate of IL .357 per dollar, with most transactions being conducted at one of the two higher rates. This resulted in an immediate doubling of the (average) nominal exchange rate, with further depreciation occasioned by a gradual shift of transactions to higher rates. In 1953, an even higher rate—IL 1.800 per dollar—was added to the system, and by the end of 1954 almost all transactions were conducted at this rate, which in early 1955 became the new, uniform official exchange rate. Thus, within a period of about two and a half years, a nominal devaluation of 400% (that is, a fivefold increase of the rate) took place. The real devaluation was lower, of course, but very impressive nevertheless, at 150% between 1951 and 1955—a factor of two and a half.[6] This represents a more than doubling of the real rate from 1949 to 1955—an outcome that, in a rough way, might have been yielded by an unrestricted foreign-exchange market.

Again, the black-market exchange rate may provide an indication of the attenuation of the disequilibrium. On the eve of the February 1952 devaluation, this rate was more than six times higher than the official rate.[7] In the first few months after the devaluation, the ratio of the two fell by half, to around 3. In early 1955, when the devaluation process was completed and a new uniform rate was established, the black-market rate exceeded the official rate by a factor of only 1.2–1.3. This ratio was maintained, amid some fluctuations, for several years.

Partly Free, Compartmentalized Foreign-Exchange Markets: The 1950s

During the 1950s, the government established several segregated markets in which foreign exchange (directly or through immediate proxies) was transacted legally (or semi-legally) at freely determined rates (that were nevertheless subjected, at least occasionally, to government intervention in the market).[8]

Table 3.1. Black-Market and Formal Exchange Rates, Quarterly, 1949–56 (Israel pounds per dollar)

Period[a]		Black-Market Rate (1)	Formal Rate[b] (2)	Ratio of (1) to (2) (3)
1949	Q1	0.379		1.1
	Q2	0.425	0.333	1.3
	Q3	0.419		1.3
	Q4	0.498		1.4
1950	Q1	0.573		1.6
	Q2	0.635		1.8
	Q3	0.748		2.1
	Q4	0.862	0.357	2.4
1951	Q1	1.349		3.8
	Q2	1.221		3.4
	Q3	1.183		3.3
	Q4	2.402		6.7
1952	Q1	2.583	0.460	5.6
	Q2	2.663	0.700	3.8
	Q3	2.544	0.800	3.2
	Q4	2.240	0.790	2.8
1953	Q1	2.511	0.770	3.3
	Q2	2.400	0.800	3.0
	Q3	2.314	0.880	2.6
	Q4	2.442	0.890	2.7
1954	Q1	2.763	1.240	2.2
	Q2	2.613	1.420	1.8
	Q3	2.553	1.680	1.5
	Q4	2.495	1.710	1.4
1955	Q1	2.300		1.3
	Q2	2.225		1.2
	Q3	2.263		1.2
	Q4	2.423		1.3
			1.800	
1956	Q1	2.407		1.3
	Q2	2.379		1.3
	Q3	2.476		1.4
	Q4	2.748		1.5

Source: M. Michaely, 1975, p. 46, table 2–9.

[a] Most rates given are for end-of-period.

[b] For the 1952–54 period, when a formal multiple-rate system was in effect, the rates are averages weighted by the size of imports.

These mechanisms were intended to partly relieve acute problems that the low level of the official exchange rate created. Here we discuss three such schemes (leaving aside others of lesser importance): "imports without payment," the PAMAZ market, and the NATAD market.

"Imports without Payment"

The popular term "imports without payment" stood for the more technical and more accurate term "imports without allocation of foreign exchange."[9] The permits for such imports specified that they would not require, and would not be entitled to, an allocation of foreign exchange. (For this reason, as noted above, they were not included in the foreign-exchange budget.) Such imports obviously had to be financed from some other source, which, in turn, was exempt from selling foreign exchange to the Treasury, was available for these imports, and was allowed to finance them. Sometimes this was inherent in the nature of the transaction. Thus, gifts of goods from abroad or personal imports by immigrants could not involve any transfer of or payment in foreign exchange. However, there were some schemes that allowed imports of goods through payment by what would have been a foreign-exchange transaction, such as various unilateral transfers. Moreover, even a "pure" movement of goods was occasionally, through one device or another, a transferable transaction for which a market was formed. Thus, the "imports without payment" schemes were characterized by three facts: transactions conducted under their terms were transferable, they involved a market, and such markets specified an explicit or implicit price of foreign exchange.

The establishment of this group of compartmentalized markets was intended to serve several targets. On the foreign-exchange receipts side, the purpose was to encourage unilateral transfers (donations to private or semi-public organizations, immigrants' capital, etc.) and private capital imports (primarily foreign investment in Israeli companies) by offering a higher exchange rate than the official one. On the expenditure side, the main goals were to facilitate the importation of goods that were considered "essential" (certain raw materials and capital goods) yet were not granted an allocation in the foreign-exchange budget, and to allow some imports of "luxury" goods without appearing to do this explicitly through foreign exchange allocations. Associated with this target was the intention to absorb some private-sector income.

The exact regulations—who was entitled to sell foreign exchange (directly or embodied in goods), who was entitled to buy, the nature of the mechanism, and the manner of setting the exchange rate—varied frequently, sometimes every few weeks. Generally speaking, most of the time the exchange rates in these markets were determined freely in each compartmentalized market. Episodes in which the government itself set the rate—at a submarket level— were short-lived because the market then tended to disappear. The market exchange rate always exceeded the official rate by a wide margin and usually resembled the black-market rate due to the bidirectional relationship of these two rates.

Table 3.2. Imports with and without Allocation of Foreign Exchange, 1949–54 (in percentages of aggregate imports of goods)

	1949	1950	1951	1952	1953	1954
Aggregate imports	100.2	100.0	100.0	100.0	100.0	100.0
With foreign-exchange allocation	84.7	82.9	81.2	79.7	78.7	87.0
Without foreign-exchange allocation	15.3	17.1	18.8	20.3	21.3	13.0
Thereof (ratio to aggregate imports)						
Capital transfers	6.8	7.0	8.3	9.1	8.6	2.9
Imports by immigrants	6.3	5.0	3.2	3.0	1.1	.5
Gifts	2.2	5.1	7.3	8.2	7.4	6.3
Other[a]	—	—	—	—	4.2	3.3

Source: R. Gronau, 1970, p. 59, Table 1.

[a] Data for "other" imports without allocation are missing for 1949–52, resulting in underestimation of the aggregate size of the "without allocation" category for these years.

In the first half of the 1950s, the magnitude of transactions in the market (or markets) was significant (table 3.2) and amounted to roughly 20% of total imports in 1949–54. Capital imports always accounted for a large share of market sources. Imports by immigrants declined steadily—as might be expected, since mass immigration ended by late 1951—and almost disappeared by 1954 as immigration tapered off to inconsequential levels. "Gifts," on the other hand, increased in size during the period, largely because a specific mechanism for the importation of gifts (the so-called "scrip" scheme) facilitated the transfer of some capital, as well as some unilateral transfers, in the disguise of "gifts."

The steep decline in the importance of the "imports without payment" category in 1954, and particularly its capital-transfers component, gave early indication of the drastic contraction of this market after the mid-1950s. The massive devaluation in 1952–54 and the establishment of an official exchange rate that presumably approximated an equilibrium level made this special market almost redundant. The two other schemes described below, on the other hand, emerged in the second half of the 1950s. They were partly related to the development of a new disequilibrium in the system during a period in which the nominal exchange rate remained unchanged for a rather long stretch of seven years (early 1955–early 1962).

PAMAZ

The PAMAZ program (Hebrew acronym for "Foreign Currency Deposit") was essentially a retention quota for exporters.[10] Exporters were allowed to withhold a certain proportion of their export proceeds—instead of selling them to the Treasury—and to use this part to pay for imports of raw materials that they needed for the manufacture of additional exports (instead of applying for a foreign-exchange allocation).

The scheme was presumably designed to relieve the bureaucratic inconvenience (and the cost) to exporters of having to obtain foreign-exchange allocations. However, it developed quite naturally into something beyond that. Often, the allowed quota of retention exceeded the value of raw materials actually required to produce the specified amount of exports. Furthermore, since the nature of these intermediates was not always easy to ascertain, other goods that had especially high profit margins in the domestic market (i.e., quota profits) were imported as well. Closely related to the foregoing, importation rights were often transferable de facto, although not de jure. (A full-fledged market for PAMAZ rights was never established.)

The exact details and the requisite size or nature of the export transaction in the PAMAZ scheme varied over time. Some of the variations were significant, for example, the fraction of the value of exports entitled to inclusion in the retention quota (sometimes this was 100%) and the degree of restrictiveness of the requirement that imports should be "in the line of production" of the exports that gave rise to the import entitlement. In addition, of course, the quota profits varied with the nature of each import product. Thus, the implicit exchange rate in the PAMAZ market varied substantially over time, among industries, and often among individual exporters, despite the limited de facto transferability of the importation rights. Naturally, information about these rates was hard to come by. Estimates of major industry averages in the mid-1950s pointed to a range of IL 2.50–IL 3.80 per dollar and an overall average of IL 3.00 in 1954–55 and IL 3.10–IL 4.80 and IL 3.50, respectively, in 1957. (The official exchange rate during these years, as we recall, was IL 1.80 per dollar.)

The PAMAZ program was introduced in 1953. At its peak, in 1955–56, it applied to some 15% of Israel's aggregate export transactions. In 1957 and 1958, however, it gradually lost its importance. Two events in 1956 contributed to its decline and, later on, to its demise. First, most export transactions became eligible for an alternative to the PAMAZ scheme: direct premiums. Second, imports of intermediates were liberalized; imports of raw materials were freed of quantitative restrictions and quota profits were eliminated. (See below.) Thus, the PAMAZ entitlement lost most of its value. Consequently, the scheme was discontinued by the end of 1959.

The NATAD Market

This market originated mainly in an important source of foreign exchange, German restitution payments to Israel residents.[11] These payments started in 1954 and assumed significant proportions in the latter half of the 1950s.[12] Although the size of restitution payments themselves must have been almost completely inelastic to the rate of foreign exchange, the size of transfers to Israel was responsive to this rate (or so, at least, was widely believed by the government). This prompted the government to offer a concessionary exchange rate to recipients of restitution payments.[13]

First, the sale of such receipts to the Treasury entitled the seller to a 20% bonus.[14] Second, the recipient was allowed to retain a given fraction of these receipts in the form of a foreign-exchange deposit. Such a deposit could serve, effectively, as a foreign-exchange-indexed liquid asset. More important, however, it could be used for purposes for which, at that period, virtually no foreign exchange-allocation was provided at all—mainly foreign travel, the importation of some "luxury" goods such as passenger cars, and investment in foreign securities. The fraction of this allowance started as 20% of the total transfer in each transaction but increased later on, incrementally, to 35%.

An important change in this scheme, which led to the establishment of a separate foreign-exchange market, took place in December 1958, when holders of restitution foreign-exchange deposits were allowed to sell them to any Israeli resident at a freely determined price (i.e., an exchange rate).[15] More important, the buyer in such transactions acquired the same specific rights of use of the foreign exchange that the original owner had held.

The size of the NATAD market was not overwhelming; in 1960, total sales in the market were less than $13 million.[16] In some categories of transactions, however—mainly foreign travel, for which nearly half of total transactions were made—it was a major source of foreign-exchange supply.[17]

The exchange rate in the NATAD market was freely determined and fluctuated. The actual fluctuations, however, were rather moderate because banks were entitled to buy NATAD foreign exchange for their own portfolios and, in practice, functioned as stabilizing speculators. The average exchange rate in the NATAD market (average of twelve monthly observations) was IL 2.31 per dollar in 1959 and IL 2.23 in 1960, as against the base rate of IL 2.16 (i.e., the rate at which all restitution receipts could be sold to the Treasury, and black-market rates of IL 2.62 and IL 2.47 in 1959 and 1960, respectively. These prices probably indicate that "shortages" of foreign exchange (i.e., the intensity of disequilibrium of the official exchange rate) were not overwhelming at this period.

The NATAD market operated for a three-year period (1959–61). In February 1962, in the wake of an official devaluation (from IL 1.80 per dollar to IL 3.00), the mechanism that established this market was abolished.

Relaxation of Foreign-Exchange Controls on Current Transactions

As noted, the major impetus for the initial dismantling of foreign-exchange controls was the radical devaluation of 1952–54 (and its accompaniment, rather restrictive macroeconomic policies). This drastically reduced disequilibrium in the foreign-exchange market and made the controls less restrictive if not redundant. The process of easing the controls, however, lasted many years and was long confined to current-account transactions, with few changes concerning transactions on capital account.[18]

The first declared act of liberalization took place in early 1956. From then on, most raw materials could be imported freely.[19] Within several years, this became true for most capital goods. Thus, foreign-exchange controls became almost ineffective for most imports of goods. Even for consumer goods, from the late 1950s the rules dictating the granting (or withholding) of an import permit had little to do with the availability of foreign exchange. Instead, imports were prohibited—partly or completely—if an Israeli manufacturer claimed that the goods could be provided from domestic manufacture. Thus, the principle in regulating imports was the protection of domestic manufacture rather than the availability of foreign exchange. Indeed, from the late 1950s onward, liberalization was debated in terms of lifting the protection granted by import restrictions.

Although foreign-exchange controls became largely ineffective on imports of goods by the late 1950s or early 1960s, little further relaxation of controls was undertaken during the next fifteen years. Control of imports of services—mainly foreign travel—remained in effect and, more importantly, the strict control of capital movements hardly changed. Similarly and relatedly, the general requirement to sell all proceeds of foreign exchange to the Treasury was maintained throughout. The next major step in the decontrolling of foreign exchange came in late 1977, and we will turn to this presently. First, however, we digress for a brief discussion of the fate of the mechanisms that protected domestic activities from competing imports. Strictly speaking, this is not part of the process analyzed here, the liberalization of the foreign-exchange market. Reference to it, however, complements the analysis thus far of the removal of constraints on current-account transactions.

By the end of the 1950s, as noted, most imports were admitted with hardly any foreign-exchange constraints. Imports that competed with domestic manufacture, however, were strictly regulated and often prohibited outright.[20] High tariffs were often imposed on such imports, but quantitative restrictions were the predominant means of protection. The requirement for import permits led to severe restriction of imports if not total ban.

The second "new economic policy," introduced in February 1962, led to a major change. This policy consisted of three major elements. The first was a large formal devaluation of about 67% (from IL 1.80 per dollar to IL 3.00). This was meant partly to create real depreciation in order to prevent balance-of-payments disequilibrium,[21] but mostly to compensate for the second major element of the policy, the elimination of export subsidies and import levies. Thus, the changes in the effective exchange rates—primarily the rate applying to export transactions—were much smaller than the change in the formal rate. The third element, perhaps the most important in the long run, was a decision in principle to lift the quantitative restrictions on imports, leaving only tariffs as the instrument of protection.

The implementation of this last policy measure was drawn-out and incomplete. First, it was decided to replace the quantitative restrictions (QRs) with equivalent tariffs, that is, tariffs at levels that would leave imports at the same level as that achieved by the abolished QRs. Separate committees were established to handle each area of activity; they were to decide whether to make the change at all (despite the declared general policy) and, if the QR were removed, to determine the level of the equivalent tariff. These committees were slow to form and slower in their deliberations. Thus, even after three years, by mid-1965, the conversion process was only partial. It was suspended altogether in 1965, with the onset of the major recession that lasted through 1967, and was completed only in the early 1970s. Even then, major exceptions remained, two of which are noteworthy: agricultural goods, in which most imports remain subject to QRs to this day, and imports from "third countries"—those other than the United States and the European Common Market (later the E.C. and the E.U.)—for which QRs were often stepped up instead of removed as these countries became cheaper sources. Not until the 1990s was the process of replacing QRs with tariffs applied to imports from these countries.

Gradually, tariffs were also lowered or abolished. Major stages in this process were associated with agreements with Israel's major trade partners. A set of agreements with the European Common Market and its successors, starting in the late 1960s and culminating in a free-trade agreement in 1977, led to the gradual abolition (over a decade) of tariffs on imports from this area. Similarly, a Free-Trade Area Agreement with the United States, concluded in 1985, resulted in the phaseout of tariffs on imports from this partner, again over a decade. Thus, by the end of the 1980s, protection by tariffs (and by QRs) was applied predominantly to imports from other countries, mainly those in eastern Asia. Starting in 1991, a new liberalization policy gradually lifted most protection from this trade as well. Thus, by the end of the 1990s, import protection was largely a thing of the past. Like the liberalization of the foreign-exchange market, a slow and steady process of freeing imports, nearly fifty years in duration, transformed a state of nearly hermetic protection into one of almost complete freedom.[22]

LIBERALIZATION OF THE CAPITAL ACCOUNT, 1977–2002

The "Ehrlich Liberalization," 1977–84

The first major act of liberalization that largely concerned the capital account was introduced by Minister of Finance Simcha Ehrlich, shortly after he assumed office following the accession of Israel's first non-Labor government.[23] The move, announced dramatically on October 28, 1977, was heralded as the dawn of a new era of economic liberalization. Although it proved to be less than that, it was nevertheless an important first step toward capital-account liberalization.

The reform consisted of two major components that were somewhat interrelated: relaxation of foreign-exchange controls and a change in the exchange-rate system (and in the rate). The main components of the reform were the following: (1) external borrowing, short- or long-term, was decontrolled (until then, restrictive permits were required); (2) nonresidents were allowed to hold domestic liquid assets including bank accounts; (3) residents who did business with the outside world were allowed to hold external deposits for the purpose of such transactions; (4) unilateral transfers abroad became easier; and finally, and not related to the capital account, (5) residents were allowed to buy substantial amounts of foreign exchange for foreign travel—up to $3,000 dollars per trip. This amounted to the relaxation of major controls on current-account transactions that had survived during the 1960s and most of the 1970s.[24]

The exchange-rate regime changed from the crawling-peg system that had been in effect since mid-1975 to a floating rate. This also involved some unification of the set of formal rates, as various special rates for some categories of transactions (e.g., Israeli organizations' unilateral receipts from abroad) were abolished. A further unification of the effective rate system was introduced with the elimination of subsidies, mainly the export-premium scheme that, after being dismantled with the February 1962 devaluation, resurfaced and became significant from the late 1960s. The new and presumably "free" rate that the market established immediately after the liberalization announcement was IL 15.25 per dollar, representing a formal devaluation of some 48%. The devaluation of the effective rates was much smaller, particularly for exports, where it amounted to only a few percentage points. The large formal devaluation, however, was of critical importance for the fate of the liberalization. (See below.)

The liberalization set out from an inauspicious point of departure. During the five preceding years, the country was beset by large fiscal deficits and high (around 30% per year) inflation, although both were rather steady. The immediate impact of the liberalization was a large capital inflow, particularly of a short-term nature. This became a self-reinforcing process: the inflow led to (real) appreciation that, by creating expectations of more of the same in the future, resulted in a (perceived) lowering of the (foreign) interest rate on external borrowing relative to the interest rate on domestic borrowing. This, in turn, led to increased demand for external borrowing. For a while, the process seemed to be self-sustaining. A few key numbers illustrate the extent of the change in short-term capital inflow. Commercial banks' borrowing from foreign banks increased from around $600 million at the end of 1977 (and an average of about $400 million in each of the two preceding years) to more than $1.7 billion at the end of 1978. Quarterly data show clearly that the escalation began in the last quarter of 1977, exactly when the liberalization was introduced. To give an impression of the significance of this inflow, the change between 1977 and 1978 alone—some $1.1 billion—amounted to roughly the size of total demand deposits denominated in Israeli currency in the banking system at the end of 1978, or about 1.5 times the banking system's domestic-currency deposits with the Bank of Israel.

Additionally and probably even more important, the massive formal devaluation (almost 50%) that accompanied the liberalization led to an equally large increase of the domestic-currency value of the economy's foreign-exchange-denominated liquid assets. Thus—again, to illustrate significance—the public's foreign-currency-denominated deposits with commercial banks increased from IL 28.6 billion at the end of the third quarter of 1977 to IL 49.7 billion by the end of the year, as against a money supply of IL 17 billion at the end of September 1977, or close to IL 16 billion of the "broad" monetary base.

Thus, the (partial) liberalization of the capital account and the large-scale formal devaluation that accompanied it evidently led to a dramatic monetary expansion. We pay some attention to this development here because it appears to have been crucial in determining the fate of the liberalization itself. By late 1978, it had become clear that this exceptionally large monetary expansion was detrimental to the country's macroeconomic stability. The annual rate of inflation soared from 28% in the first three quarters of 1977 to 53% over the following year (Q4:1977–Q3:1978). It leaped again in the next three quarters, to an average of 78%, and then almost doubled, to an average of about 137%, by the end of 1980. By that time, inflation had become a self-reinforcing process through currency substitution and continuously falling demand for IL-denominated money.

The rapid acceleration of inflation (which had been stable on average, despite fluctuations, during the five years preceding the liberalization) and the realization of its relationship with the size of capital inflow, led to the curtailment of this inflow—a step back that marked the beginning of partial retrogression from (although not the complete reversal of) the liberalization. In February 1979, the Bank of Israel (to which the controller of foreign exchange now belonged) issued an order (valid for sixty days) prohibiting Israeli firms and households from taking short- or medium-term credit in foreign exchange, which was soon extended to a total ban on foreign-currency loans. This was considered an emergency measure and was replaced in April 1979 by a penalty system: a surcharge of 12% per year on all external borrowing by resident commercial banks and a compulsory deposit with the Bank of Israel (carrying a negative interest rate of 17% per year) of 30% of the size of such borrowing.[25]

The partial repeal of the 1977 liberalization was, in effect, the only significant setback to the continuous fifty-year process of liberalization of current-account or capital-account transactions. The retreat may be traced mainly to the unanticipated nature of the monetary impact of, and the monetary authorities' inadequate response to, the liberalization. With hindsight, it appears that the implementation of the two-step combination—liberalization of capital movements and changes in the exchange-rate regime—was problematic. Specifically, the replacement of the "informal" components of the effective exchange rate by a formal devaluation was excessive. Similarly, it seems that for an appropriate liberalization (particularly of short-term capital flows) the Bank of Israel should have been better prepared for the conduct of monetary policy after the country's money market was stripped of its insulation from the rest of the world.[26]

By mid-1979, only a few tangible vestiges of the Ehrlich liberalization remained and several lessons had been learned. The most important vestige was the partial freedom of capital movements—even though the government intervened in the form of interest surcharges (and in determining what was ostensibly a freely floating exchange rate). Similarly, in current-account transactions, much more foreign exchange was allocated to foreign travel than before the liberalization. The main lesson learned was that capital flows cannot be liberalized successfully without the accompanying adjustment of the financial system and the instruments and mechanisms of the conduct of monetary policy.

In the following years, inflation (arguably originating with the liberalization attempt) continued to gather momentum and attained levels that started to be considered "hyperinflation." Additionally and relatedly, the banking system went through a serious upheaval in the share-manipulation crisis in autumn 1983. Predictably, no progress in the liberalization of capital movements was contemplated during those years. In fact, several additional steps of retrogression, albeit minor, took place during this period. On November 20, 1979, a ninety-day total freeze on foreign-currency credit was imposed. The system of penalties against foreign borrowing, however, became less restrictive, as the rate of surcharge, the negative interest rate on compulsory deposits with the Bank of Israel, and the fraction of such deposits in total foreign-exchange credit were lowered gradually. Controls on the acquisition of liquid foreign assets and on foreign investment were loosened. Resident purchases of foreign exchange for purposes other than foreign travel were discontinued in 1983. The travel allowance was lowered from the $3,000 level introduced in the 1977 liberalization to $2,000 in January 1984 and $1,000 in November of that year.

In mid-1985, the highly successful Economic Stabilization Program lowered the annual inflation rate drastically and stabilized it for several years at around 20% (somewhat lower than the inflation rate preceding the 1977 liberalization). The financial system regained its stable and solvent stature in the late 1980s. These circumstances made the liberalization of capital movements feasible again. Indeed, the process was rekindled in 1988. It is to this (final) stage in the liberalization of the foreign-exchange market that we turn now.

Progress toward Complete Freedom, 1988–2002

The Starting Line

By the end of 1987, the foreign-exchange control system had become somewhat less restrictive than it had been a decade or two earlier. As noted, capital movements were freer than they had been before the Ehrlich liberalization. Significant restrictions, however, still prevailed, particularly in regard to the capital account. The following is a capsule description of the main attributes of the system at that point in time.[27]

Current-Account Transactions

- Payments and receipts had to be effected in the currency and the manner prescribed by the exchange control authorities.
- Banks automatically allocated foreign exchange to pay for authorized imports (upon the presentation of the relevant documents) and for payback of suppliers' credit.
- With a few exceptions, exports did not require licensing.
- Export proceeds had to be received in foreign currency and surrendered to an authorized dealer or held in a PATAM (resident foreign-currency-denominated) account. Exporters could retain a specified fraction of their receipts in a bank deposit abroad or a special foreign-exchange account with a local bank. Proceeds from exports of services were subject to similar rules, for the most part.
- Any resident could accept payment on account of customary tourism services and purchases in specified convertible currencies.
- Currency for Israelis traveling abroad was sold in a limited amount per trip ($2,000 at the end of 1987, up from $1,000 until April of

that year). Most often, this was also the maximum amount of foreign exchange that a resident might possess.

Capital-Account Transactions

- Nonresidents could hold funds either in foreign-currency accounts or in domestic-currency accounts. They could open nonresident foreign-currency accounts without prior approval. They could use their foreign-currency accounts freely, including conversion of funds into a domestic-currency account at the market rate of exchange.
- Nonresidents could freely open domestic-currency accounts and use them for permitted local transactions, including transfers to domestic-currency accounts of other nonresidents.
- Residents could maintain PATAM accounts with local banks. Such an account earned interest only if it was a time deposit for a term of at least one year. New accounts could be opened only for term deposits as defined.
- Exporters and recent immigrants were allowed to maintain nonresident deposits with local banks.
- Recipients of restitution payments could maintain PATAM-restitution accounts with local banks and use them, up to specified limits, for foreign travel (in addition to the general travel allocation) or for the acquisition of foreign securities, which could, in turn, be sold to other residents.[28]
- Proceeds from the realization of foreign investments (principal and profits) were transferable abroad in their entirety if the original investment was made through an authorized foreign-currency dealer or from State of Israel Development Loan bonds.
- Residents were not normally permitted to hold real estate or financial assets abroad and were not allowed to keep the income from such assets abroad (the main exception being immigrants for a period of twenty years after their official date of immigration).
- Capital transfers abroad by residents (other than immigrants) required a special permit from the controller of foreign exchange. Emigrants were allowed to transfer domestic assets abroad up to the equivalent of $2,000 per year.
- Direct loans from residents to nonresidents, in whatever form, were subject to licensing.
- Resident borrowing in foreign currency was restricted. At that point in time, all such borrowing was suspended except suppliers' credit and loans of average maturity of at least thirty months. Loans from abroad other than the latter might carry an interest charge not exceeding LIBOR+1.5% and were subject to a 3% levy.
- Residents were allowed to perform forward transactions in foreign exchange provided that they were intended to hedge the exchange-rate risk arising from authorized trade and capital transactions and were conducted through authorized dealers.

Deregulation

On January 1, 2003, a dramatic announcement was made: the liberalization process had been completed. All restrictions on transactions in or possession of foreign exchange, and on any transaction between residents and nonresidents, had been abolished. Thus, the final stage of liberalization took about fifteen years from beginning to end—although its essentials were completed within the shorter period of ten to twelve years.

The process was gradual, consisting of perhaps hundreds of changes. Most were bureaucratic measures, many of which were intended to eliminate constraints of a "nuisance" nature. Here we indicate only those actions that may be considered, partly due to their symbolic nature, landmarks in the process. The appendix reports policy measures of considerable significance but again does not resort to exhaustive detail.

In July 1993, the export-premium program and a general surcharge on imports were abolished. Both provisions, although quite minor by then, were formally regarded by the IMF as maintenance of multiple exchange rates. Thus, the abolition of these schemes established Israel's currency regime as one that stipulated a uniform rate and presented no restrictions on current-account transactions. This made it possible for the Israeli government to declare that it was abiding by Article VIII of the IMF Articles of Agreement, rather than resorting to Article XIV. This step in itself was largely devoid of substance and had little to do with capital-account transactions. For the international financial community, however, moving from the Article XIV category to Article VIII signifies the adoption of currency convertibility and is considered a major indication of liberalization.[29]

The next landmark was the amendment to the Foreign Exchange Control Law, adopted on May 14, 1998, that was mentioned in the introduction. Its essence, as we recall, was a move from a "positive list" to a "negative list." Before the amendment, anything related to foreign exchange was prohibited unless expressly permitted; afterward, everything was permitted unless expressly prohibited. Beyond the radical difference in the concept of control,[30] the change was accompanied by an important easing of constraints: the new "negative" list was not the "complement" of the replaced positive list but was much less restrictive. In fact, almost all transactions in foreign exchange, on either the current account or the capital account, became unrestricted after the amendment. With a few exceptions, the only transactions subject to restrictions were those involving financial institutions—provident funds, pension funds, and insurance companies. Forward transactions (involving foreign exchange) between residents and nonresidents also remained proscribed.[31]

The liberalization was effectively completed in October 2000.[32] The only remaining restriction applied to institutional investors (such as provident funds), which were allowed to invest abroad only 20% of total assets. On January 1, 2003, this vestigial constraint was also removed and full liberalization and full currency convertibility were announced. Israel's foreign-exchange regime had become as free as any in the world.[33] Thus, Israel's "regime change," from one that was about as restrictive as they come in 1950 to one of full freedom, reached its conclusion.

Manifestations of Liberalization: The Extent of Capital Movements

Although it is not the purpose of this chapter to analyze and assess the impact of the liberalization, it will provide several measures—probably the most important ones—of how important the capital-account liberalization of the 1990s was. The following, then, is a concise quantitative description of the extent of capital movements between Israel and the rest of the world during these years.[34]

Table 3.3 and its diagrammatic representation, figure 3.1, illustrate the size of private-sector foreign investment in Israel from 1988—the start of the final liberalization episode—to 2002. The data are shown both in absolute terms (billions of dollars) and as a fraction of GDP. The increase in foreign investment during the period, in real as well as in financial assets, is remarkable indeed. Needless to say, the capital-market liberalization did not *create* these capital movements. One factor that did play such a role was the expansion of the economy and, particularly, the fast growth of the high-tech sector, a major magnet for foreign investment. Another causal factor was the global expansion of foreign investment (particularly in emerging-market economies). These factors do much to explain the expansion of private-sector foreign investment in Israel. (It is no coincidence, of course, that this investment declined—that is, the annual flows became negative—in the last two years of the period

Table 3.3. Private-Sector Foreign Investment in Israel, 1988–2002 (end-of-year balances)

	$ Billions		Percent of Israel's Annual GDP	
	Real investment (1)	Portfolio investment (2)	Real investment (3)	Portfolio investment (4)
1988	.3	3.5	.2	2.4
1989	.3	4.0	.3	2.9
1990	.4	4.6	.3	3.3
1991	.3	8.3	.2	6.2
1992	.4	8.1	.3	6.8
1993	.4	7.7	.4	6.6
1994	4.2	10.8	3.5	9.0
1995	5.7	13.5	4.6	11.0
1996	7.0	16.2	5.6	13.0
1997	9.5	21.9	8.1	18.6
1998	10.7	21.4	10.4	20.7
1999	20.4	38.1	19.2	35.8
2000	24.1	44.1	20.5	37.6
2001	25.1	31.7	23.6	29.8
2002	24.7	28.1	25.2	28.6

Source: Bank of Israel.

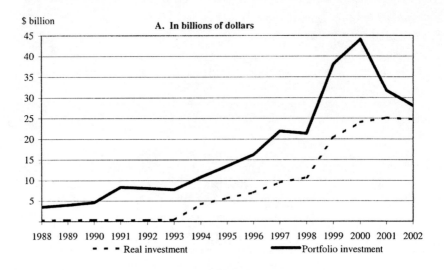

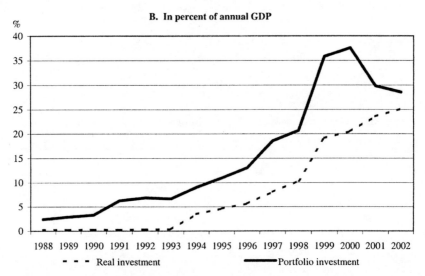

Figure 3.1. Foreign Investment in Israel, 1988–2002 (end-of-year balance).

surveyed.) It is equally clear, however, that without the liberalization most of this investment could not have taken place.

Table 3.4 and figure 3.2 show, similarly, the movement in the opposite direction, that is, the magnitude of external investment by Israel's private sector. The expansion was just as phenomenal as that of foreign investment in Israel, although the two were not equal: the excess of the latter over the former—the balance of "net" foreign investment—was roughly $16 billion or 16% of Israel's GDP in 2002 (as against only $4 billion in 1988). Notably, the powerful escalation of external investment began not immediately upon the start of this phase of capital-market liberalization but in 1995 or 1996.

**Table 3.4. External Investment by the Private Sector, 1988–2002
(end-of-year balances)**

	$ Billions		Percent of Israel's Annual GDP	
	Real investment (1)	Portfolio investment (2)	Real investment (3)	Portfolio investment (4)
1988	0	0	0	0
1989	0	0	0	0
1990	0	0	0	0
1991	0	4.7	0	3.5
1992	0	4.2	0	3.6
1993	0	4.8	0	4.1
1994	0	6.6	0	5.5
1995	2.9	6.2	2.3	5.1
1996	2.3	5.9	1.9	4.8
1997	3.1	7.5	2.6	6.3
1998	4.1	10.7	4.0	10.3
1999	4.8	16.4	4.6	15.4
2000	8.0	20.4	6.8	17.4
2001	8.1	23.4	7.6	22.0
2002	9.1	27.9	9.2	28.4

Source: Bank of Israel.

Finally, table 3.5 and figure 3.3 illustrate the significance of short-term capital inflow by presenting the fraction of credit granted in foreign exchange in aggregate credit in Israel. The increase in this fraction is also impressive—from roughly 25% in 1988 to some 40% in 2002. However, two observations should be made. First, the entire increase took place through the expansion of foreign-exchange credit from domestic banks; the share of aggregate credit issued in the form of direct credit from abroad (presumably suppliers' credit, to a large extent) was roughly unchanged throughout the period at around 14%. Second, the expansion of foreign-exchange credit occurred during only part of the period surveyed—1990 to 1998—and has not expanded further in recent years.

In sum, by all these quantitative indicators, this phase of the capital-market liberalization, which began in 1988 and ended in late 2002 with the establishment of complete freedom, led to a remarkable expansion of Israel's transactions on capital account with the rest of the world, that is, to Israel's integration into the global capital market.

CONCLUSIONS: PACE, TIMING, AND SEQUENCING

The process of liberalizing Israel's foreign-exchange market was lengthy. From beginning to end—from an overall restrictive regime to one of complete

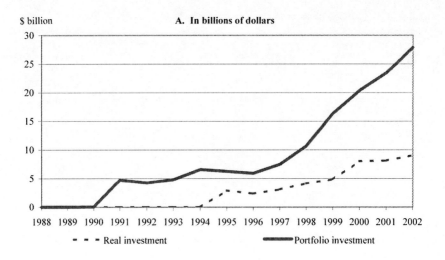

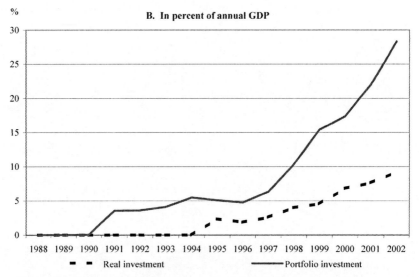

Figure 3.2. Israel's Private-Sector Investment Abroad, 1988–2002 (end-of-year balance).

freedom—it took about half a century. It has occupied practically the whole lifetime of Israel's existence as a state, thus surpassing somewhat the existence of the Bank of Israel. Even were we to mark the end of the process somewhat earlier and assert that total freedom was basically achieved by 1998, the lengthof the liberalization process would not change much. The process may be divided into two distinctly different subperiods, each quite long. A quarter-century of liberalization mostly in regard to current-account transactions, from 1952 to 1977, was followed by another quarter-century, until 2002, to liberalize the capital account.

Table 3.5. Composition of Credit, Domestic Currency, and Foreign Exchange, 1988–2002 (in percentage of total credit, end-of-year data)

		Foreign-Exchange Credit			
Year	Domestic-Currency Credit[a] (1)	From Israeli Banks (2)	From Abroad (3)	Total (=(2) + (3)) (4)	Total (= (1) + (4)) (5)
1988	75	11	14	25	100
1989	76	10	14	24	100
1990	74	13	13	26	100
1991	70	11	19	30	100
1992	69	11	20	31	100
1993	74	9	17	26	100
1994	75	11	14	25	100
1995	67	19	14	33	100
1996	67	20	13	33	100
1997	63	23	14	37	100
1998	60	25	15	40	100
1999	60	26	14	40	100
2000	63	24	13	37	100
2001	62	25	13	38	100
2002	60	26	14	40	100

Source: Bank of Israel.
[a] Including credit denominated in foreign exchange (a gradually disappearing item).

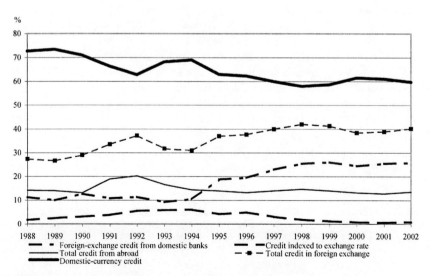

Figure 3.3. Composition of Credit, Israeli Currency, 1988–2002 (end-of-year data, in percent of total credit).

By and large, as the total length of the period would tend to indicate, the process was gradual rather than a stop-and-go set of changes. The "active" periods of policy change lasted about a dozen years in the stage of current-account liberalization—from 1952 through the mid-1960s—and nearly twenty years (1977–83 and 1988–2000) for the capital-account liberalization. Thus, fewer than twenty years during the relevant half-century (1963 or 1964 through 1977; and 1984 through 1987) were marked by almost no action. As the length of the periods of activity suggests, the process consisted mostly of a long series of small measures rather than a few bold and radical steps. Two exceptions stand out, both marking the start of the two major phases of liberalization. One was the dramatic policy change—"the new economic policy" that began in early 1952 and lasted for some two and half years—that introduced massive devaluation followed by radical liberalization of current-account transactions. The other was the Ehrlich liberalization, undertaken in late 1977, which involved a basic change of perception and which, despite some reversals, augured the beginning of capital-account liberalization. One may, perhaps, add the 1998 amendment that, by introducing a change in concept and a more radical change of substance, shortened the lengthy liberalization process that had been implemented through many small changes during the preceding decade.

Although the overall process was lengthened by the smallness of the policy measures taken, the consistency and persistence of these measures should be noted. Except for one partial retrogression, in the case of the Ehrlich liberalization, the liberalization process never retreated—certainly a mark of achievement. Although some pauses occurred, they represented an absence of further progress rather than retrogression. This may definitely be regarded as a measure of success.

What were the sources of this success? One, the most fundamental, to which we shall return soon, is that basically the policies were introduced in the "right" way. One may infer this from the experience of other countries (judging from Israel's own experience would make such statement a tautology) and from a priori analysis. Beyond this, however, the persistence of the liberalization policy, particularly in regard to current-account transactions, owes much to the intensity of the crisis that preceded it. Before the "new economic policy" of 1952, the population generally perceived Israel's economic situation as desperate and blamed this on pervasive government involvement, particularly in foreign trade. The strong reflection of this stance of public opinion in the political arena clearly made an impression on policymakers. This was a defining experience, much like Germany's experience with hyperinflation in the early 1920s, that served as a warning against recurrence.

Prime among the things that were done "right" was the overall sequencing of the liberalization process—goods first, capital movements later. The vast literature on this subject seems to have led to a consensus.[35] It is accepted today that liberalization of current-account transactions should come first and should be largely completed before serious liberalization of the capital account begins. Current-account liberalization amidst unrestricted capital movements faces a dual risk. First, a capital outflow may lead to the rapid depletion of foreign reserves and hence may inspire policymakers to reimpose restrictions on imports of goods and services. Second, conversely, a large-scale capital inflow may cause real currency appreciation and, by so doing, may discourage the production of tradables and, in particular, may prevent stimulus to exports to counter the expansion of imports following trade liberalization. Both risks have come to pass in the experience of other countries and have often led to the reversal of trade liberalizations. Israel avoided this danger by undertaking its current-account liberalization while capital movements were still controlled.

Another important contribution to the success of liberalization was its combination with other policies. One of the most important lessons from world experience is that durability and further progress of liberalization depend crucially on its being accompanied by appropriate macroeconomic policies that prevent inflation and real currency appreciation following its introduction. This accompaniment by the "right" macroeconomic policies was most remarkable, perhaps, in the radical policy transformation in 1952–54, when fiscal deficits and real money balances contracted drastically. Another important example was the introduction of a (limited) currency float in the early 1990s, which, by reducing the risk of runs on the currency and large-scale drawdown of foreign reserves, must have helped to ensure the survival and progress of the last phase of the foreign-exchange liberalization process. Although actual reversals of liberalization were, as noted, rare, the "pauses" in the process largely coincided with macroeconomic imbalances, that is, the severe recession of the mid-1960s and rapid inflation in the first half of the 1980s.

The only major episode in Israel's liberalization history that cannot be termed successful was the Ehrlich liberalization in the late 1970s. Indeed, rules crafted on the basis of theoretical considerations and the study of other countries' experiences would not have predicted success in this episode. The first important step in the capital-account liberalization, in this case, involved *short-term* capital movements in the main. By all accounts, this is the category that should have been left to the end of the process.[36] Indeed, some analysts would recommend the continued regulation of short-term capital movements (preferably by price measures rather than quantitative restrictions) even in an otherwise fully liberalized market. These movements are fraught with danger. Avoidance of this danger should require, at the very least, the existence of a fully developed financial system and a central bank that possesses a large arsenal of policy tools, proven ability to use them, and a high degree of alertness and awareness. These preconditions were not in place in late 1977, when this stage of liberalization was introduced. Moreover, the act of liberalization was not accompanied by appropriate macroeconomic policies. The expansionary fiscal policy that followed the liberalization and the monetary policy, flawed by the shortcomings of the Bank of Israel and the banking system, allowed a dramatic monetary expansion to ensue. Thus, the Ehrlich liberalization was doomed ab initio; the remarkable thing is that it only suffered a partial reversal rather than total collapse.

From the perspective of international experience, Israel has done quite well. In persistence, consistency, the almost complete absence of reversals, and the sequencing of trade versus capital-movement liberalization, Israel's liberalization resembles that of the Western European countries in the postwar era although it was somewhat slower. It is radically different from liberalization in most Latin American economies, where (at least until the late 1980s) the process was often reversed and restarted from scratch every so often. The Latin American experience demonstrated a situation in which, in order to succeed, liberalization must be performed in a big leap that transforms the regime in one stroke. Israel's experience, on the other hand, may be characterized as gradual, although major phases did start with distinct rather than trivial acts of liberalization. In retrospect, it appears that if everything had been done "right," the road from extreme restrictiveness to complete freedom might have been shortened materially. Nevertheless, in the context of world histories of liberalizations over the last half-century, Israel's foreign-exchange liberalization should definitely be judged a success.

APPENDIX: SALIENT CHANGES IN FOREIGN-EXCHANGE REGULATION 1987–97 ("1997" GOES THROUGH MAY 1998)

Residents

Table A3.1. Possession of Foreign Exchange

1987	• The limit on possession of cash ($500 out of $2,000 allowed to be held) is abolished.
1990	• The structure of resident foreign-exchange deposits is simplified. Later in the year, all categories of deposits are unified. Deposits become transferable among residents. • The interest ceiling of LIBOR+1.5% is abolished.
1992	• The possibility of holding a foreign-exchange account is extended to all residents.
1993	• Residents are allowed to hold and trade in gold. • Various restrictions on PAMAZ-restitution accounts (e.g., interest rates and type of currency) are lifted.
1994	• The amount of foreign exchange allowed to be held (or acquired for travel abroad) is increased from $3,000 to $7,000. • The definition of "foreign exchange" is expanded to "all legal tender that is not Israeli currency." • Various changes toward unification of foreign-exchange accounts are made.
1996	• Residents are allowed to deposit the proceeds of foreign loans and of the sale of securities for foreign exchange in foreign-currency accounts.
1997	• Residents are allowed to purchase foreign exchange from an Israeli bank and deposit it in a type of account called PAMAH ("foreign-currency deposit"). • Further unification of foreign-exchange accounts is made. • Proceeds from restitution and similar payments may be deposited abroad.

Table A3.2. Investment in Foreign Securities

1989	•	Provident funds are allowed to invest in (and trade in) foreign securities, subject to regulations and provided that the securities are deposited with an authorized dealer.
1992	•	The range of foreign securities that residents may acquire is expanded.
1994	•	Provident funds are allowed to transact in the market for options.
1995	•	Israeli firms are allowed to invest in all foreign securities (i.e., in addition to those issued by subsidiaries of other Israeli firms). The investment is limited to 5% of the firm's annual sales or 10% of its net worth, whichever is higher.
	•	Israeli firms are allowed to acquire and invest in foreign firms.
1996	•	The definition of "recognized securities" (in which residents may invest) is extended to almost all tradable securities.
1997	•	The ceiling on holdings of foreign securities by Israeli firms is raised to 15% of annual sales or 25% of net worth. In January 1998, the ceiling will be abolished altogether.
	•	The ceiling on provident funds' investment in foreign securities is raised to 5% of each fund's total assets.
	•	The ceiling on mutual funds' investment in foreign securities is raised to 50%. In January 1998, it will be removed altogether.

Table A3.3. Borrowing from Abroad

1987	•	The interest-rate ceiling on credit from abroad is lowered from LIBOR+2.2% to LIBOR+1.5%.
1989	•	The minimum term for borrowing from abroad is shortened from 30 to 18 months; then to 12 months and, finally, to 6 months.
	•	Exporters entitled to financing from export funds are allowed to borrow directly from abroad.
1990	•	Importers are allowed to make payments directly from proceeds of foreign loans instead of having first to deposit the foreign-exchange proceeds in Israel.
	•	Direct borrowing from abroad is allowed.
1992	•	Residents are allowed to borrow from foreign branches of Israeli banks.

Table A3.4. Other

1989	•	Banks are allowed to conduct forward transactions on their own accounts, provided that they are financed by foreign exchange earmarked for investment.
1991	•	Permission to perform forward transactions is extended to all transactions intended to hedge financial and trade risks.
1994	•	An emigrating resident is allowed to transfer abroad the proceeds of sales of assets up to an annual amount of $20,000–$50,000.
1995	•	Israeli firms are allowed to invest in real foreign assets.

Continued

Table A3.4. Continued

| 1996 | • | The ceiling on external transfer by emigrating residents is raised to an annual amount of $50,000 or 20% of the value of the assets, whichever is higher. |
| 1997 | • | Constraints on the conduct of forward transactions are greatly relaxed. |

Nonresidents

Table A3.5. Holding of Deposits with Israeli Banks

1987	•	Foreign exchange received from the sale of goods and services to residents or from the sale of foreign securities may be deposited in a PATAH (nonresident) account.
1988	•	A nonresident deposit in domestic currency is established (parallel to the PATAH), from which domestic investments may be made.
1989	•	A ceiling of LIBOR+1.5% on the interest rate for foreign-exchange deposits is imposed.
1990	•	Nonresidents may deposit funds in a resident foreign-exchange account.
1991	•	The possibility of transferring funds from a resident to a nonresident account is eliminated.
1997	•	Significant steps are taken toward further unification of categories of non-resident foreign-exchange accounts.

Table A3.6. Holding of Israeli Securities

| 1990 | • | In transactions between nonresidents and residents in Israeli securities, the requirement that the price should be no lower than the stock-market price is abolished. |
| | • | Israeli firms are allowed to issue securities abroad or to transfer the place of issuance from Israel to abroad. |

Table A3.7. Repatriation of Investment

1987	•	A nonresident may repatriate various assets acquired in Israel, such as foreign exchange or securities, through a PATAH account.
1989	•	Repatriation rights are extended to investment in domestically traded Israeli corporate bonds (other than those of banks).
1992	•	The possibility of repatriating the proceeds of sales of Israeli securities, or of income therefrom, is expanded.
1996	•	Firms operating in Israel and registered as foreign are allowed to repatriate profits created in Israel or the proceeds of liquidation.

Table A3.8. Other

1992	•	Nonresidents are allowed to borrow from an Israeli bank and deposit the proceeds in a PATAH domestic-currency account.

Notes

I am indebted to Haim Barkai, Micky Eran, Nadav Halevi, Shalom Hersko, and Assaf Razin for their advice and comments.

1. In fact, the wording of the 1978 statute remained in effect without change. However, the new legislation included a general permit allowing all transactions except those specifically restricted.
2. Exceptions to this rule, under one scheme or another, are discussed shortly.
3. The description of this mechanism draws on Sussman (1959) and Halevi (1971).
4. That is, unless the import permit specified that it was provided "without an allocation of foreign exchange"—a category of transactions to be discussed shortly. In such transactions, neither the imports nor their source of finance was included in the foreign-exchange budget.
5. In general, the black-market price is not the equilibrium price that would prevail in an uncontrolled market. In this specific case, movements of the black market rate were strongly associated with changes in the market (or markets) for "imports without payment," which will be discussed shortly.
6. Moreover, just as the use of official prices leads to an underestimate of the real appreciation that preceded February 1952, it must lead to an underestimate of the real depreciation in the next few years. With domestic prices largely liberalized, the official price indices must have overstated the true rate of price increase during this period.
7. It was sometimes asserted that the large increase of the black-market rate during the half-year preceding the devaluation—from around IL 1.2 per dollar in mid-1951 to IL 2.6–IL 2.7 by early 1952—reflected rising expectations of an imminent official devaluation. This explanation, however, would be reasonable only if the anticipated devaluation would be from the existing official rate of IL .357 per dollar to a level exceeding the existing black-market rate, i.e., a devaluation that would raise the official rate by a factor of seven, eight, or even more. It is hard to believe that economic agents anticipated such a change.
8. Throughout the 1950s, it was generally believed, although never fully admitted or documented, that the government also intervened occasionally in the black market for foreign exchange.
9. This section is based on Kochav (1953) and Gronau (1970).
10. This section draws primarily on Michaely (1963).
11. This section draws on ibid.; and on Ben-Porath (1970).
12. In 1958–59, for instance, foreign-exchange receipts on account of restitution amounted to $171 million, as against $914 million in imports of goods and $387 million in total exports.
13. The monetary impact of restitution payments and of the mechanisms involved in their transfer and holding is discussed by H. Barkai in Part I of Volume I of this book.
14. Given in the form of securities; the bonus also applied to some other, more minor, forms of transfers.

15. The technique of such transactions was somewhat intricate. Foreign exchange could not be transacted legally and freely. This would have established a new, legal exchange rate which, by the ruling of the courts, would be "the" rate (rather than the official one) to serve in the government's foreign-exchange linked obligations. Hence, the seller would have, first, to buy foreign securities, to be sold to the buyer who, finally, would sell the securities for foreign exchange. This is the source of the term "the NATAD market"—NATAD standing for the Hebrew acronymn of "Securities for Dividends" (a term which refers to the scheme from which the securities originated). All transactions, it should be mentioned, had to be carried out through authorized Israeli banks.

16. The maximum possible size—that is, had the restitution recipients sold all their allowed rights—would have been almost three times that much (35% of roughly $100 million). It should be noted that the magnitude of "sales" did not include additions to holdings by banks, mentioned shortly.

17. The amount of foreign exchange that could be bought (and used) for this purpose could not exceed $120 per passenger per trip. This was usually far below the actual amount required, thus leaving ample room for the black market—the major alternative source of foreign exchange.

18. The category of foreign travel, however, was consistently excluded from the process of liberalization of current-account transactions; in effect, it seems to have been treated similarly to capital movements. Interestingly, the amount of foreign exchange allowed for a trip abroad and the amount that a resident could hold legally were often identical.

19. An import permit was still required. It was, as a rule, granted, and it implied the allocation of foreign exchange, but it could specify the identity of the foreign currency, terms of payment and the like. It often directed the buyer to a supplying country with which Israel had a payments agreement.

20. An imported product could be regarded as competing even if not manufactured in Israel at all. It sufficed for a domestic entrepreneur to declare that he could, and intended to, produce it.

21. This disequilibrium was not yet evident then (for instance, there was no decline of foreign reserves). It was, rather, anticipated, in view of the large-scale reparations from Germany soon to be exhausted.

22. For a more thorough discussion of the import liberalization, see Barkai and Michaely (1963), Halevi and Baruh (1991), Halevi (1994), Gabai and Rob (2001).

23. See also Gross's chapter in this volume.

24. Another component of liberalization was the introduction in March 1978 of the new Foreign Exchange Control Law (replacing the 1941 ordinance).

25. The Bank of Israel also augmented its instruments of monetary control at this time by imposing domestic credit quotas.

26. Gottlieb and Blejer (2001) give a somewhat different interpretation of the reason for the (partial) failure of the Ehrlich liberalization. They assign the failure to an upturn in macroeconomic instability prior to the introduction of liberalization. This, however, was not quite the case. The rate of inflation during the year or two years preceding the liberalization, although quite high, was somewhat lower than in the few years preceding it. Similarly, the fiscal deficit was lower than before (see Michaely, 1981). According to the interpretation proposed here, it was the liberalization itself that led to macroeconomic destabilization. Thus, with the same prior conditions, the liberalization might have succeeded had it been implemented differently—specifically, without lifting the constraints on short-term capital flows.

27. This description draws primarily on the IMF *Annual Report on Exchange Restrictions*, which, in turn, is based on information provided by the controller of foreign exchange at the Bank of Israel.

28. This is still, basically, the arrangement described in the "Liberalization of Current-Account Transactions, 1950–77" section, pp. 66–77.

29. Article VIII states, in its major outlines, that the member country shall "[not] impose restrictions on the making of payments and transfers for current international transactions . . . [not] engage in any discriminatory currency arrangements or multiple-currency practices . . . [but] shall buy balances of its currency held by another member" [provided these are balances created through or needed for current-account transactions].

   Article XIV, intended to provide for a transition period upon the formation of the IMF, states that "In the post-war transitional period members may, not withstanding the provisions of any other articles of this Agreement, maintain . . . restrictions on payments and transfers for current international transactions. . . . Members shall withdraw [such] restrictions as soon as they are satisfied that they will be able, in the absence of such restrictions, to settle their balance of payments. . . . A member availing itself of the transitional arrangements shall notify the Fund as soon thereafter as it is prepared to accept the [obligations of Article VIII]."

   By the late 1950s or early 1960s, nearly all OECD countries accepted the obligations of Article VIII. Most developing countries, in contrast, resorted to Article XIV for lengthy periods.

30. Notably, the conceptual change not only represents a change of ideology but also has important manifestations in the practice of controls. After the amendment, for example, any transaction could take place without the transactor having to prove ab initio that it is permitted; it could be prevented only if the controlling authority could show that it is not permitted.

31. Back in August 1992, the controller of foreign exchange recommended what he described as a "forward leap" (rather than further gradual change) from a positive to a negative list. This proposal included a major relaxation of controls but would have left a more substantial list of prohibitions than the one actually retained when the change was made six years later.

32. At that time, it will be recalled, the function of controller of foreign exchange was abolished; the Department of Foreign Exchange Control at the Bank of Israel was renamed the Foreign Exchange Activity Department.

33. Gottlieb and Blejer (2001) report Israel's score and relative position on the IMF's composite index of foreign-exchange restrictions, which is essentially an enumeration of existing restrictions (a score of 0 indicating perfect freedom and 1 representing no freedom whatsoever). The lowest indexes recorded (i.e., the highest levels of freedom), at the end of 1997, were practically 0. (The Netherlands actually scored 0.) Israel's score at that point was .43, ranking it in the middle of the group of forty-one countries for which the index was estimated. By the end of 1998, with the substantial liberalization that took place that year, Israel's index fell to .15, advancing it to around tenth place on the list of top liberalizers. It is safe to guess that by January 2003, Israel's index was at or near 0, placing it among the countries with perfect foreign-exchange freedom.

34. Gottlieb and Blejer point to several additional measures of the effectiveness of the liberalization: the narrowing of three gaps—between risk-discounted rates of interest on credit in Israel and abroad, between (real) yields in the stock markets, and, in Israel itself, between credit and debit interest rates in the commercial

banking system. All these gaps indeed narrowed during the 1990s—indicating an increased impact of capital transactions with the outside world on Israel's economy. See Gottlieb and Blejer (2001), particularly pp. 307–18.

35. See, for instance, Edwards (1984, 1986); Harberger (1986); Krueger (1986); McKinnon (1982, 1991); Michaely, Papageorgiou, and Choksi (1991); Rodrik (1987).

36. See McKinnon (1991), particularly chaps. 9–10.

References

Barkai, H., and M. Michaely. "More on the New Economic Policy." *Economic Quarterly* 39 (1963): 232–310 (Hebrew).

Ben-Porath, Y. "The Exchange Rate in Realization of Foreign Securities." In *Israel's Foreign-Exchange Rate System,* part 3—Annexes, by M. Michaely, 72–102. Jerusalem: Maurice Falk Institute for Economic Research in Israel, 1970 (Hebrew).

Edwards, S. "The Order of Liberalization of the External Sector." *Princeton Essays on International Finance* 156 (1984).

———. "The Order of Liberalization of the Current and Capital Accounts of the Balance of Payments." *In Economic Liberalization in Developing Countries,* ed. A. M. Choksi and D. Papageorgiou, 185–211. Oxford: Basil Blackwell, 1986.

Gabai, Y., and R. Rob. "The Import-Liberalization and Abolition of Devaluation Substitutes Policy: Implications for the Israeli Economy." In *The Israeli Economy 1985–1998: From Government Intervention to Market Economics,* ed. A. Ben-Bassat. Cambridge, MA: MIT Press, 2001.

Gottlieb, D., and M. Blejer. "Liberalization in the Capital Account of the Balance of Payments." In *The Israeli Economy 1985–1998: From Government Intervention to Market Economics,* ed. A. Ben-Bassat. Cambridge, MA: MIT Press, 2001.

Gronau, R. "The Exchange Rate in Imports without Payment Transactions." In *Israel's Foreign-Exchange Rate System,* part 3—Annexes, by M. Michaely, Jerusalem: Maurice Falk Institute for Economic Research in Israel, 1970.

Halevi, N. "Exchange Control in Israel." in *Israel and the Common Market,* ed. P. Uri, 29–65. Jerusalem: Weidenfeld and Nicolson, 1971.

———, ed. *Import Policy and Exposure of Israel's Industry.* Jerusalem: Maurice Falk for Economic Research in Israel, 1994 (Hebrew).

Halevi, N., and J. Baruh. "The Experience of Israel." In *Liberalizing Foreign Trade,* vol. 3, *Israel and Yugoslavia,* ed. D. Papageorgiou, M. Michaely, and A. M. Choksi, 1–156. Oxford: Basil Blackwell, 1991.

Harberger, A. C. "Welfare Consequences of Capital Inflows." In *Economic Liberalization in Developing Countries,* ed. A. M. Choksi and D. Papageorgiou, 157–81. Oxford: Basil Blackwell, 1986.

Kochav, D. "Imports Without Payment," M.A. thesis, Hebrew University of Jerusalem, 1953 (Hebrew).

Krueger, A. O. "Problems of Liberalization." In *Economic Liberalization in Developing Countries,* ed. A. M. Choksi and D. Papageorgiou, 15–31. Oxford: Basil Blackwell, 1986.

McKinnon, R. "The Order of Liberalization: Lessons from Chile and Argentina." In *Economic Policy in a World of Change,* ed. K. Brunner and A. Meltzer. Amsterdam: North-Holland, 1982.

————. *The Order of Economic Liberalization*. Baltimore: Johns Hopkins University Press, 1991.

Michaely, M. *Foreign Trade and Capital Imports in Israel*. Tel Aviv: Am Oved, 1963 (Hebrew).

————. *Foreign Trade Regimes and Economic Developments: Israel*. New York: Columbia University Press, 1975.

————. "Inflation and Money in Israel following the 1977 Liberalization." *Economic Quarterly* 109 (1981): 115–36 (Hebrew).

Michaely, M., D. Papageorgiou, and A. M. Choksi. "Liberalizing Foreign Trade: Lessons of Experience in the Developing World." In *Liberalizing Foreign Trade*, vol. 7, ed. D. Papageorgiou, M. Michaely and A. M. Choksi. Oxford: Basil Blackwell, 1991.

Rodrik, D. "Trade and Capital Account Liberalization in a Keynesian Economy." *Journal of International Economics* 33 (1987): 113–29.

Sussman, Z. "The Foreign-Exchange Budget as a Forecast of Imports to Israel." M.A. thesis. Hebrew University of Jerusalem, 1959 (Hebrew).

4

Economic Policy in Israel as Viewed by Leading Officials of the Bank of Israel, 1954–2000

Nachum T. Gross

For this survey of opinions and developments, we interviewed personalities who belong to three categories:

1. Former governors of the Bank of Israel (BOI): Moshe Sanbar (November 1971–October 1976); Arnon Gafny (November 1976–October 1981); Moshe Mandelbaum (January 1982–June 1986); and Jacob Frenkel (August 1991–December 1999).
2. Directors of the BOI Research Department (RD): David Kochav (April 1953–December 1961); Zvi Sussman and Eliezer Sheffer (codirectors, January 1962–March 1972, Sussman until March 1980); Mordechai Fraenkel (April 1980–July 1987); Avi Ben-Bassat (August 1987–March 1992); Leora Meridor (April 1992–June 1996); and Leo Leiderman (July 1996–June 2000).
3. Experts on specific issues: Meir Heth, Yakir Plessner, and Sylvia Piterman.

Interviewing the RD directors was particularly rewarding for two reasons. First, the RD has long been the BOI department most involved with economic policy and its agents. Second, most directors of this department had long tenures with the bank, the majority having started out as research assistants during their student days. Thus, they have a long-term perspective and are able to discuss the bank's policies and achievements under various governors, including the deceased (David Horowitz [who served 1954–71] and Michael Bruno [1986–91]) from a comparative and distanced perspective.

Below the views expressed in the interviews are summarized by main topics. The opinions were retrospective and the facts and issues discussed by each interviewee were sometimes selected arbitrarily. Systematic chronological surveys and discussions of BOI history are presented in other parts of this study.

THE BOI CONSTITUTION

The personalities most involved in framing the BOI Constitution and, thus, the chief founding fathers of the BOI, were David Horowitz, Dr. Ernst Lehmann, and Eliezer S. Hoofien, all three deceased. Horowitz, an erudite self-educated economist, had for many years served the Jewish Agency as an economic advisor and as director of the Economic Department, and the State of Israel as director general of the Ministry of Finance and in delicate diplomatic missions. Lehmann was a key figure in the Bank Leumi group and the manager of its Issues Department in 1948–54. Hoofien was general manager (from 1914) and, from 1947 on, chairman of Bank Leumi, the leading Jewish bank in pre-Israel Palestine, which also performed some functions of a central bank until 1954. Generally viewed as the country's "Mr. Banking," he was the first chairman of the BOI Advisory Committee.

David Kochav was appointed by Horowitz in April 1953 to assist in establishing the Bank of Israel and its Research Department. He laid the foundations of the RD and its structure and regime. (See "The Research Department," pp. 116–120.)

To prepare the BOI constitution, Horowitz consulted foreign—especially American—experts. Members of the government and the Knesset also had their say, of course. It seems, however, that Horowitz's own preferences and experience had a large impact. These were apparently among the factors that influenced the decision to place control over monetary policy in the exclusive hands of the BOI governor. In early 1950s Israel, Kochav believed, it would have been very difficult to find suitably qualified members for a BOI council.

The bank was equipped, however, with two associated panels: an advisory committee and a council. This reflected not only the demands of various political parties and economic interest groups but also the original conception of Israeli economic policy as the shared responsibility of the government and the BOI. This cooperative view and the absence of a clear-cut separation of fiscal policy from monetary policy were also reflected in the appointment of the BOI governor as economic advisor to the government. The most veteran interviewees regard the current view—that fiscal and monetary policy should be separate and the BOI and the Ministry of Finance are potential adversaries—as anachronistic when applied to Israel's early decades.[1]

The heads of the BOI were fully aware of the constraints imposed on monetary policy by the perceived needs of development policy and the government's domination of the capital and loan markets. Importantly, too, at the time "modest" inflation was considered not detrimental and perhaps even conducive to growth. However, they viewed themselves as partners in the implementation of overall economic policy and their chief task as restraining the inflationary tendencies of fiscal measures. In this capacity, they often had to oppose specific budget provisions and government action or inaction, in the spirit of shared responsibility.[2]

The Advisory Committee, whose approval was necessary for certain BOI measures, was comprised of leading bankers, manufacturers, and agriculturists. The intention in their appointment was to represent both the private and the Histadrut sectors,[3] although in theory they were chosen on personal merit only. The influence of the committee depended on its members' personalities and, in particular, the standing of its chair. Horowitz was adept at inducing the committee to make its decisions by consensus and was aided in this by the two leading figures of the early years, Hoofien and the manufacturer Simon Bejarano. Over time, the importance of the Advisory Committee seems to have diminished.[4] In August 1982, the minister of finance, Yoram Aridor, arranged for the Knesset Finance Committee chair, Avraham Shapira, to be appointed head of the Advisory Committee. His intention was to strengthen support for his fiscal policies in the Knesset.[5] After a two-year interval without an advisory committee, a panel under Shlomo Lorincz was appointed in 1987. It served until 1989; after that, there was no advisory committee until 2000.

Conflicting views were expressed about the dual functions of the BOI governor. Kochav criticized this institutionalized dualism in retrospect, arguing that the function of economic advisor interfered with the conduct of monetary policy. Three former governors—Sanbar, Gafny, and Mandelbaum—concurred. Mordechai Fraenkel, however, noted that their activities were consistent with the dual function and that they apparently enjoyed their role as advisor to the government. (Sanbar's difficulties in this respect are described below.) Several governors in particular immersed themselves in general economic policy by participating in meetings of the government, the Ministerial Economics Committee, other government committees and councils, and various ad hoc commissions. Noteworthy in this respect was the late Michael Bruno, who is reported to have not only fully enjoyed the role but also to have increased its scope and importance without detracting from his concern with BOI affairs.[6] Several former directors of the Research Department, citing numerous examples that will be discussed below, stressed the importance of the advisory role, coupled with a cooperative outlook, as a way to influence economic policies and become involve in the planning and preparation of specific measures.[7] Critical views about the dual functions were expressed by Plessner and Piterman and emphatically by Leiderman. Jacob Frenkel believed it essential, although impractical in the short term, to strictly separate the role of the BOI governor from any formal advisory status. Even in the immediate term, he said, the new BOI Law should not include a government advisor function. Instead, he proposed, the governor should advise the government by dint of his or her position and personal authority until a council of economic advisors could be established.

The BOI also has a deputy governor (or two)—appointed for a renewable five-year term—as stipulated in Articles 10 and 11 of the BOI Law. The duties and competences of deputy governors, except the function of pro tem, depend solely on the governor. Legal opinions about whether the law requires or merely permits the appointment of DGs have oscillated over time. Horowitz and his successor, Sanbar, did not implement this provision of the law, apparently with the implicit consent of the political establishment. The situation was changed by legal action against the BOI (beginning in 1975) by relatives of the bankrupt banker Yehoshua Ben-Zion, who blamed the BOI for his failure and conviction in the collapse of the Israel-Britain Bank and sought a way to attack the legitimacy of the bank's actions.[8] This raised, among other issues, the question of Article 10 and following a recommendation from the attorney general, Aharon Barak, the article was implemented in 1977, after Sanbar's tenure.

Arnon Gafny, succeeding Sanbar as governor, found himself in a quandary, as he assumed that any government appointment would be political. He fended off this possibility "creatively" by proposing that Sheffer and Sussman, director general of the bank and director of the RD, respectively, be appointed DGs. Although this action—a government appointment—would terminate their secure tenure as professional officials, both men agreed. Gafny easily persuaded Y. Rabinowitz, the minister of finance, to approve the appointments, and the government followed suit. There was no de facto change at the bank, since Sheffer and Sussman had been Gafny's closest consultants to begin with.[9]

As it happened, in mid-1981, when Yoram Aridor was minister of finance, the government did not renew Sheffer and Sussman's appointments as DGs and forced both officials to leave the bank. In September 1981, Aridor engineered the appointment of Moshe Mandelbaum, his preferred candidate for the governorship, as deputy governor. In January 1982, Mandelbaum was indeed promoted to the governorship, and in April 1982 Aridor filled the vacancy in the DG's office by appointing his part-time advisor, Yakir Plessner, to the post in order to provide him with a full-time position. Plessner, however, was a relative outsider at the bank, more involved in Aridor's policies than with BOI affairs. Plessner left the bank in 1985 and the DG position remained vacant until 2002.

BOI INVOLVEMENT IN ECONOMIC POLICY, 1954–85

Monetary Policy

There is a broad consensus among the interviewees that until 1985 the BOI was not really able to conduct monetary policy as such. In effect, it acquiesced in the lack of separation between the conduct of monetary and fiscal policy. Today, this acquiescence is criticized as a sign of the BOI's lack of independence during those years. Specifically, the bank had very little direct influence on the money supply via the monetary base, which was chiefly determined by the "twin deficits" (budget and balance-of-payments). Kochav and Sheffer believe that, on the whole, the bank did have a strong impact on the money market by restraining policy measures that increased the money supply; Sussman and Heth are more skeptical. Sanbar opined that even today, when the BOI can control the interest rate, influencing the quantity of money would be the preferable tool, both achieving the same result. Quantity changes are less conspicuous and operate at a longer time lag—advantages in his view. He concedes, however, that this method is less applicable today than a generation ago, due to the current, exceedingly low reserve requirements.

Even on commercial banking credit the BOI had very little influence. All changes in reserve requirements had to be approved by the government. The BOI gradually managed to raise the reserve requirements steeply and also established quantitative ceilings for bank credit. These restrictions, however, were officially circumvented by the system of "directed credit," in which restriction-exempt loans were granted to firms that were considered important for economic growth and, especially, exports. Directed credit was allocated in two phases: (1) on the basis of yearly quotas to main economic sectors, as recommended by a joint committee of the Ministry of Finance, the Ministry of Industry and Trade, and the BOI, and (2) at the level of specific loans, at the discretion of BOI officials following government guidelines. Thus, the bank's restrictions affected only the unrestricted-credit capacity of the commercial banks. The larger banks and firms partly circumvented those limits by borrowing from abroad on the basis of permits from the Ministry of Finance.[10]

The BOI leaders considered it their duty to try to restrain the twin deficits and the system of directed credit. According to Sheffer, they had a sense of being "keepers of the flame" of sane economic policy against various vested interests and the politicians. The first three directors of the RD have no doubt that their department and the governor had considerable influence on economic policy. First, their *Annual Report* and periodical reports on changes in money supply not only provided data and analyzed economic developments but also included policy recommendations that often criticized government policy. Second, the governor and also (sometimes) the RD directors participated in government economic deliberations and committees, consulted with the minister of finance and/or senior ministry officials, and appeared before relevant Knesset committees. On all these occasions, the leading economists of the BOI presented their views on economic policy and often urged changes and reforms.

The third channel of influence was public opinion. Sheffer, in particular, stressed this approach, even arguing that during his term "monetary policy was limited to persuasion." Edification and persuasion, applied in appearances before the Knesset Finance Committee and other committees, and in public lectures in relevant forums, were the bank's power and "weapon." The press, Members of Knesset, and officials in economic organizations recognized the BOI officials as well-intentioned apolitical figures who had no personal axe to grind. Individual MKs asked the heads of the RD to instruct them in the principles of economics and economic policy. "We enjoyed public sympathy," Sheffer said, and "a good, supportive press." Although the BOI lost this advantage during the 1970s, Gafny also used the "weapon" of turning to public opinion.

Horowitz, much admired for his broad erudition as well as his political and diplomatic skills and extensive network of domestic and international connections, was not part of the Mapai (Labor Party) establishment that ruled the country until mid-1977. Nevertheless, he was much involved in economic policy in general and had some successes in restraining its inherent expansionary bias. Since most of his governorship was noted for rapid growth and modest inflation, BOI policy could be accommodating.

Sanbar was much appreciated at the bank as an economist—by academic training and by intuition—and for his lengthy experience in public service and the private sector. He was admired even more for his independent stance and "fighting spirit." He had been a right-hand man and close confidant of Pinhas Sapir, the veteran Mapai functionary and actor in economic affairs, for so long that when he reluctantly accepted the appointment to the governorship, the BOI staff was fearful for its relative independence. To everybody's surprise, however—not the least Sapir's—Sanbar felt free to criticize fiscal policy and to reject Finance Ministry demands that he considered detrimental. For some time, he also cultivated his old connections with senior officials at the Ministries of Finance and Industry and Trade. All this evoked Sapir's ire and crimped the BOI's policy options more severely than under "normal" conditions.

Sanbar evaded the restrictions in ingenious ways. For example, unable to obtain the government's consent to changes in the reserve requirements, he developed roundabout methods to limit "unrestricted" bank credit. As the government's economic advisor, he recommended to Yehoshua Rabinowitz, Sapir's successor as minister of finance, the introduction of a value-added tax, after reading the arguments of the Jerusalem professor Amotz Morag. He also was involved in the major income-tax reform proposed by the Ben-Shahar Committee and participated in the decision to peg the Israel pound (IL) to a currency "basket" instead of to the U.S. dollar.

Arnon Gafny brought to the governorship training in economics and a long and variegated public-service career. His forte was his excellent relationship with Rabinowitz, whom he had served as director general. On this basis, the BOI and the Finance Ministry continued to cooperate closely. Inside the BOI, he established an informal forum for regular consultations with Sheffer, Sussman, and Heth.

Nevertheless, inflation accelerated during the governorships of both Sanbar and Gafny; for lack of policy tools—and perhaps also limited theoretical understanding—the BOI did not manage to stem the tide. (See below.)

Moshe Mandelbaum, succeeding Gafny as governor in January 1982, did not consider the function of economic advisor to the government appropriate to his concept of the role of BOI governor. Utilizing his theoretical expertise and practical experience, he concentrated on monetary-policy matters and established a Monetary Department (MD) at the bank, under Victor Medina, for this sole purpose. This meant, first, that various aspects of monetary policy—reserve requirements, limited open-market operations, and rediscounting, which had been dispersed among various BOI departments and insufficiently coordinated by the monthly meetings that Sheffer had established—were gathered under one umbrella. The basic idea was to develop tools for a future time when normal conditions and an independent BOI would make effective monetary policy possible. One problem resulting from the inflationary situation and previous measures, especially credit quotas, was the extensive use of nonbanking financial intermediaries for credits denominated in IS.[11] The BOI also had changed reserve requirements and interest rates to the detriment of IS versus dollar reserves, which greatly widened the interest spread between IS and dollar bank deposits. The innovative approach of Medina's MD was to develop IS financial instruments and, at the general level, to make domestic-currency deposits attractive to the public again. Thus, the BOI introduced unindexed bank deposits in 1982, induced the Ministry of Finance to make them attractive by exempting them from income tax, and cooperated with the Finance

Ministry in reestablishing short-term Treasury bills (MAKAM) in 1983. The BOI also began to use reserve requirements and stiff penalties for exceeding them as an alternative to the setting of quotas ("ceilings") for unrestricted bank credit, introduced monetary lending as an alternative to reserve requirements for commercial banks, and gradually discontinued the manipulation of market prices for government bonds.[12]

Mandelbaum and his MD were well aware, however, that all these efforts could have only a very limited effect under the prevailing inflationary conditions and fiscal policies. Therefore, they pinned their hopes on far-reaching reform and, particularly, on liberating the BOI from its de facto unlimited obligation to monetize the fiscal deficit.

Relations with Prime Ministers and Finance Minister

As long as the system of cooperative economic policy remained in effect, harmonious relations between the BOI governor and prime ministers and finance minister were of paramount importance.

Whenever the governor and the minister of finance strongly disagreed about something, the former brought his case to the prime minister. According to Kochav, this worked quite well with Ben-Gurion and Levi Eshkol. During Ben-Gurion's premiership, there was a triangle of forces composed of Horowitz, Eshkol, and Sapir. The last-mentioned—director general of the Finance Ministry and, from 1955, minister of industry and trade—was Horowitz's main adversary. The chief disagreements concerned the periodic need for currency devaluation and the extent of directed credit, especially in connection with Sapir's policy of managed (and often discriminatory) industrialization. Although Eshkol and Sapir were close friends, Eshkol often sided with Horowitz, having been convinced that the latter was right.

Ben-Gurion (and even more so his "alternate" in the premiership, Moshe Sharett) usually relied on Eshkol's judgment and leadership in economic affairs, but extreme cases of disagreement were brought before him as mentioned. Kochav remembers in particular a fierce conflict with Sapir about the 1962 devaluation, over which Sapir, who had the backing of then Foreign Minister Golda Meir, threatened to resign. After hearing senior officials from both sides (separately), Ben-Gurion decided that a significant devaluation was indeed necessary. "Without Ben-Gurion's support, Eshkol could not have wrested a positive decision from the government," Kochav remarked. The BOI itself was not involved in the top-secret preparations for the devaluation, but Kochav (both before and after leaving the BOI) chaired, and Nurit Wahl of the RD participated in, the small ad hoc team that prepared the policy change.

During her premiership (1969–74), Golda Meir was minimally involved in economic policy; she relied on her finance minister (Sapir).[13] However, Sanbar persuaded her to have monthly meetings with him so that he could apprise her of matters that he considered important. Yitzhak Rabin, in his first premiership (1974–77), relied on his finance minister, Yehoshua Rabinowitz, but major proposals were presented to him before government discussions. Gafny as governor made a point of keeping Rabin informed and on good terms.[14]

Both Sanbar and Gafny maintained excellent cooperation with Rabinowitz, whom they regarded highly. Sanbar emphasizes that Rabinowitz had been involved in budgetary affairs for many years, first in the Histadrut apparatus and later in the Municipality of Tel Aviv, before he was elected mayor. Gafny had maintained working relations with Rabinowitz for many years and found that he had an open mind and was interested in reforms and innovations. Indeed, several important innovations—the aforementioned income-tax reform and value-added tax, and the crawling peg exchange-rate regime—resulted from close BOI—Finance Ministry teamwork.

Mandelbaum had been appointed at the initiative of Finance Minister Aridor as part of the latter's effort to change the BOI management and was considered "Aridor's man" at the bank. Once in office, however, Mandelbaum kept his distance and concentrated on BOI work, although he participated in cabinet meetings as the government's economic advisor.

Specific Disagreements

Both before and after establishment of the BOI, Israel's foreign-exchange regime was based on two mechanisms. One was a system of discreet currency devaluations that aimed to narrow the gap between the domestic and foreign purchasing power of the Israeli currency. The BOI staff, concurring with Israel's academic economists in general, seemed to favor more frequent and less dramatic devaluations. The second was a system of multiple "effective" exchange rates for different types of exports, imports, and capital inflows, achieved by an array of subsidies and imposts that became increasingly varied and complicated. Until 1954, even the formal exchange rate was multiple. The BOI staff, opposing this discriminatory and often arbitrary system as a mechanism for influencing foreign trade and economic development according to government priorities, advocated the adoption of a uniform rate.

The leading and most consistent opponent to the BOI's recommendations on both counts was Pinhas Sapir, who served as minister of industry and trade for nearly ten years and as minister of finance for eleven. Sapir's opposition to a uniform exchange rate is easily understood, since such a rate was diametrically opposed to his view of how to manage the Israeli economy. His stance against more frequent devaluations probably stemmed from the fact that these ideas were usually bundled with the demand for unification of the exchange rate. Be this as it may, the topic of devaluation elicited recurrent and very emphatic disputes between Horowitz and Sapir, which Eshkol mediated with difficulty until they came to a boil in 1962, as related above.

Devaluation expectations abounded during 1961; there had been a general feeling that the exchange rate was far from equilibrium and that too many "effective" rates existed. Thus, there was no genuine element of surprise at what happened, except for its exact timing and the extent of the change.[15] The bank also argued for abolishing all import quotas. This measure and the end of the system of subsidies and imposts were achieved only partly in 1962, but Sussman believes that the actions at that time marked the beginning of foreign-trade liberalization by touching off a cumulative process of changes in the foreign-trade and exchange-rate regime that continued even during the difficult times of 1974–75. Sussman also notes, however, that some economists thought that greater reliance on quantity restrictions might cause less inflation pressure than devaluation would. When the 1962 change in trade policy resulted in accelerated inflation, even though the growing balance-of-trade deficit decreased the money supply, the BOI tried to institute a more restrictive policy within its limitations. Sussman, however, does not remember any explicit government decision to subject domestic demand to drastic restraint, that is, to cause a recession.

In an interesting observation, Sussman notes that despite the close control of foreign-currency movements, large speculative capital movements preceded and followed most discreet devaluations, especially those in 1974 and 1977. Generally speaking, he concludes, devaluations were determined endogenously but the timing was sometimes forced by growing speculative capital outflows.

BOI–Finance Ministry collaboration was quite close during the tenures of Eshkol and Sapir and very close under Rabinowitz (whom Arnon Gafny served as director general until he was appointed BOI governor). Some of the tension between Sapir and Sanbar developed before the 1962 devaluation (which Sapir opposed vehemently), when Sanbar was a member of the small devaluation committee. The rupture in their relations, however, came in 1972, when—as was customary before elections—the Ministry of Finance prepared to inject money into the economy by enlarging the budget deficit even amidst full employment and rising prices. The BOI, led by Sanbar, spoke out against this intention and refused to monetarize the added expenditure. Sapir, who abhorred opposition to and criticism of his policies, considered this an act of "treason" and broke off contact with Sanbar. Still, Sheffer and Sussman report that they themselves had "very good" professional and even personal relations with Sapir. "There were stormy debates and shouting," Sussman recalls, "but close relations." Sanbar, however, felt that part of his world had been shattered.[16] The 1973 war occasioned a reconciliation that enabled Sanbar to arrange for emergency credit without collateral, guaranteed by the BOI, for manufacturers whose workforce was partly mobilized.

During the 1960s, in addition to the exchange-rate and directed-credit issues, the BOI was intensely concerned about efforts to contain the maximum legal rate of interest. An Ottoman law (1887) that limited interest to 9% had remained in force during the Mandate era and in Israel until 1957, when new legislation authorized the minister of finance to set the maximum legal rate. In March 1957, this maximum was set at 10% for agriculture and manufacturing and 11% for other borrowers. In view of the rate of inflation and the limited supply of unrestricted bank credit, however, these rates were below the market equilibrium for nonsubsidized short-term loans.

A black market in credit began to develop in the mid-1950s and a loophole in the 1957 statute made it quasi-legal for borrowers to offer bills at the maximum interest rate plus a commission, part of which was passed on to private lenders by the intermediate bank. Thus a "gray" market of "bill brokerage" took shape. Even though this activity eroded the growth of deposits and other banking business, it expanded due to a growing supply of liquid funds and growing demand, especially during the boom of the 1960s.

From 1960, if not earlier, David Horowitz waged an information and lobbying campaign in government, Knesset, and public forums, for the repeal of the Interest Law. The opponents of the repeal, citing moral and "social" arguments, represented partly the public's abhorrence of "usury" but mainly the perceived interests of the borrowers, chiefly those in agriculture and manufacturing. Thus, the opposition cut across the line ordinarily separating the private and the Histadrut sectors and was strongly supported by the ministers of agriculture and of industry and trade and by a broad front in the Knesset.

Kochav is convinced that in the 1950s or the 1960s Eshkol could not have engineered the repeal of the Interest Law. Probably Eshkol himself was not only influenced by personal sentiments and political calculus but also impressed by the prediction that the rate of interest would actually rise after repeal, thereby increasing the cost of government borrowing. This reasoning also explains why he persistently denied the BOI permission to engage in "open-market operations."

The BOI (and the Ministry of Finance) became increasingly aware of bill brokerage and tried to restrain the practice. By all indications, however, the volume of this type of credit grew steadily, even in the first year of the 1966–67 recession. In the late 1960s, the law became increasingly ineffective. It did not apply to CPI- or dollar-indexed loans and, with respect to unindexed bank credit (not to mention nonbanking lenders), it encouraged more and more ways of evasion—of which Kochav gave several examples. Concurrently, the campaign for repeal of the Interest Law intensified. In September 1968, the *Banking Quarterly Review* published a debate on the issue (in Hebrew), in which Eliezer Sheffer summarized the reasons for regarding repeal as urgently necessary. The arguments, however, were not new; what decided the issue and led to the repeal in March 1970 was a change in circumstances. Several interviewees expressed this view; Kochav thought that the policy in Israel might have been affected by a change in economic theory that attributed increased importance to interest rates. The repeal, however, did not automatically enhance the BOI's ability to use the key rate as a policy tool.

Control of foreign exchange was assigned to a department of the Finance Ministry. The original draft of the BOI Law empowered the governor to set the exchange rate, but Horowitz renounced this prerogative—due to its political character—after his consultations in America. The bureaucracy that dealt with foreign currency controls was so large and cumbersome that it would have been impractical if not counterproductive to transfer it all to the BOI. The Ministry of Finance circumvented limits on BOI lending by borrowing abroad. (However, this was not the decisive consideration in keeping the foreign-currency control within the ministry's purview.) Another way of circumventing BOI restraints—borrowing by Israeli banks from abroad—became a significant problem only in the 1970s.[17]

Policies 1966–77

As far as the RD was aware, the 1966–67 recession was not a planned and preconceived development. As noted, Sussman remembers the intention to restrain excess demand that had been occasioned partly by the effects of the 1962 devaluation. When the balance-of-payments began to balloon again, liquidity in the economy from this source was also reduced. Furthermore, efforts to improve the "structure" of the economy and induce export-led growth were not a novelty of the mid-1960s. As the recession developed, however, the lag in obtaining "real-time" statistical data on the economy became crucial. M. Fraenkel recalls that the recession took the bank by surprise and that the BOI still spoke and wrote about the need to restrain demand even two months after the recession was under way.[18]

After 1973, the Israeli economy found itself in tremendous difficulty due to the expenses of the war and the arms race that followed it, the effects of the oil crisis on world markets and particularly on economies lacking oil, the rise in prices of all basic commodities, and, not least, the desire to preserve employment and wages.[19] Inflation accelerated. Monetary policy was supposed to apply restraint but currency devaluations undermined its efforts. The appointment of Rabinowitz as minister of finance strengthened cooperation between the ministry and the BOI. Henceforth, devaluations were the results of joint decisions, as was the pegging of the domestic currency to a "basket" of currencies instead of the U.S. dollar.

The next step was the adoption of a crawling-peg exchange rate. Sanbar still thinks that this was a correct decision, as was later the sliding-rate ("diagonal") band. The message of such a measure is a declaration of intent aimed at investors in export industries, although the changes in the exchange-rate regime in the 1970s were also influenced by the breakdown of the international regime at the time. Plessner thinks that the purpose of instituting the crawling peg was to erode the real wage. He points to the report of the Sussman Commission on COLA reform as a source that mentions this intention—which proved impossible due to the opposition of the still-powerful Histadrut. Be this as it may, additional inflation pressure undermined the system by forcing accelerated adjustments of the pace of the "crawl."[20]

In Fraenkel's view, limited understanding of the devaluation-inflation mechanism was a major problem at the time, not only among Israeli economists but also in the general economic literature. The effects of short-term capital movements on the equilibrium exchange rate were underrated if not ignored. The main theoretical difficulty, in Fraenkel's opinion, was insufficient understanding of the forces that determined the *real* exchange rate, including underestimation of the effect of the budget deficit. Two articles by Bruno in 1978–79, on economies with and without indexation, were an important theoretical step in the right direction. These, however, were preceded by the "Erlich liberalization."[21]

Before every general election, it was the BOI's practice to prepare a macroeconomic plan that would be presented to the new government. Gafny and his deputies followed this practice in early 1977. Ben-Bassat recalls having been assigned by Sussman to draw up such a plan in conjunction with Jacob Lavi. One of Gafny's main proposals was to cut the defense budget—a process that was already under way—and to prune government expenditure in general. The surprise came after the election, when the BOI heads met with Simcha Erlich, the new minister of finance, and his deputy, Yehezkel Flomin. At the meeting, the ministry leaders revealed their intention to abolish all foreign-currency controls, a measure that the platform of their party, the Liberal Party, had prescribed for many years. They asked the BOI to prepare—under extreme circumspection—a detailed plan for this regime change. The BOI "triumvirate" (Gafny, Sheffer, and Sussman) sat down with Amiram Sivan, the director general of the Finance Ministry, and did as requested. Secrecy was kept so successfully that Fraenkel recalls attending a two-day meeting of senior economists from the BOI, the Ministry of Finance, and academia in Tiberias without anyone getting an inkling of the brewing "revolution." Back in Jerusalem, Fraenkel was assigned by Sussman to prepare a plan for liberalization of the foreign-exchange market and movements. Although he combed the literature thoroughly, he found it of little assistance. In particular, it offered him no advice about what to liberalize first, the nonfinancial or the financial markets. He felt unable to write the requested paper and had the general feeling that the economy lacked the preconditions for such a reform.[22]

Gafny, Sheffer, and Sussman, in collaboration with Meir Heth, worked up the plan. The document stressed the need for additional reforms, specifically drastic reduction of the government deficit. In the final stage, several additional officials from the Finance Ministry and the BOI were co-opted onto the preparatory team. In Sheffer's estimation, a sudden total elimination of the budget deficit would cause a liquidity shortage. He wanted to recommend an annual deficit of around IL 6 billion but was persuaded by Gafny and Sussman not to elaborate on the subject. The matter came up at a summarizing meeting with Erlich and Flomin, in which the finance minister declared his intention of demanding a "zero deficit." Gafny apprised the press of this intention on several occasions. He also prepared an emergency guarantee from the Bank of International Settlements in case the regime change precipitated too large a loss of reserves.

Eventually, the government decided not only to forgo a zero deficit but also to refrain from cutting its expenditure at all, even though all ministers had been informed and lobbied by the BOI people. Prime Minister Menachem Begin had warned Erlich beforehand that considerations of his coalition prevented him from adopting the recommendation. Thus, the government accepted the foreign-currency liberalization plan, which Begin viewed as the last step in the dismantling of the Mandate-era regime, but without the provision of cutting the budget deficit. When the minister of finance informed his colleagues and the BOI officials of this development, Gafny saw no choice but to appeal to the government in public. Thus, he immediately went to an economic forum in which he was scheduled to lecture, declared there that the government had approved an excessively large budget that would undermine the foreign-exchange liberalization, and urged the government to reconsider. Begin reprimanded him for this public performance.[23]

In retrospect, Ben-Bassat—who was not personally involved at the time—considers the liberalization a major failure on the part of the BOI. If the RD directors thought that conditions were not ripe for such a dramatic change, especially in view of the massive twin deficits and an annual inflation rate of 40%, they should have refused to cooperate and made efforts to abort the project. Ben-Bassat thinks that the idea of introducing dollar-indexed resident deposits (PATAM) was one of several indications that the officials responsible for the detailed plan were apprehensive about its chances of success.

Toward Stabilization

Yigael Hurwitz replaced Erlich as minister of finance in November 1979 and, after briefly and unsuccessfully trying to reduce the deficit, was succeeded by Yoram Aridor in January 1981. Aridor's director general was the economist Ezra Sadan. One of the results of the change in ministry leadership was an outright crisis in relations between the Finance Ministry and the BOI. Sheffer felt that Aridor considered Gafny and his deputies "enemies." Taking a more balanced view, he and Sussman think that Aridor rejected the "conventional wisdoms" of the bank, particularly its strong emphasis on the balance of payments. In any case, in July 1981, when Sheffer and Sussman's term as deputy governors ended, they were not reappointed but rather replaced (several months later) by Moshe Mandelbaum and then by Aridor's advisor, Yakir Plessner. After Gafny's term expired in October 1981, Mandelbaum was appointed BOI governor in January 1982.

The BOI and its RD were not invited to take part in several of the new policy initiatives of the Aridor-Sadan-Plessner team. Mandelbaum, in turn, was not motivated to try to influence economic policy, especially in fiscal affairs.

The exception, in a roundabout way, was Aridor's idea in 1983 of "dollarizing" the economy. When consultations about this idea began, Aridor invited Leora Meridor, a member of the RD staff, to join them. He knew her personally and also knew about her views on the need for a monetary "anchor." As a loyal employee of the BOI, Meridor asked Aridor to let her bring her superior, Mordechai Fraenkel, aboard as well. Thus, Fraenkel, Ben-Bassat, and Meridor joined the team that discussed the dollarization project. (Sadan later informed Mandelbaum, who gave his ex post facto blessing to the participation of BOI officials in the discussions.) Meridor also recalls that to keep the project strictly secret, and since there were no personal computers yet, she wrote all the position papers on the subject by hand.

In addition to the three RD staffers, the team included four officials from the Ministry of Finance (Aridor, Sadan, Plessner, and Jacob Neeman, director general during Hurwitz's tenure), and several economists: Nissan Liviatan, Eitan Berglas, Elhanan Helpman, Pinhas Zusman, and Meir Kohn, a friend of Plessner's and a visiting scholar at his department. Ben-Bassat recalls two versions of the dollarization proposal—to introduce "green" U.S. dollars as Israel's legal tender or to peg the IS to the dollar. The issue was not definitely settled. Fraenkel thinks that the position taken by Liviatan and the RD members, seconded by Mandelbaum, was based on what was taken to be the moral of the failure of the Erlich liberalization, which was that the "fundamentals" had to be taken care of first, that is, the budget deficit had to be drastically decreased, largely because pegging the exchange rate would cause the balance of payments deficit and the foreign debt to balloon. Meridor believes that Aridor was willing to accept a cut in the budget deficit because he had become convinced that the inflation subsidies occasioned by lagged tax revenues (the "Tanzi effect") and nominal interest rates on directed credit outweighed the inflation tax. Only Plessner, Meridor recalls, rejected the necessity of a cut, arguing that the public, with perfect rational expectations, would understand that dollarization would take care of the deficit. Plessner himself denies this version of affairs, referring to a memo he wrote dated December 1983 that included budget cuts as part of the proposed reform. As it happened, the dollarization project was leaked to the press and thereby aborted before fiscal measures could be taken. As a result, Mandelbaum persuaded the prime minister, Yitzhak Shamir, to convene the government in order to make a decision on aborting the project. In view of the prime minister's intention, Aridor resigned in November 1983.

Several commentators regard the Bank of Israel's "passivity" in view of the inflationary spiral from the 1970s to 1985 as a tremendous failure. One may counter this perspective by claiming that this view disregards the BOI's extremely limited ability to conduct monetary policy, on the one hand, and the (global) lag of theoretical and institutional developments in response to changes in economic trends—"stagflation," high inflation, globalization—on the other hand. Still, Israel's adjustment to the new circumstances may have been too slow.

Be this as it may, "heterodox" ideas, which underlay the dollarization proposal and, eventually, the stabilization in 1985, were beginning to develop in Israel in the early 1980s. The main realization was that the twin deficits, the nominal price and wage levels, the monetary accommodation, and the inflation rate were all increasing and mutually reinforcing in a rudderless economy and that a monetary anchor—such as a fixed exchange rate—was needed. Within the BOI Research Department, a small group—Meridor, Amos Rubin, Tsippi Galyam, and Uri Litvin—led the way. Ben-Bassat stresses that these economists did not believe that fixing the exchange rate only, without concomitant fiscal measures, would stop inflation, as Plessner was believed to have thought. Other RD staffers, led by Piterman and Meir Sokoler, were more conservative and "orthodox," viewing elimination of the fiscal deficit as a sufficient anti-inflation measure. They came around to the new way of thinking only gradually and in the course of lively, thoroughgoing debates that took place regularly at the RD and the economics departments of the Hebrew University and Tel Aviv University.

In early 1981, Michael Bruno gave an interview to a monthly journal of the Labor Party that outlined his plan to "shock" the economy, including the institution of an exchange-rate anchor and a fiscal cut.[24]

A semi-formal step for advancing the discussion was initiated by M. Fraenkel in July 1981, when the bank convened a group of first-class economists to propose policies for the government that would take office after imminent general elections. Invited were two American friends of Israel, Stanley Fischer (who had published an article on monetary policy in the *BOI Review*) and Jacob Frenkel; Don Patinkin, Bruno, and Liviatan from the Hebrew University; and Berglas and Helpman of Tel Aviv University. Gafny, Sheffer, Sussman, Fraenkel, and Fraenkel's deputy Freddy Wieder represented the BOI. This group composed a draft stabilization program and Fischer and Frenkel published a summary in the September 1982 issue of the *Economic Quarterly* (in Hebrew).[25]

In December 1983, after what was widely considered the dollarization fiasco, M. Fraenkel, Piterman, and Sokoler moved on to the next phase by publishing an article in the *Economic Quarterly* that contained most elements of the 1985 stabilization plan. Mandelbaum, then governor, takes credit for the inclusion of a drastic decrease in government expenditure in this "blueprint." He presented its basic ideas to the government and the Knesset Finance Committee in the preceding report on changes in the money supply,[26] that is, before the December 1983 article.

It would be futile to assign "original authorship" of the stabilization program to any single person. Many developed its ideas over time: Bruno, Liviatan, and the four aforementioned RD staffers; the BOI Monetary Department; and the participants in the dollarization debates. They were influenced by the professional literature, foreign models, and the American consultants. Bruno, soon to become the BOI governor, and Peres, as prime minister, led the implementation, and public opinion gave them the credit for it.

The Bank-Shares Episode

As a result of accelerating inflation and stricter capital-ratio rules, most major commercial banks started to issue additional (nonvoting) shares in large quantities and to market them aggressively to the public.[27] To compete with CPI-indexed government bonds and dollar-indexed PATAM deposits, the banks guaranteed that their shares' market price would rise *at least* as vigorously as the CPI plus interest. They kept their word by manipulating the prices of their shares, increasingly with the aid of foreign credit. Vast quantities of private savings were invested in these bank shares. Naturally, this competition hurt government bond issues and made the government more dependent on the BOI and external borrowing to cover its deficit. Since the banks were the main channels for fiscal borrowing from abroad, the government tacitly acquiesced in the share-price manipulation. Just the same, the gap between the banks' net worth and the market prices of the shares widened continuously.

By the late 1970s, the dangers of the bank-share manipulation, to the bank themselves and to the credulous public, dawned on the BOI and the Ministry of Finance. Arnon Gafny, then governor, asked Shaul Bronfeld to study the matter, and the resulting memorandum caused him great concern. Believing in persuasion and relying on some previous experience, he arranged several meetings with the CEOs of the five largest banks and with each executive separately. Four of the five stubbornly refused to phase out the manipulation, perhaps partly because the banks did not trust each other enough to terminate the practice in concert. Mainly, though, they probably believed that the BOI or Finance would bail them out in a crisis by providing them with loans. Consultations at the BOI and with the managers of the Securities Authority and the Stock Exchange, as well as with senior Finance Ministry officials, led Gafny to believe that a sudden forced cessation of the issue of bank shares might cause a severe financial panic and crisis.

Attempts at persuasion remained the approach of the BOI under its next governor, Mandelbaum, and of the Finance Ministry under Aridor, but to no avail. Even after a stock-exchange bubble burst in late 1982 and early 1983 (without affecting the bank shares), both authorities remained hesitant and passive accomplices in the "crime." They were probably unwilling to pay the political price of forcing an end to the manipulations and thereby causing the bank shares to collapse. The banks clearly understood that they were riding a tiger but were afraid to get off.

The inevitable crash came in the autumn of 1983, when expectation of a major devaluation caused the public to sell large quantities of bank shares in order to buy dollars or create PATAM deposits. According to Plessner, Aridor postponed the necessary devaluation in September, knowing well that such a move would bring the bank-shares situation to a head. The banks were unable to absorb the massive sales in their portfolios and the government—fearing a major run on the banks by domestic and foreign depositors—gave in to the pressures. The four leading commercial banks were subjected to de facto nationalization and the public was guaranteed a certain price—minimizing the losses of most—for the bank shares over the next ten years. In 1985–86, an investigative commission under Supreme Court Justice Moshe Bejski recommended the dismissal of the major banks' managements and of BOI Governor Mandelbaum and also reprimanded several leading figures no longer in office, such as Gafny.

The government decisions about the bank-share settlement, engineered by Avraham Shapira (who chaired both the Knesset Finance Committee and the BOI Advisory Committee) were severely criticized by several interviewees, such as Ben-Bassat and Plessner. The latter thinks that the available statistical data would have made it possible to compensate only the genuine losers, that is, those who had bought bank shares shortly before the crash. Those who had held shares for lengthy periods, he says, would have lost only part of their potential gains from appreciation of the shares and did not deserve aid. Ben-Bassat is even more extreme, asserting that no shareholders deserved protection. In the main, however, he criticizes the details of the quasi-nationalization, particularly the decision to leave the banks' managements in control. This gave the banks excessive influence on the subsequent choice of directors representing the government.

The general view today is that the passivity of the Bank of Israel—that is, the examiner of banks and the governor—in face of the growing severity of the bank-share manipulation was a salient failure that the ostensible assent of the Ministry of Finance does not really mitigate.

Stabilization

The general elections in July 1984 resulted in a draw that was resolved by the formation of a National Unity Government with a revolving premiership.[28] In its first phase it was headed by Shimon Peres, with Yizhak Moda'i as finance minister. Moda'i began his tenure with a 9% devaluation and a cut in subsidies.

Then, when prices shot up, he negotiated a three-month "package deal" with the Histadrut (representing labor) and the Manufacturers' Association (representing management), freezing wages and prices—but not the exchange rate, the budget, and interest rates. This type of agreement was renewed twice more, probably because Peres wished to preserve relative tranquility at least until after the Histadrut elections in May 1985.

Moda'i also appointed as director general Emanuel Sharon, an economist well versed in political economy. (This was really a reappointment, since Sharon had briefly held this office under Yigal Cohen-Orgad, who had succeeded Aridor in late 1983.) Sharon was authorized to prepare a comprehensive stabilization plan and proceeded with purpose and political skill. He also renewed contact with the U.S. administration, which had already been approached during the dollarization planning with the request for a standby loan.

A consultative body named the U.S.–Israel Joint Economic Development Group (JEDG) was established on the basis of an agreement between Secretary of State George Schultz (a prominent economist) and Shimon Peres. The American chair was Allen Wallis, Undersecretary of State and an academic economist himself, joined by Professors Stanley Fischer and Herbert Stein. The chair of the Israeli team was Sharon, joined by Berglas, Bruno, Liviatan, and (unofficially) Mordechai Fraenkel. Much of the preparatory work relied on the services of Fraenkel and the BOI Research Department. The Israeli members of the team met informally on their own.

Ahead of the first JEDG meeting in December 1984, the Israeli team adopted a proposed comprehensive monetary reform plan and disclosed it at the Washington meeting, in connection with a request for an aid package for the project. The U.S. Department of the Treasury, however, opposed the aid and Peres remained hesitant and continued to pursue the package-deal approach. His attitude was backed by Sanbar and Gafny, former governors of the BOI. What is more, several economists, particularly Haim Ben-Shahar (the Labor Party's candidate for minister of finance before the elections) expressed objections to an exchange-rate freeze. Fraenkel considers the package-deal approach mistaken and traces it to Peres's political bias and "anti-economic nature."

By mid-1985, inflation seemed to be spiraling completely out of control and the foreign reserves were dwindling. Peres understood that his political survival depended on stemming inflation by drastic measures; the JEDG team added external pressure by paying a visit. On June 5, Peres and Moda'i authorized an informal expert team to present a detailed plan of action within three weeks. Its official members were Sharon (chair); Mordechai Fraenkel of the BOI;[29] Amnon Neubach (Peres's economic advisor); and, as informal, independent, and unpaid consultants, Eitan Berglas and Michael Bruno. Several potential members of the team were abroad at the time. Liviatan was vacationing in Europe.[30] Sanbar and Haim Ben-Shahar were also out of the country; in Fraenkel's opinion, this helped to present Peres with a consensus plan. At a late stage, several Treasury officials from professional divisions joined the preparations. The group, meeting in various unconventional places (such as Bruno's study at the Israel National Academy of Science and the Humanities and an apartment made available by the Secret Service), composed the plan in its final form. There was disagreement on one topic in particular: pegging the IS to the U.S. dollar. Berglas opposed the idea of a fixed exchange rate; Bruno favored it and eventually won the day. The final program was presented to Peres on June 29 and to the government the next day.

The government debated the plan in a stormy twenty-hour session. Since it had proved politically impossible to carry out the fiscal part of the plan as a first step, it was now crucial to have it approved en bloc. Some ministers strongly opposed this and Peres began to waver. Fortunately, Berglas and Bruno attended the government meeting and threatened not only to resign from the team in the event of nonpassage but also, and immediately, to speak out in public against such inaction. Under this pressure, Peres rallied and the government—reportedly half-asleep by then—endorsed the critical mass of the proposed measures on the morning of July 1. The resolution decision included the provisions that all monetary policy aspects of the stabilization would be conducted exclusively by the BOI and that "printing of money" would be banned by law.[31] (The monetary policy that complemented the plan was indeed conducted by the BOI Monetary Department and made an important contribution to the plan's success.)

Michael Bruno, who had joined the RD as an advisor in 1984, was named to the stabilization team and mobilized the department's resources for all preparations. His participation on the team, along with Fraenkel's, enabled the team to receive inputs from the RD without endangering the secrecy of the plan.[32] Ben-Bassat counts this case as one of the RD's outstanding contributions to government economic policy-making.

Sylvia Piterman provided an interesting comment about the stabilization success. Not only was it planned elaborately by brilliant minds but it also had considerable good luck. Oil and commodity prices were declining and the U.S. dollar—to which the domestic currency was pegged—depreciated, to the benefit of Israeli exports to Europe. The Erlich liberalization, in contrast, had run into bad luck; apart from its faulty planning, it collided with the second "oil shock" (1979). Piterman also emphasizes a clause in the stabilization plan to the effect that the pegging of the currency would depend on holding the general wage level constant (in effect, via the real exchange rate).

An exceedingly important complement to the stabilization plan was the passage of the so-called no-printing law, which released the BOI from its erstwhile obligation to monetize fiscal deficits by the practically unlimited purchase of government bonds. Like other components of the reform, this legislation had been proposed or demanded by several players. A memorandum from Plessner to Aridor in December 1983 about dollarization included the idea. Medina's MD advanced the idea repeatedly. The law was based in part on a memorandum on the topic, titled "A 'Non-Printing Arrangement,'" by Meridor and Akiva Offenbacher of the RD, at the initiative of M. Fraenkel, which was presented to the governor, Mandelbaum, on December 29, 1983.[33] Mandelbaum included the need for such legislation in his January 1984 monetary report and subsequently presented Moday with a detailed draft on the subject. The principle of the statute was also included in a memorandum that Stein and Fischer presented to Peres in March 1985, subsequently referred to as "Herb's Ten Points." In a sense, the memo constituted U.S. pressure to proceed speedily with a drastic reform. The bill that the government approved in early August 1985, however, left the government with the loophole of (partly) monetarizing deficits by borrowing from abroad. This lacuna, in Mandelbaum and Fraenkel's opinion, resulted from Israel's weak credit rating at the time and insufficient forethought.

THE RESEARCH DEPARTMENT

The RD was established as an organic part of the newly created BOI. It and the Department of the Examiner of Banks, taken over from Treasury, constituted for years the chief components of the bank's administration. The BOI also "inherited" two veteran economists from previous Jewish Agency and government posts, who, due to their seniority, were formally not part of the RD: Arieh Ludwig Gaathon (Gruenbaum) and Fanny Ginor. Another veteran, Robert David Ottensooser, was included as well.

The Department of the Examiner—whose chief was appointed by and reported solely to the governor—seems to have been run as something of a separate fiefdom. Eventually, it created its own research division and RD personnel had almost no contact with its work.[34]

The functions of the RD were derived from the responsibilities tasked to the bank. Article 59 of the Bank of Israel Law provides for the publication of an annual report on the bank's activities and policies and on "economic and monetary conditions" during the past year. Horowitz and Kochav, who laid the foundations of the department, chose to interpret this article broadly. Accordingly, the bank's *Annual Report* soon became the main source of information on all aspects of the Israeli economy and its development, as well as on fiscal and monetary policies. The needs of the BOI also spurred the Central Bureau of Statistics to improve its gathering and reporting of economic statistics. Until around 1980, preparing and developing the *Annual Report*—and amplifying its database—was the main concern of the RD. Fraenkel and Ben-Bassat, finding this concern too exclusive, broadened the research activities to include, in the main, the writing of policy-oriented position papers. Meridor considered this policy orientation too narrow and worked to redress the tendency by encouraging more theoretical work. The BOI governor also issues occasional special reports on extraordinary increases in the money supply.[35] Since these reports had to include analysis of the causes of the monetary increase and relevant policy recommendations, they became an important forum for advocacy of greater government restraint in increasing the monetary base.[36] This type of report was succeeded by the Inflation Report, introduced in the late 1990s under J. Frenkel and Leiderman pursuant to an earlier proposal by Sokoler.

To a large but varying extent, the RD geared its activity toward helping the governor in his function as economic advisor to the government. The extent of this activity and of the involvement of the RD directors in economic policy depended on the governor's inclination to involve himself in this field, his standing in so doing, his and his staff's relations with the minister of finance and the senior ministry staff, and the bank's own initiatives.[37] As for abolishing the governor's function as economic advisor to the government—and, by extension, that of the RD—Ben-Bassat emphasized, more strongly than some others who expressed a similar view, that only if the Ministry of Finance or the Office of the Prime Minister had a research capacity of comparable scope and independence could such a move be justified. Meridor stressed the tendency of politicians to preoccupy themselves with short-term problems and noted that the BOI and its RD viewed the economy from a long-term perspective. The bank's history, with the ups and downs of its advisory activity, seems to bear these views out.

The RD developed gradually and consistently, its attention continually drawn to innovations in theory and practice abroad. Zvi Sussman, Kochav's first recruit, joined the department in 1954 while still a student—a practice that many young economists would adopt. Sheffer, who joined in 1959, was an exception, since he came aboard with a doctorate from the London School of Economics. Three years later, a division of labor ensued—one section, led by Sussman, concentrating on the "real" (nonfinancial) aspects of the economy and another, headed by Sheffer, focusing on monetary affairs. In the early 1960s, Michael Bruno worked on his project of an Israeli input-output schema,[38] which also contributed to the training of junior researchers at the department. Bruno's project benefited from the advice and guidance of Hollis Chenery of Stanford University, who spent a full year at the RD as a visiting scholar. By then, the RD's staff already counted more than twenty economists of varying grades.[39]

By that time, the department was involved in constructing a national budget, following an initiative by Kochav for the introduction of long-term analysis in the yearly planning of the state budget by analyzing the budget's effects on the various economic sectors. A Norwegian expert, Odd Aukrust, was invited to instruct the project team in the relevant methodology and stayed for several months. The project was undertaken in conjunction with the Ministry of Finance, in which Kochav served as advisor to the minister (Levi Eshkol) from 1959 on, concurrent with his work at the BOI, until he organized the Economic Planning Authority in the autumn of 1961. The first national budget, formulated with Aukrust's assistance, was presented in 1958. It became a permanent feature of the RD's work. In this connection, the late Carmela Moneta developed a flow-of-funds scheme for the RD. Realizing the value of this approach during her two-year stay with the National Bureau of Economic Research, she established the conceptual framework and the RD's data-collection system for this purpose. The flow-of-funds schema debuted in the BOI *Annual Report* for 1959 and became a permanent feature.[40]

An important element in the atmosphere at the BOI was the RD's nearly total academic freedom. The bank allowed the department to express itself uninhibitedly in its policy evaluations and recommendations, the *Annual Report*, and the occasional reports and position papers that it prepared for the governor or for meetings with Finance Ministry officials.[41]

Since the reports were the governor's responsibility, he read their various sections and, especially, the summary closely and referred his comments and questions to the RD. Horowitz established the pattern of giving the RD free rein. He never demanded that the RD change its views but only asked the department's writers to tone down their phrasing if he thought it would be more "political" and more effective for them to do so. Sanbar, while maintaining this liberal tradition, endeavored to initiate his younger colleagues in the principles of political economy and emphasized that monetary policy must take micro-level responses into account. He also established a Monetary Division within the RD, headed by Sheffer and later by Shaul (Sam) Bronfeld.[42] Gafny went one step further in recognizing the talents of the RD staff by relying on the directors of the department, Sheffer and Sussman, as his close consultants even before they became deputy governors.

The democratic atmosphere was suspended during the four-plus years of Mandelbaum's governorship. Tension between him and the RD developed during his first months at the bank, as deputy governor, and escalated later due to his strong preference for the (new) Monetary Department and the RD's sense of having been demoted. According to the independent testimony of several interviewees, backed by numerous examples, Mandelbaum tended to limit the RD's freedom of expression and to "censor" views expressed in the draft annual reports, resulting in much frustration and bitterness. Mandelbaum emphatically denies this allegation, holding M. Fraenkel responsible for having restricted freedom of expression in the RD. The examples quoted, however, pertain not only to sections of the draft annual reports but also to several position papers and a collection of articles called *Issues in Monetary Policy in Israel*, which was presented to Mandelbaum in December 1982. The governor ignored all these writings and thwarted their distribution. Mandelbaum's excitable temperament and tendency to raise his voice amplified disagreements of substance on both sides by adding personal antagonism and sensitivity that persisted in relations between the RD and the governor afterwards as well. Such was also the case with relations between the RD and the MD, which led to the disruption of contacts between the two entities. The constant tension caused Fraenkel to take a leave of absence for part of 1984. The department still continued with most of its work, even if much of it was not expressed in the bank's recommendations and positions, and with its contacts and consultations with the Ministry of Finance.[43] Relations between Mandelbaum and Medina (head of the MD), in contrast, were noted for understanding and good chemistry.

In the 1950s and 1960s, most RD staff members had only bachelor's degrees in economics, and gifted third-year students were recruited as well.[44] By the 1970s, as the BOI staff—like that of general government at large—was expanding rapidly, the supply of qualified economists had grown considerably and the RD could be more selective.[45] From its early days it was the RD's practice to recruit academic advisors. The first in this capacity were Michael Michaely, who served as general advisor in 1955–59 at Kochav's invitation, and Jacob Paroush, who was econometric advisor in 1962–67. In the 1970s, Fraenkel invited three university professors as long-term advisors: Giora Hanoch and Reuben Gronau (advising mainly in econometrics) and Nissan Liviatan (who is still there today). He also added "research associates" for specific projects: Rafi Melnick and Professors Benzion Zilberfarb and Leo Leiderman.

In the 1980s, Fraenkel and Ben-Bassat (his deputy from 1981 and his successor in 1987) reduced the time allotted to the *Annual Report* and developed specific inducements for other research activities. Salary-grade rewards were conditioned on output. Fraenkel sequenced the priorities: monetary policy first, macroeconomic matters second, and microeconomic topics (e.g., individual industries) that had previously been stressed only third. An academic editorial board for the BOI series *Economic Review,* an important forum for academic discussion from early on, was established. In late 1981, Ben-Bassat organized a departmental research seminar that quickly went over to a weekly schedule. It contributed to the RD's work by facilitating interaction and discussion under the leadership of a designated staff member and by monitoring adherence to agreed timetables. Shortly afterwards, a Discussion Papers series became the forum for revised (and refereed) presentations at the seminar.[46]

Leora Meridor, as head of the RD, took a critical view of the Fraenkel regime, deeming it too narrowly oriented toward position papers and cooperation with the Ministry of Finance. She traces this tendency partly to Bruno, who as governor utilized the RD's services for his involvement in policy. Be this as it may, considering theoretical research analogous to investment, Meridor increased this type of activity, hired a larger number of part-time academic advisors, and encouraged gifted youngsters to study for a Ph.D. degree—if advisable even abroad. This was mainly a shift in degree and emphasis, since these patterns—including the allotting of time to doctoral dissertations—had been established long ago. The competitive tension between the Research and Monetary Departments that had developed during Mandelbaum's governorship continued—though less acutely—during Meridor's tenure, with certain personal undertones.

Competitive spirit was also evident inside the RD. The internal atmosphere in the department changed. Kochav had set the department on a democratic, egalitarian footing, conducting uninhibited discussions and consultations about the drafts of annual reports, position papers, and so on. As the RD staff swelled, not all members took part in every discussion. All interviewees remember Zvi Sussman as extremely liberal and democratic, even at the expense of "output." This approach applied to freedom of expression both inside and outside the bank and to the encouragement of independent thinking and a variety of views. Although this probably stemmed from Sussman's nature and weltanschauung, they were probably also influenced by the Horowitz-Kochav foundation. Fraenkel, as noted, introduced greater emphasis on research output and tight management. He also demanded that staff members refrain from criticizing BOI measures and recommendations to outside parties, especially the press. Still, the last-mentioned rule was applied less strictly than in most similar institutions abroad. IMF missions admired the BOI for the variety of views and nuances that were presented to them and compared this favorably with other countries' behavior.[47] In any case, Ben-Bassat relaxed the "gag rule" when he took over as chief of the RD.[48] Although the degree of liberalism in the RD's management fluctuated in subsequent years, the extreme Sussman style never returned.

During Jacob Frenkel's governorship, the role and activity of the Research Department underwent changes. The leading RD economists strongly opposed Frenkel's policies, whether for reasons of principle or of conservatism. Even today, Ben-Bassat and Meridor strongly criticize the very restrictive interest-rate policy, which by completely disregarding the effect of high interest on nonfinancial aspects of the economy, deprived the economy of growth and potential output and aggravated unemployment and socioeconomic inequality. They also consider Frenkel's de facto resignation from the function of the government's economic advisor (see below) detrimental not only to the BOI but also to the economy.

Partly in connection with these strong disagreements, and partly because several senior economists left for other BOI departments during Meridor's tenure as RD director (1992–96), the Monetary and Foreign Exchange Departments developed their research activities including the publication of quasi-independent research reports. The purpose of these activities, led by David Klein and Meir Sokoler, was to support Frenkel's policies and supply him with current research products. The critics felt that all these changes undermined the standing of the Research Department.

Leo Leiderman was a key player during Frenkel's tenure as part-time advisor to the RD and the governor from the summer of 1992 on and director of the RD from July 1996 to June 2000. He was much involved in Frenkel's policy decisions.[49] Leiderman argued, for example, that the newly developed variety and diversity in economic research within the BOI did not necessarily cause friction and was in fact conducive to interdepartmental cooperation. Defending Frenkel's tight interest policy, Leiderman notes its goal—preventing the resumption of the inflationary process of the 1970s and 1980s—and states that the resumption of an inflationary spiral would have hurt the low-income sector first of all, especially in the long run. Leiderman introduced several changes and improvements in the RD, including an improved and more "reader-friendly" format of the *Annual Report*. More important, perhaps, was the introduction of the semiannual Inflation Report (replacing the report on money-supply changes, as had previously been proposed by Meir Sokoler). In research matters, Leiderman first developed econometric models tailored to the new policies and circumstances and provided support services in the periodic discussions on changes in the key rate. He also organized a series of international conferences at the BOI on current developments in the global economy and relevant theories. In general, he emphasized the importance of international comparison and—where advisable—emulation, thereby reinforcing a tendency that the RD had long evinced.

THE BOI UNDER MICHAEL BRUNO AND JACOB FRENKEL

Michael Bruno, June 1986–August 1991

Michael Bruno, appointed to the governorship in June 1986, brought with him his prestige as an outstanding theoretical economist and a successful economic politician. After a period of internal tensions and difficulties and reduced authority among the Israeli public, he provided a boost to BOI morale. All interviewees who worked with him or whose terms coincided with his speak of Bruno with admiration if not a trace of adoration. Personalities as diverse as Leora Meridor and Mordechai Fraenkel describe themselves as having been his personal friends. Bruno, in turn, was dedicated to, and very conscientious about, his duties at the bank.

Bruno, reportedly an excellent administrator, introduced order and discipline in a staff that had been growing rapidly and diffusely. He also downsized the staff and, at a certain point, tried to cut salaries—leading to an unpleasant interval. He appointed a strict director general, Yitzhak ("Izzi") Rahav, and "senior directors" as the superordinates of two or three department directors instead of having deputy governors. He reduced tensions among departments and encouraged cooperation by establishing interdepartmental committees. Relations with the Ministry of Finance were excellent during Bruno's term, except for the two years in which Victor Medina was director general at Finance.[50] Still, in his academic publications he remained true to his theoretical preference of real macroeconomic issues over monetary ones.[51]

Bruno construed his duty as economic advisor to the government as a serious obligation and interpreted it broadly. During his term, the BOI—and often Bruno himself—was involved in a number of important economic policy measures and proposals, many of which had been initiatives of the bank. Ben-Bassat and others regard this period as the height of BOI policy involvement.

As an example, in August 1986 Bruno appointed a BOI interdepartmental committee to compose a detailed plan for capital-market reform. The initiative related to government involvement and taxation, ownership of the banks, shareholders' voting rights, nonbanking financial intermediaries, and so on. The first part of the panel's recommendations was implemented in April 1987 with the support of the Finance Ministry. Several additional provisions followed gradually. Another outstanding instance was a set of BOI recommendations for a new approach toward immigrant absorption, a project that continued in cooperation with the Finance Ministry.

Most of the BOI's policy initiatives and proposals were based on preparatory research by the RD. A significant example is Bruno's emphatic support of the view that the Lavi warplane project should be aborted, a government resolution in which he was instrumental. This case also exemplifies Bruno's willingness to take a stand and defend his opinion on controversial issues of public policy (such as full implementation of the Bejski Commission recommendations).

In October 1986, the exchange-rate peg was shifted from the dollar to a five-currency "basket" and in January 1987 a 10% devaluation was carried out.

In early 1989, following a 13.5% devaluation after heavy pressure on the BOI, a narrow exchange-rate band was adopted with a floating rate within the band. The BOI was involved in the market every day but intervened strongly only in cases of intense pressure. The band was horizontal but was raised from time to time, for example, by 6% in June 1989 and again in March 1990, when it was also widened. This recurrent raising of the band was later severely criticized by Jacob Frenkel as insufficiently transparent.[52]

In the wake of the stabilization plan, the bank achieved a substantial increase in its independence and its ability to conduct monetary policy and had considerable initial successes. Although inflation had been slashed, the bank (still under Mandelbaum), doubting the success of the policy, conducted an extremely cautious policy in the first poststabilization year. Thus, it kept the real interest rate at record levels. Afterwards, the BOI tried to apply an interest-rate policy that would support the policies of a stable economy and a fixed exchange rate. Since the reduced fiscal deficit provided an environment conducive to reforms, the Finance Ministry and the bank implemented a policy of capital- and money-market reform, first by decreasing government control of the use of savings and of long-term credit. Thus, the weight of directed credit in total lending by the banking system was reduced from 60% to 28% in the early post-1985 years and tended to zero during J. Frenkel's governorship. The BOI also encouraged, in various ways, increased competition in the short-term credit market. The oligopolistic structure of the banking sector remained a major obstacle to reforms and improvements. Thus, in 1989 Bruno successfully applied direct pressure to the banks to narrow the spread between debitory and creditory interest rates.

Despite his initial popularity, Bruno's monetary policies came under severe pressure from business interests and their advocates among politicians and in the media. Thus, in 1988 Bruno appointed Gideon Schurr—who had just returned from service with the IMF—as the first spokesperson of the Bank of Israel in order to counter the criticism and improve the bank's public image. He also invited Schurr to attend the deliberations of senior management in order to be better able to convey the bank's message to the public and politicians alike.

Sylvia Piterman, although appreciative of Bruno, views his monetary policy critically—perhaps because she looks at it from the perspective of the 1990s. Her main point is that inflation remained "stuck" at the 17%–20% level without anyone really understanding why. She believes that the BOI actually conducted an accommodating exchange-rate policy, depreciating the currency whenever the real exchange rate eroded somewhat, with the corresponding monetary effects. Although this policy may be defended in view of the traumatic balance-of-payments difficulties that Israel had endured in preceding years, she views it as effectively perpetuating inflation. Ben-Bassat thinks that the causes, of which Bruno was well aware, were the rigid structure of the capital and money markets, which had been only partly and gradually reformed, and of the labor market. Labor-market rigidity, in any case, was greatly eased in the 1990s by mass immigration from the former Soviet Union.

In 1987, Victor Medina, senior director in charge of the Monetary, Foreign Exchange, and Credit Departments, resigned from the BOI—reportedly in anger—due to "professional disagreements."[53] Bruno—in an unusual step—replaced him with an outsider, David Klein of the management of Bank Leumi le-Israel. It was Klein who continued to liberalize the foreign-exchange market and to reform the money market, proceeding in gradual, cautious, but persistent steps. By persevering in these activities during Jacob Frenkel's tenure, he supported the governor's policy. He used monetary lending (in effect, a form of rediscount) as the chief tool of monetary policy, finding it better suited Israeli conditions than open-market transactions, even though short-term Treasury bills (MAKAM) and reserve requirements were used as secondary tools. These tools were constantly refined and diversified. In November 1989, the BOI also introduced three-month forex call options; twelve-month options were introduced later. The purpose was twofold: to smooth fluctuations in demand for foreign exchange and to encourage the use of transactions in future assets in other financial markets. The monetary loans, Treasury bills, and options were increasingly sold by auction rather than by quotas.

Additional measures were taken to decrease the segmentation of the financial markets, to narrow differentials between various types of interest—NIS versus dollars or dollar-indexed instruments, bonds versus long-term deposits or saving accounts, creditory versus debitory, and so on—and to liberalize the rules governing credit from abroad, both to banks and to nonfinancial firms. By moving in these directions, BOI policy dovetailed with changes in Finance Ministry rules and tax policies.[54]

Bruno concluded his term as governor in mid-August 1991, as required by the BOI Law, and displayed no interest in renewal. Several interviewees speculated about his reasons for this; none of their suggestions was conclusive.

Jacob Frenkel, August 1991–January 2000

Jacob Frenkel returned to Israel after a brilliant career at the University of Chicago and the IMF, pursuant to an invitation by the government of Israel to become BOI governor.[55] His acceptance of the invitation, entailing the renunciation of attractive job offers (e.g., from Harvard's Kennedy School), was based on a deep Jewish-Zionist commitment. In particular, he felt that the expertise and experience that he had amassed in the integration of emerging markets into the globalizing world economy and stabilization programs would enable him to contribute to the absorption of mass immigration from the FSU.

Frenkel had been developing connections with Israeli personalities and institutions for years. He had served several stints as visiting professor at the Hebrew University and Tel Aviv University and had advised the BOI on two or three occasions. Thus, his own "absorption" could have been smooth and gradual.

It was not. Shortly after his term began, demand for foreign exchange pushed the exchange rate against the upper bound of the trading band. Apart from having to respond to the pressure, Frenkel considered this a test case for his policy and fortitude as governor. Thus, instead of adjusting the band upward as had been done several times before, Frenkel convinced the BOI monetary-policy team to fight the demand for dollars by raising the interest rate enough to make borrowing for exchange speculation uneconomical. He also informed the prime minister and finance minister (Shamir and Moday, respectively) of his intention and warned them that a brief period of dramatically high interest rates and public outcry were in the offing. Indeed, several significant rate hikes followed until the market turned around and the exchange rate receded.

Frenkel realized, however, that this had been a once-and never-again maneuver and that the exchange-rate regime had to be replaced. After considering similar cases in other countries and consulting with Leiderman, he decided to change the horizontal exchange-rate band to a sloping one. This brought up the question of the slope of the band, which had to be the difference between inflation expectations in Israel and those in the global market. Thus, on December 16, 1991, the Finance Ministry and the BOI jointly announced that the regime was to be changed and that—since domestic inflation in 1992 was expected to remain at the 14%–15% level experienced in 1991—the slope of the band would be determined in accordance with the expected difference in inflation rates.

Gradually, the use of inflation expectations to determine the slope of the band led to a conceptual change: the setting of an inflation target. The process was facilitated by a government decision to adopt, from the 1992 budget on, multiannual policy targets including a forecast of inflation expectations. Step by step, the BOI began to treat these outlooks as target rates and to determine the slope of the band accordingly. The BOI also had some influence on the inflation target decisions. In these respects, the BOI acted like leading central banks abroad and sometimes even preceded them.

BOI intervention in the foreign-exchange market, meant to smooth fortuitous fluctuations, was discontinued in May 1995 after the band was widened. Frenkel considers this a matter of propitious timing, since the restrained behavior of Israeli financial markets during the international financial crisis of 1997 justified the decision.

The principal change in course, however, was toward viewing the reduction and the eventual elimination of inflation, by means of the interest rate, as the central if not the exclusive goal of BOI policy. The purpose was to "modernize" the Israeli economy and promote its integration into global markets. The background factors that made this urgently necessary, in Frenkel's view, were the mass immigration, the high-tech revolution, and the change in foreign and defense policy that were brought about mainly by the Israel-Palestinian accords. Clearly, under complete liberalization of the currency and, especially, of short-term capital movements, a significant rate of inflation, or even the expectation of one, would deter the desired level of investment and impede the development of sound financial markets. Furthermore, a fixed exchange rate, pegged by whatever system, could not be maintained and effectively defended under such a regime.[56]

Frenkel felt that the Research Department, an excellent team that had stood firmly behind the 1985 stabilization, was slow in adjusting to the conceptual shift of emphasis. This reflected in part a degree of conservatism on the RD's part but, in the main, the RD's intensive concern with the nonfinancial aspects of the economy as against Frenkel's focus on the financial aspects. Thus, the MD was a closer ally than the RD in his aggressive war on inflation and also provided better research support, at least until Leiderman became director of the RD in July 1996.

These changes in emphasis touched off disagreements and policy debates within and among BOI departments, largely concerning the detrimental effects of a very tight monetary policy on output, employment, and growth. Unfortunately, the disagreements were tainted by personal antagonisms and sensitivities.[57] Frenkel argues adamantly that the difference between viewing the exchange rate as a financial and monetary variable and considering it a "real" variable is immaterial, since in the medium and long terms sound and stable financial conditions are absolutely necessary for full employment and economic growth. In an open economy, in contrast, monetary policy cannot have much direct influence on employment and growth. Good sense eventually prevailed, Frenkel says, as all—or almost all—BOI economists accepted his approach. He discerned a similar development among the public and in academia.

These changes were supported by the possibility of lowering the interest rate and accelerating growth as inflation abated. Frenkel points to the experience in 1999–2000 as bearing out his contention—until the eruption of the Second Intifada in late 2000 forced a policy reversal.

Relating to a different aspect of his activities, Frenkel stresses his avoidance of all involvement in domestic politics, on the one hand, and his close and regular contacts with all prime ministers under whom he served, on the other. Yitzhak Rabin, in particular, avoided all intervention in BOI policy decisions but appreciated being fully informed of impending changes, particularly those that might cause friction with the finance minister and, perhaps, others. Rabin also highly valued Frenkel's discretion and trustworthiness. Yitzhak Shamir, Shimon Peres, Benjamin Netanyahu, and Ehud Barak shared these attitudes.

Frenkel's concentration on the promotion of his exchange-rate and interest policy, against (at least initial) wide opposition in the public, the Knesset, and the government, led to his gradual withdrawal from the function of economic advisor to the government. During his first term (August 1991–July 1996), he continued to be involved in policy as Bruno had been and supported Ben-Bassat's activity in various commissions and projects. One example was the "committee of four" that proposed a plan for increasing competition in telecommunications. Another instance was the adoption in 1995 of long-dormant BOI recommendations about forcing commercial banks to divest themselves of holdings in nonfinancial corporations. Frenkel himself, however, participated less and less in meetings of the government and its committees on economic affairs and privatization, delegating this function to Ben-Bassat.[58]

During his second term, Frenkel effectively discontinued all BOI activity in nonmonetary economic policy. He seemed to withdraw from situations that were conducive to confrontations concerning his policies.[59] Frenkel himself recalls having placed emphasis on influencing the views and enhancing the economic understanding of politicians and the public, not the least as an indirect way of affecting attitudes in the government and the Knesset. For this purpose, he maximized his appearances in the media and in all sorts of public forums, not because he loved the limelight (as his avoidance of publicity after leaving the governorship ostensibly shows) but because he regarded these as effective vehicles for the attainment of his goals.

Frenkel also highly valued Israeli membership and involvement in international institutions, such as the Bank of International Settlements, and encouraged such membership and activities. Since 1985, the domestic media was becoming increasingly active in investigative and critical reporting, and monetary policy became progressively more effective and influential. This confluence of developments made it more important to emphasize public relations and present uniform opinions of BOI staff to the public. Thus, Frenkel added the functions of international affairs and information to the Public Relations Department and in 1993 appointed the head of the department, Gideon Schurr, to the management.

As his term as governor neared its end in the summer of 1996, Frenkel felt that his mission had been accomplished and that he should move on to new challenges. Inflation had been stamped out, foreign-currency controls abolished, and the conceptual transition to globalization and integration into the world economy achieved. The new approach toward monetary policy, emphasizing the key rate as the chief and almost exclusive tool and the maintenance of monetary and fiscal stability as the predominant goal, had been largely accepted as had the need for multiannual targeting.

However, the political turbulence following the assassination of Prime Minister Rabin in November 1995 and the swift succession of elections frustrated Frenkel's intention to end his tenure in an orderly fashion. When Ehud Barak was elected prime minister in mid-1999, Frenkel thought that a new and stable regime had taken over and expressed his desire to leave his post. Barak accepted this regretfully but asked Frenkel to help him to pass his new budget and, later on, to stay until after the Y2K hurdle—the adjustment of all computer systems to the new millennium—was surmounted. Barak also asked Frenkel to recommend his successor. Frenkel refrained from suggesting a specific name, agreeing only to indicate several persons who seemed to have the desired combination of qualifications and characteristics. Barak interviewed most of them, but each turned down the appointment for reasons of his own. Finally, Barak nominated David Klein as, in Frenkel's words, a "natural choice" and a guarantee of policy continuity.

It was under these circumstances that Frenkel stepped down in January 2000.

In sum, the proposal for a new BOI Law (authored by the Levin Commission and currently tabled) strongly reflects Jacob Frenkel's views and policies. Furthermore, the main criticisms of this draft reflect the criticism of these policies. Frenkel himself fully supports the proposal, viewing it as following the European Central Bank model.

All interviewees who were asked about the matter agree that the existing fifty-year-old BOI Law should be replaced. Some, however, favor the specification of a single goal for monetary policy ("stability") or, at least, a major and a secondary, subordinate goal (full employment and growth). The others consider the present formulation of the bank's tasks as generally correct and reinforce their view by citing various foreign models. Similarly, there is disagreement about the composition of the new committee tasked with making the principal policy decisions and about the method of its appointment. The main apprehension is that the committee members will all think alike and conform to the governor's views. Alternatively, some fear that the committee will be dominated by politicians and vested interests. The debate seems to be concentrating on policy issues, resulting in the neglect of "prosaic" matters of administration and setting of the BOI budget and salary scale. Since most of these questions are still the subjects of lively public debate, we forgo a detailed discussion of the various opinions. Even without a new law, however, the Bank of Israel in its jubilee year is quite different from the institution originally established.

Notes

1. Kochav explicitly and Sheffer and Sussman implicitly.
2. Kochav, Sheffer, Sussman.
3. The Histadrut—the General Federation of Labor in Israel—represents organized labor and owned a wide range of economic and industrial enterprises at the time.
4. Later interviewees expressed this view but Meir Heth, Examiner of Banks in 1969–75, recalled that the committee had been intensively involved and helpful in drafting an Israeli banking bill in 1971–73.
5. Plessner, Deputy Governor in 1982–1985.
6. Fraenkel, Ben-Bassat.
7. Fraenkel, Ben-Bassat, Meridor.
8. The Israel-Britain Bank was owned mainly by Nahum Zeev Williams, a wealthy British businessman, and managed by his son-in-laws—Yehoshua Ben-Zion in Palestine/Israel and Harry Lundy in London. In 1968, the London branch became a separate subsidiary, but collapsed after the bankruptcy of the Israeli bank. Both banks raised money on the Tel Aviv Stock Exchange and in financial markets, and invested much of it via anonymous Liechtenstein corporations. The bank ran into trouble during the mid-1960s recession and deteriorated further by getting involved, from the late 1960s on, in speculative activities on European currency and gold markets. After intricate attempts to obtain assistance by means of guarantees from a Swiss private bank and from Mr. Williams, and despite generous loans from the Bank of Israel and various untrue presentations to the BOI, the bank conceded that it could not honor its obligations, especially toward creditors in Europe. It could not be sold to any large Israeli bank without unlimited BOI guarantees and was therefore seized for liquidation by the BOI in July 1974. Various interested and/or misinformed persons and institutions, in Israel and in the Anglo-Jewish community, intervened on Ben-Zion's behalf and also attacked the BOI and its governor in public and in the Knesset.
9. Sanbar, Gafny, Sheffer, Sussman.
10. Kochav, Sheffer, Heth.
11. Israel Sheqel.
12. The views and actions of Medina's Monetary Department are detailed in the "Monetary Policy" section of chap. 9 of the BOI *Annual Reports* for 1983–86.

13. Sheffer, Sussman.

14. Sanbar, Gafny.

15. Sussman. The BOI based its arguments partly on an extensive study by a Falk Institute team titled "One Hundred Exchange Rates," which in Hebrew comes out as *Meah She'arim*—the name of the famous Jerusalem neighborhood.

16. Sheffer, Sussman, Sanbar.

17. Kochav.

18. The economy was turned around by the 1967 war and its aftermath, as is well known.

19. Plessner emphasizes the last-mentioned factor.

20. It is not clear who devised the crawling-peg system. Plessner ascribes it to Michael Bruno, Rabinowitz's advisor. Sanbar claims to have been the originator; he borrowed the idea, he says, from a rudimentary proposal by a Finance Ministry economist, Asher Shlain, based on practices in several Latin American countries. Leiderman confirms Sanbar's account and believes the issue was already being discussed in the literature. Liviatan also recalls Shlain's proposal.

21. See also Michaely's chapter in this volume.

22. Gafny, Sheffer, Sussman, and Fraenkel.

23. Gafny, Sheffer, Sussman.

24. M. Bruno (1993), p. 88n. Details from this retrospective book are utilized here in lieu of an interview.

25. Since the BOI governor had already been replaced, the bank's own *Review* could not be used for this purpose (Fraenkel, Frenkel).

26. Article 35 of the BOI Law provides for a special report by the governor on any extraordinary increase in the quantity of the economy's money supply ("means of payment," in its conventional M1 definition) by 15% or more during the preceding 12 months. Until the Monetary Department was established, the RD prepared these reports as well.

27. See also Michaely's chapter in this volume.

28. This subsection relies chiefly on the interview with M. Fraenkel, augmented by details from Bruno (1993), and focuses on BOI involvement.

29. "Without implicating a reluctant Governor" (Bruno, 1993, p. 100 n. 34).

30. He was surprised at not having been recalled.

31. Mandelbaum.

32. Ben-Bassat.

33. Therefore, Fraenkel claims authorship of the nickname given to the legislation: the "No-Printing Law."

34. Kochav, Sussman, Heth, and Fraenkel. Ben-Bassat adds: until the late 1980s.

35. See n. 26 above.

36. Sheffer and others.

37. For developments in these respects, see examples in the sections entitled "BOI Involvement in Economic Policy, 1954–85" and "The BOI under Michael Bruno and Jacob Frenkel."

38. Bruno (1962).

39. Kochav, Sheffer.

40. Kochav, Sussman.

41. Sussman vividly remembers a meeting with Pinhas Sapir about a specific policy issue, to which Horowitz invited him (Sussman) and Sheffer and asked them to present Sapir with their own, separate, opinion as well.

42. Sheffer, Sussman, Sanbar.

43. Fraenkel, Ben-Bassat, Piterman, Meridor, and Plessner, who tried to restrain the "censorship."
44. Fraenkel.
45. Piterman.
46. M. Fraenkel, Ben-Bassat.
47. Ben-Bassat.
48. Fraenkel, Ben-Bassat, Meridor.
49. Although Piterman thinks that he did not give them sufficient support when in his public appearances he discussed macroeconomic issues rather than monetary policy.
50. Fraenkel, Ben-Bassat, Meridor, Piterman.
51. Fraenkel.
52. Piterman.
53. He never disclosed their nature.
54. Piterman and MD reports.
55. This subsection also uses parts of the interview with Leiderman.
56. Several interviewees made the latter point. Furthermore, there was a broad consensus against a fixed exchange-rate regime—as proposed, for instance, by Rafi Melnick—under the prevailing circumstances.
57. Cf. discussion of similar matters in "The Research Department" section.
58. Ben-Bassat. Frenkel generally confirmed this description and expressed strong appreciation of Ben-Bassat's dedication to structural reforms.
59. Ben-Bassat, Meridor; and Leiderman claims that demand for Frenkel's advice also decreased.

References

Bruno, M., *Interrelations, Utilization of Resources, and Transformations in the Development of the Israeli Economy*. Jerusalem: The Bank of Israel, Research Department, 1962. (Hebrew).

———. *Crisis, Stabilization, and Economic Reform*. Oxford: Clarendon Press, 1993.

5

Banking Supervision in Israel

Jacob Paroush

The word "supervision" carries the negative connotation of intervention in and penetration of the business of an unwillingly supervised entity. This immediately raises questions about the nature and purpose of banking supervision, which are among those that we will try to answer here. Thus, in addition to providing a historical description of supervision over the past fifty years, this chapter explains what Israel's supervisory authority does, whom and what it supervises, the means employed, its aims, its benefit for the public, and its connection with the Bank of Israel and monetary policy. The chapter also provides background for some issues that are relevant today, such as deposit insurance, financial stability, bank fees and charges, the Basel 2 rules, and conflict of interest in securities consultancy.

The chapter is divided into six parts—five sections and an appendix—each of which is independent and may therefore be read separately, with no need to refer back and forth. Nevertheless, for a complete picture and a comprehensive description of all aspects of banking supervision by the Bank of Israel, it is recommended that all the sections be read.

The first section briefly describes the historical development of the supervision of the banking industry by the Bank of Israel over the past fifty years.

The second section discusses the object of the supervision, i.e., what is supervised. It describes the Israeli banking system, its characteristics and development, and the risks in banking activities that are overseen by the Supervisor of Banks.

The third section explains how the public benefits from banking supervision, the importance of stability in the banking system and why it should be preserved, and the link between the supervision of stability and monetary policy.

The fourth section gives a historical description of five events that are viewed to some extent as supervisory failures. The events were selected because they shocked the public and because the lessons learned from them led to changes in the supervisory body's working methods.

The fifth section reviews the ways and means that the Banking Supervision Department may employ and describes how it does its work.

The Appendix presents a model describing the importance of banking supervision and the difficulty in exercising it.

The chapter refers extensively to banking research carried out in Israel, particularly papers prepared and published by the Research Unit of the Banking

Supervision Department. They provide additional sources for a more profound understanding of the subject. The references are listed in endnotes.

I have tried in this chapter to take a positive approach and to refrain as far as possible from any normative judgment.

HISTORICAL PERSPECTIVE ON BANKING SUPERVISION IN ISRAEL

The historical development of the Bank of Israel's supervision of the banking sector may be divided into two main periods—up to the late 1980s and afterward. The first period, in which Israel grew from a small developing economy into a larger, developed one, was characterized by almost absolute government control of the economy and the financial and capital markets. In fact, during this period the banking system was an agent for the government, both in raising money from the public and in issuing credit ("directed credit" and credit from deposits approved for grant of loans). Most credit extended by the banking system was steered by the government to its preferred objectives. The government set the price of this credit, dictated the payback dates, and took responsibility for the risk.

The government and the Bank of Israel controlled both the amount of credit (the money supply) and its price (interest and charges). The restrictions imposed on the banking system served not only the goal of stability but also monetary and foreign currency goals as well as, in the 1970s and the early 1980s, mainly fiscal goals. Government intervention created a system of restrictions that led to operational inefficiency. To the best of our knowledge, no other banking system in the world labored under so complex a burden of restrictions on its day-to-day activities, both in choosing allocations and in setting prices. The government's rampant intervention in the financial market partitioned banking activity into eight separate segments of operation. The segments were so independent from one another that banks were not allowed to appropriate funds from one segment and allocate it to another. The inefficiency was evident in the large variance among the spreads of the various segments.[1] In practice, the banks were allowed to set interest rates and determine spreads freely in only two very narrow segments of operation (unindexed domestic currency and unrestricted foreign currency), the total weight of which did not exceed one-tenth of total banking activity. It was this activity, however, that brought the banks most of their income.[2] The restrictions prompted the banks to increase their foreign activities; in one decade—from the mid-1970s to the mid-1980s—they tripled the number of external representations (subsidiaries, branches, and agencies) from fifty to 150.

In the mid-1980s, the capital market and the banking system underwent two financial upheavals. One was the bank-share crisis—due to a lengthy process in which several banks manipulated the prices of their shares—and the other was the mass bankruptcy of kibbutzim and moshavim (collective and cooperative rural settlements) due to indiscriminate and generous lending to them by the banking system. Although inflation at that time was not the main cause of these crises, it was clearly a comfortable underpinning for their occurrence.

It is important to bear in mind that the responsibility for these occurrences belonged not only to the banking supervision system; it also lay at the door of the government.[3] In both of these cases, the government found a way to prevent the crisis from spilling from the financial sector into the nonfinancial sector. In the first case, it nationalized the banks by purchasing the shares from the public at an exorbitant price; in the second case, it bail out the banks by setting up a "kibbutz debt settlement board," which wrote off much of the debt and restructured the remainder while partially compensating the banks for their losses. Both solutions were immensely expensive and it was the taxpayer who bore the burden. (For greater detail, see the "Instability" section, pp. 148–153.)

The government's solution for the kibbutz crisis seems to have taught the banks not to be afraid to lend to bodies that are highly regarded by the government. Thus, twenty years later, the banking system has again found itself in a similar situation after having lent to municipal authorities irrespective of their payback abilities. The chances are that the problem will be solved in a similar fashion.

To some extent, the financial crises of the mid-1980s undermined the safety and soundness of the banking system and led, in addition, to the de facto nationalization of the banks (following the share manipulation crisis) and to a series of supervisory measures designed to increase stability. The measures were reflected in raising entry barriers to the industry, the promulgation of regulations for capital adequacy, and the introduction of arrangements previously unknown in the system. Reporting requirements were broadened and auditing was intensified. All in all, it amounted to a substantial reform in the means of supervision.

We call the first period, from the establishment of the Bank of Israel up to the late 1980s, SD (Supervisory Dominance), when on-site auditing was the rule, and the second period RD (Regulatory Dominance), when regulatory rules were added and became an important means of supervision. (For a more detailed discussion of the means of supervision, see "Means of Supervision," pp. 154–158.)

In 1985, hyperinflation set in, the external debt swelled almost to the size of GNP, and economic growth tended to zero. This set the stage for the kibbutz crisis that occurred about two years later. In particular, too, it provided the motive for devising the economic stabilization plan that was implemented in July of that year. The architects of the plan clearly had in mind the bank-share crisis, which had developed against the backdrop of inflation and had driven the capital and financial markets to the brink of collapse less than two years earlier.

The 1985 Economic Stabilization Plan was a milestone in the transition of the Israeli economy from government involvement to a market economy.[4] It also marked the change that occurred in the banking system as it was gradually released from government involvement and the reform of banking supervision in the changeover from SD to RD.

In the late 1980s, but more noticeably in the early 1990s, the government started to apply a capital-market reform that reduced its operations via the banking system, narrowed its directed credit, and lowered the barriers among the banks' segments of operation. In monetary policy, the Bank of Israel replaced its fixed exchange-rate regime with one based on an inflation target and renounced the reserve requirement (the reserve ratio or the "monetary tax") as a policy tool.[5] Notably, the reserve requirement is a traditional tool, in addition to open market operations, that central banks use to control the money supply. In the Israeli case, the central bank abandoned this tool and replaced it with the monetary auctions. Concurrently, liberalization of the money, capital, and foreign-exchange markets got under way, culminating in a convertible NIS and a Tel Aviv Stock Exchange that trades in external as well as domestic assets. As the banking system was freed from the government's grasp, banks were able again to focus on domestic banking activities. Thus, within ten years—from the mid-1980s to the mid-1990s—the number of banking representations abroad was reduced by about one-third, to about one hundred.[6] As all these changes occurred, the supervision of banking stability was toughened by means of regulation.

In addition to the existing single-borrower restriction, a total capital restriction of 3% was imposed. Eventually, the latter restriction was adjusted to risk assets according to an international key (Basel 1) and raised first to 8% and after a while to 9%.[7] Today, the minimum risk-adjusted capital ratio is 9%. These capital-adequacy rules, as well as others, restrain the banks' ability to issue credit.

During the SD period, when supervisory considerations on amount of credit and rate of interest were mainly fiscal, the principal means of supervision were: visits by the staff of the supervisory body to the banks, followed by periodic audit reports to the examiner of banks. In the RD period, which began when true reform of the means of supervision commenced, the standard auditing tools were augmented by capital requirements; restrictions on lending to single borrowers, groups of borrowers, related persons, and individual industries; and Proper Conduct of Banking Business rules were drafted. In addition, accounting rules were established to define precisely the types of problem loans and the provisions that must be made for them. As the liberalization process progressed, banks were also required to limit their exposure to foreign-exchange risks.

It is no coincidence that the SD period corresponded to the time when government macroeconomic policy was characterized by budgetary considerations, fiscal targets were attained not by means of a monetary anchor but with the aid of an inflation tax, and monetary policy was tasked with keeping the system in equilibrium. During this period, when most banking activity was subjugated to budget policy, there was no need to base supervision on regulatory rules.[8] After the stabilization plan went into effect, the economic policy of the government became mainly monetary. Its goal now was to attain a predefined inflation rate by maintaining budget restraint. The exchange rate would no longer serve as an immovable anchor; it would be free to move within the bounds of a predetermined and known band. This regime released the banking system from the government's grip, making it necessary to add regulatory rules to the existing means of supervision. It is this that distinguishes the RD era from its predecessor.

As an analogy, consider a driver who responds to a wet road and poor visibility by slowing down. To prevent an accident, he must also be sure that the car is mechanically sound and that his lights are properly adjusted. To prevent an accident in good weather, however, regulations such as a speed limit are needed as well. Notably, in addition to the influence of the government's policy on the transition from SD-type supervision to RD-type supervision, there was global trend of such transition into which Israel was integrated.[9]

Sizeable bank failures have occurred in Israel about once a decade and each was handled in a way that maintained public trust in the system. The maintenance of trust was achieved mainly by de facto deposit insurance, that is, whenever a bank failed, depositors received full compensation at taxpayer expense. (De jure deposit insurance is discussed in "The Need for Supervision," pp. 144–148.) The banking supervisory body studied each bankruptcy carefully and learned and applied the lessons. To further stabilize the system, weak banks were encouraged to merge with stronger ones or with one another.

Notwithstanding its benefit for the public, supervision of banking-system stability has been costly. Stringent supervisory methods and entry barriers, official and other, have kept down the number of banks in the system. They have also prevented the government from selling the controlling interest in banks that it still retains. The government has not been able to find a suitable buyer who is willing to pay the asking price, even though for almost twenty years it has been its declared policy to seek such buyers. This, along with other contributory factors, explains the absence of foreign banks. It has also, and mainly, created a sector with that has a clearly oligopolistic if not duopolistic structure. Indeed, more than 60% of all banking activity is concentrated with the two largest banks.[10]

This concentrated power is reflected both in high prices of credit,[11] manifested mainly in steep penalties and surcharges for overruns of credit facilities, and in the wide range of fees and charges that banks invoke for commercial-banking and capital-market services.[12] The fees and charges, more than two hundred in number, have created a labyrinth in which the public cannot find its way. In addition, the banks have a policy of "cross-pricing" between their operating and financial domains.

It is difficult to estimate how much this structure has cost the economy in "consumer surplus" terms,[13] due to occasional changes in direct price control (interest and bank fees and charges) during the SD period and the threat of contestability from outside the sector, which has escalated in the RD period as a result of foreign-exchange liberalization and has somewhat reduced the harm to the public from the absence of internal competition in the industry. The first factor created movement on the credit-demand curve; the second made the demand curve more elastic. Since the early 1990s, the Banking Supervision Department has acted to stimulate competition in the banking industry and place more information in consumers' hands. This is most evident in proper-disclosure directives that have forced banks to improve "market discipline" and to make switching banks less costly. Furthermore, the liberalization exposed the system to competition from external banks and the first indications of foreign banking in Israel have recently come into sight. Just the same, the domestic banks' market power has not diminished, particularly vis-à-vis customers who cannot exploit the banks' market discipline and benefit from the external competition, such as small businesses and households.[14]

The main cost to the economy of supervision during the SD period stemmed mainly from the absence of competition among banks and inefficiency occasioned by direct government intervention in the allocation and price of credit. The main cost of supervision in the RD period, in contrast, stems from the regulatory rules that restrict system activity (restrictions on capital, sectoral concentration, and nonfinancial activities, and loan-loss provision rules). This cost is manifested in lost production and other nonfinancial activities for lack of suitable financing due to the contraction of credit.[15]

In this respect, the Banking Supervision Department faces a typical dilemma, especially in times of recession, that afflicts all economies but is particularly severe in Israel, where the credit market is quite narrow and insufficiently competitive. On the one hand, in a recession the economy needs available and inexpensive credit to facilitate its ability to survive; on the other, credit and liquidity risks mount at such a time, leading to a tendency to restrict credit and reduce the banking system's sensitivity to "contagion" from bankruptcies in the banking sector. There is also a tendency to make credit more costly, as the risk-premium component of interest rises. A resolute supervisor would act to limit credit and increase loan-loss provisions in order to preserve stability. These measures would hurt the nonfinancial sector during a recession, as indeed has occurred in Israel in 2003–2004.

In principle, every means of supervision has a cost because it limits the ability to attain the goals of activities financed by the credit given by the bank, just as every constraint imposed on an optimization process has a "shadow price."

From a historical perspective, Israel's banking-supervision system may be deemed a success story in that it has attained the goal of keeping the system stable. For some fifty years, the banking system—which deserves credit for its significant contribution to the country's economic development and growth—has indeed been stable and trusted by the public. Evidence of this success is, first, the good reputation of Israel's banking system around the world and the recognition that leading international rating companies have given it and, second, the volume and stability of external deposits in the domestic system, which underlie the foreign reserves.

The actual capital adequacy of the system (capital base/total assets), an important yardstick for banking stability, never fell below that of similar systems in other countries during the SD period, when there was no formal minimum capital ratio,[16] and it has never failed to meet the minimum requirement during the RD period. The system's performance, foremost in terms of profitability and return on capital, has been impressive even in times of recession and has proved its survivability in times of crisis. This success may be attributed partly to the examiners and supervisors of the banks, who were alert to potential bank failures during most of the period, and partly due to prudent and responsible management of most of the banks during most of the period.

The foregoing capsule historical review of banking supervision in Israel emphasizes the inevitable "flipside" of successful supervision: the cost involved. Optimal banking supervision is the kind that balances the marginal benefit to the public from the stability with the marginal cost that the public pays for it. This is by no means an easy task, and here we must conclude that the Bank of Israel's supervision of banks over the past fifty years has not always performed this balancing act without interruption. There have been bouts of instability (described in the "Instability" section) and the cost of the stability attained has usually been too high.

THE OBJECT OF BANKING SUPERVISION IN ISRAEL

The Israeli Banking System

The market structure, the segmentation of Israel's banking industry, the universal character of its business, and its special historical development are an interesting combination that differentiates this industry from its counterparts elsewhere. This combination also illuminates some of the problems that face the Banking Supervision Department.

Market Structure

In May 1948, when Israel was established, there were about a hundred cooperative credit associations in the financial intermediation system. Over the next twenty years, almost all of them merged with commercial banks, presumably because scale economies precluded their continued independent existence. Israel also had branches of foreign banks in 1948, but they disappeared, probably due to unwillingness to be part of a sector so completely controlled by government. The most noteworthy feature of Israeli banking, however, is that the number of Israeli commercial banks has remained more-or-less unchanged— between twenty-two and twenty-nine—for almost fifty years when the population has grown more than ten times. Although various banks have come and gone during this time, the level of concentration, as measured by various relevant indices, has not changed drastically.[17] If we take into consideration the negative correlation between banking-sector concentration and the size of the economy,[18] however, we find that the concentration has grown relative to the size of the economy. Furthermore, the stable number of banks does not mean that the supply of banking services has remained the same. Supply has increased, as reflected in growth of employment and office area in the banking sector and the vigorous development of banking technology: automatic teller machines, direct banking, and credit cards. Even so, the increased supply has not kept pace with demand for banking services. The increase in demand is manifested first in population growth. Second, since the demand elasticity for banking services relative to income is greater than 1, per capita demand for banking services has outpaced growth in per capita income. Thus, the banking industry's share in GNP has risen.[19] When demand grows more rapidly than supply and the number of banks remains the same, the result is an increase in the banks' monopolistic power—reflected, among other things, in declining customer-service standards. For example, Israel today has the world's fewest branches and ATMs per population and the average queuing time for a teller, an ATM, or investment advice is not getting shorter.[20] The constant number of banks is presumably the result of entry barriers, since the high return on equity in the Israeli banking system, compared with other industries, should have attracted new investors. In the SD period, foreign banks hesitated to enter the market mainly because of government involvement; during the RD period they have been reluctant due to the entry barriers, among other reasons. Another interesting result is that for some years several small commercial banks in the Israeli system reported lower net return on equity than interest on government bonds, a risk-free alternative investment, and in some years providing even a negative return. Although the survival of these banks in the system was seen as a puzzle, the owners of the banks actually behaved logically: due to the entry barriers, the value of their banking licenses climbed in a range of a few years steadily, generating an economic rent that would be foolish to relinquish. Thus, the entry barriers not only dampened competition within the industry but also created "exit barriers" for inefficient banks. One of the motives for the entry barriers, presumably, was supervisory convenience, because the fewer banks there are, the lower the cost of supervision. Perhaps we should add the reprimand that the supervision system received due to faults that were found in the licensing process after the collapse of North America Bank (see the "Instability" section).

This section on the market structure concludes with four remarks: (1) The entry barriers to the sector are not merely formal, for example, the minimum equity requirement (which has risen over time from $3 million to $30 million) but also economic, personal, and other (see the "Ex Ante Supervision" subsection). (2) Banking generally, and Israeli banking particularly,[21] is noted for economies of scale and scope. Since opening a bank requires a large fixed investment relative to demand, the constancy in the number of banks may trace not only to entry barriers imposed by the supervisory agency but also to the possibility that Israel's banking sector is largely a "natural oligopoly." An indication of this is that the number of applications to open a new bank is considerably smaller than the number of applications to acquire an existing bank. Furthermore, with the development of banking technology, the expansion of globalization, and the proliferation of risks, the scale and scope economies and the fixed investment required for opening a bank have increased over the years, reinforcing the validity of this reason. (3) The ever-increasing burden to the public of no competition, derived from the gap between demand for and supply of banking services, has been alleviated by two factors: the blurring of segmentation of the oligopolistic market that existed in the SD period (see below) and the liberalization process that began in the RD period and expedited contestability from abroad. (4) In the past few years, the number of banks in Israel has suddenly decreased by 25%—from twenty-three in 2002 to seventeen in 2004—as six small banks have left the system. Israel has never had fewer banks. This is apparently the result of coincidence: one bank collapsed when a management risk (embezzlement) was realized, another failed due to liquidity risk, three merged with larger banks, and one had its license revoked. The Bank of Israel encouraged three mergers and took the last-mentioned action on its own following the realization of risks at the first two banks. These events probably made the remaining banks more stable but also more powerful in the market.

Market Segmentation in the Banking Sector

For fifty years, Israel has had "sectoral" banks, that is, banks that focus on specific population groups. Bank Otsar Hahayal serves the security forces, Bank Massad specializes in teachers, Bank Yahav's customers are mostly civil servants, and the Arab-Israel Bank attracts the Arab sector. The names of some banks—Agriculture Bank, Shipping Bank, Construction Bank, Trade Bank, Industry Bank—indicate their focus. Union Bank used to specialize in the diamond industry. Over the years, the large banks also specialized; the agricultural sector, for example, came to be associated with Bank Hapoalim. Mortgage banks, most of which belong to the commercial banking groups, operated until recently as separate banks. This specialization—by industries, population groups, or banking operations—exists in every developed economy. It abets the operational efficiency of the bank but also, of course, exposes it to the risks inherent in its particular industry or population group. Historically speaking, however, Israeli banking has been characterized by an additional distinction that dovetails with the previous one and that, to the best of my knowledge, does not exist in other countries: political segmentation. It may come as no surprise that in Israel, where citizens have clear political leanings, the banking market is also divided by segments of the political spectrum.[22] The two largest banks, which account for most banking activity in the country—Bank Leumi le-Israel and Bank Hapoalim—originally had clear political labels: Bank Leumi's customers were associated with the political Center and Right and Bank Hapoalim's with the Left. Bank Hapoalim served the Histadrut (the General Federation of Labor in Palestine/Israel), its institutions and industries, and the kibbutz and moshav movements. United Mizrahi Bank was associated with the religious Zionist parties and their institutions. Agudath Israel Bank served the constituency of the ultra-Orthodox party of that name. Needless to say, political segmentation that is not based on principles of operational efficiency creates an oligopolistic division of the market. When this characteristic combines with the considerable market concentration that has long typified the Israeli banking industry, the market takes on a powerful monopolistic structure. Unsurprisingly, then, customer mobility in Israel tended to zero as both households and businesses were "trapped" with the bank to which they "belonged." In a reflection of this distortion, the screening system used by the banks to discriminate among customers (in quantities and prices) operated not only on the basis of the riskiness of the project up for finance or the customer's demand elasticity but also on the basis of the customer's political tag.

Most political segmentation faded away after the crises of the 1980s and became almost indiscernible after the government sold its equity in Bank Hapoalim and United Mizrahi Bank to private investors. Nevertheless, the absence of customer mobility among banks remains a peculiarity of Israeli banking.[23]

Universalism

Another typical feature of Israeli banking is its universality. There is no differentiation between commercial banks and investment banks. Israeli banks, large and small alike, do it all—from financial intermediation to intensive activity as participants, either as portfolio managers in the secondary capital market or as underwriters in the primary market.[24] In the diversity of its operations and its involvement in nonfinancial activities, Israeli banking resembles the German or Japanese systems more than it does the American or British ones.[25] Until recently, bankers sat on the boards of directors of many manufacturing firms. Here, too, the combination of universalism and severe concentration generates massive economic power. For years, Israel has had the most concentrated universal banking system in the world. Indeed, the two largest banks had considerable control of the nonfinancial sector.[26] Not until about ten years ago were limits imposed on banks' nonfinancial activities and holdings.[27] This mitigated the large banks' economic power somewhat but their control in the capital market remained unchanged.

Historical Development and Other Characteristics

From the lengthy perspective of half a century, one may say that the increase in banking activities (total credit) has outpaced product. It is also clear that the money market and the nonfinancial market are interdependent in that one sustains growth in the other and vice versa. In the short term, however, the link between these trends is tenuous. The banking system's response to business cycles or waves of immigration is neither immediate nor methodical. One reason is the banks' intensive activity in the capital market, which connects banking activity not only with nonfinancial operations but also with fluctuations in the general price level and the volume of activity on the stock exchange.[28]

Thus, increases in total credit during recessions may be explained by the component of credit that is granted not for the financing of direct nonfinancial activity but, for example, for corporate acquisitions and takeovers or for large loan-loss provisions that are unrelated to recession, that is, an immediate connection to credit risk.[29] This development may also be described by using the results of an ordinary logarithmic regression of annual data (1974–2003) of total credit per capita on per capita GDP, per capita stock-exchange activity, and inflation. We performed this regression analysis in three different versions. In version 2, we added a dummy variable that separates the SD period from the RD period; in version 3 we divided the period into six five-year subperiods and added respective dummy variables to the regression.[30] Table 5.1 shows the results.

Version 1 of the regression implies that (1) the GDP coefficient is significantly larger than 1, which indicates elasticity greater than one unit of credit demand

Table 5.1. Regression Results

Variable	Version 1		Version 2		Version 3	
	Coefficient	Standard Deviation	Coefficient	Standard Deviation	Coefficient	Standard Deviation
Constant	−1.915708	0.365508	−2.633064	0.610164	0.293801	1.143501
GDP	1.272747	0.107519	1.467134	0.170342	0.639491	0.335488
Stock exchange	0.168551	0.098637	0.169969	0.096606	0.238228	0.109469
Inflation	0.001307	0.000363	0.001442	0.000367	0.000280	0.000532
RD dummy			−0.118381	0.081543		
D_1					0.057907	0.068968
D_2					0.166167	0.092792
D_3					0.149417	0.122783
D_4					0.202151	0.165753
D_5					0.507304	0.196364

with respect to income and that (2) volume of stock-exchange activity and inflation have a significant positive effect on banking activity. Version 2 shows that (3) in addition to the aforementioned influences, there is a difference in banking activity between the RD period and the SD period. By comparing Version 3 with versions 1 and 3, we may conclude that (4) in relatively short terms, the relationship between banking activities and GDP weakens and the link between banking activity and the capital market becomes stronger.

Israeli banking has always delivered impressive business results, attesting to the safety and soundness of the system. In the past decade, for example, average annual after-tax profitability was about 9% with a standard deviation of about 1%. This shows that the banks put their monopolistic power to full use. The low standard deviation shows that profitability was very stable. Since the rate of economic growth ranged from 7% to zero during the decade at issue, this stability of profitability is very impressive indeed. It traces partly to utilization of the advantages in the diversity of the banks' activities both in the capital market and abroad, and partly to the smoothing of profits over time by sophisticated use of accounting tools to write off debts and provide for loan-loss.[31]

Wages in the banking industry are among the highest in Israel and resemble those in government monopolies, irrespective of private or public ownership of the banks' equity. Particularly noteworthy are the salaries of executives, which have swelled over the years. While in the 1960s the average wage cost of a teller was about 20% of the average wage cost a bank president, today it is less than 2%. These disparities exist irrespective of the size of the bank and the private or public ownership of its equity.

Risks in Banking Management

A bank is a financial intermediary and a large part of its operations involves trading in risk assets. If a bank aspired to minimize its risks and deal only in completely safe businesses, it would be a moneychanger, providing clearing and deposit-safekeeping services only. Even such limited activity is not absolutely safe, since risks of theft and loss would still exist. The wide range of risks related to banks' activities is customarily sorted into four main categories: credit risks, market risks (interest and indexation-base), liquidity risks, and management risks. These categories may be subdivided for greater specificity. Although some risks are substitutable and complementary so that a bank may swap one for another by using modern techniques, this categorization makes sense because various factors affect each type of risk independently of the others.[32]

Just as a bank may be exposed to these risks, so may an entire banking system. Fiscal policy may directly influence inflation-engendered liquidity risks and market risks. Monetary policy may have a direct and immediate influence on market risks—interest and exchange-rate—and an indirect influence on credit risks. Business cycles have a direct influence on credit risks and liquidity risks. Thus, in the transition from the SD period, in which fiscal policy was dominant, to the RD period, when monetary policy rose to prominence, the weight of liquidity risks declined and that of interest risks increased. More recently, however, amid lengthy recession and falling interest rates, the importance of liquidity risks has increased again and that of interest risks has lessened. When the liberalization process began, the importance of exchange-rate and management risks increased. The response to this was the imposition of stability constraints in these areas by the supervisor of banks, allowing the liberalization process to continue free of concern.

The extent of each risk related to the activities of a bank is a vital piece of information that comes under supervisory scrutiny from three directions. First, the supervisor ascertains that the bank itself is aware of the extent of risks to its assets, so that it may hedge its actions with careful and intelligent provisions. For example, a Proper Conduct of Banking Business Directive requires a bank's board of directors to discuss and rediscuss these risks, and the supervisor ascertains the existence of credit controls at the bank and internal models for risk assessment and monitoring. Second, the supervisor makes sure that the bank reports to the public and properly discloses information about the risks to which it is exposed, thereby ensuring the public's own participation in banking supervision. Due diligence to the public actually creates market discipline—where competition exists—since investors decide where to deposit their money not only in view of the interest rate but also in consideration of the extent of risk. Importantly, the public's supervision of the banks is sometimes more effective and certainly less costly than supervision by the supervisor. Therefore, it should be encouraged, not belittled. The latest regulation rules of Basel 2 focus much attention on this matter of market discipline. Third, the supervisor uses information about the extent of risks to set limits for each risk in order to restrain the bank when necessary. A modern technique called the VAR (Value at Risk) method, based on certain premises, has been used in recent times to calculate the total risk level.[33] Although the VAR method captures the bank's possibility to exchange one risk for another , it has a disadvantage in that it is not clear whether the assumptions on which the method is based actually exist in every case. Finally, where deposit insurance exists, the insurer also has an interest in knowing the risk level in order to set the insurance premium at the appropriate level. The higher the risk, the costlier the insurance. Below we define each type of risk in a somewhat more precise and more detailed way.

Credit Risk

Credit risk is the most important of the four types of risk mentioned above, not necessarily due to its size but mainly because it is one that a bank faces every day in almost every type of operation. The incidence of credit risk exceeds that of all others and the bank must deal with it constantly, since its primary activity is to solicit deposits and issue credit. The portfolio of credit to the public accounts for more than 50% of the bank's total balance-sheet assets. The banks' off-balance-sheet activities—guarantees and futures transactions— also involve credit risk, since customer liability in respect of them resembles the issue of credit. Credit risk is the possibility that a borrower will default on some or all of his or her liability to the bank (principal and/or interest), to the detriment of the bank's earnings, revenues, or market value.[34] Credit risk is categorized in terms of quality and concentration. The quality level is determined on the basis of the inherent riskiness of the projects that the credit finances. Every bank has a screening system to control credit quality. Its function is to sort loan applications and determine which of them qualify and for how much. Some of the screening system is made up of rules and standard procedures for loan approval; the rest is a sophisticated investigation matrix that entails great expertise and professionalism on the part of assessors, accountants, legal advisers, and credit-control officers. According to modern banking theory, both the interest rate on the loan and the collateral demanded are also screening tools. The higher the interest, the more adverse is the selection of borrowers and the lower the average quality of credit.[35]

The level of credit concentration is determined in accordance with the bank's level of specialization. The bank may specialize in an industry, a segment of banking activity, a market segment, or in retail banking or large borrowers. As a rule, the greater the specialization, the higher the concentration of credit and, in turn, the credit risk. Thus, operating efficiency and the credit risk derived from centralization are substitutable. If so, the optimal extent of a bank's specialization determines the desired combination of the two. The high concentration of the Israeli banking system by number of borrowers is also noteworthy. In 2002, for example, more than 70% of credit was issued to fewer than 1% of borrowers.

Market Risks

The main market risk is interest risk, to which the savings-and-loan crisis—the spate of bank failures in the United States in the 1980s—was traced.

Interest risk is derived from the existence of a "duration gap," that is, a disparity between the average life of the payment flow (liability) and that of the revenue flow (asset).[36] Mortgage banks, for example, usually have assets of relatively long duration and liabilities of relatively short life, both in average terms. Therefore, they are exposed to interest risk when the rate rises unexpectedly.

The opposite is usually the case for insurance companies, which generally have assets of relatively short average duration and liabilities of relatively long average duration and are exposed to interest risk when the rate falls unexpectedly.

One of the incentives for banks to sell insurance policies—and, conversely, for insurance companies to give loans—is to bridge this duration gap and hedge themselves against interest risks.[37] In addition, mortgage banks are exposed to "early payback risk." When the interest rate plunges, mortgagors are keen to refinance their mortgages at the lower rate, to the detriment of the bank's earnings. To prevent this, Israel's supervisor of banks allows mortgage banks to charge an early payback fee.

Another market risk is indexation-base risk, which exists when the bank's assets and liabilities are indexed to different bases and may expose the bank to an exchange-rate risk or an inflation risk.[38]

Liquidity Risks

Liquidity for a commercial bank may be likened to stock for a manufacturing firm. An unforeseen decrease in liquidity puts the bank at greater risk of insolvency. Liquidity pressure may be precipitated by unforeseen withdrawal of deposits or unforeseen excess demand for credit. The risk is usually temporary and the central bank deals with it by playing the classic role of lender of last resort. The liquidity requirement and the interest rate charged by the central bank for covering the bank's deficits are the traditional supervisory tools that the central bank uses to keep for this risk low.[39] Deposit insurance also reduces liquidity risk.

Management and Other Risks

The risks discussed in this section are mainly peculiar to individual banks and less to the system at large. Generally speaking, the more functionally distant the transactions managed by a bank are from classic financial intermediation, or the more physically distant they are from the management, the greater the management risk. It is well known, for example, that thefts and embezzlements are more common in peripheral or overseas branches than at main branches. This is why Proper Conduct of Banking Business directives regulate online banking, prohibit the signing of transactions and the provision of banking services off bank premises, and enjoin banks against involvement in nonbanking business.[40] Overseas branches come under special supervisory directives and should comply with dual supervisory systems. (of the country of origin and of the host country). Special supervisory directives address themselves to off-balance-sheet activities.

Banks are exposed to, and are expected to be aware of, many other risks. Three of them have become much more important in modern banking: operating risks, legal risk, and goodwill risks. An example of an operating risk is a faulty computer system that often crashes, has no backup, or is not protected against hackers or viruses. The Bank of International Settlement (BIS) has recently been discussing an amendment to the Basel 2 regulations that would require banks to set aside capital not only for credit and market risks but also relative to total gross income, as a safety net for the realization of operating risks. Due to their involvement in the capital market, Israeli banks are heavily dependent on nonlending revenue. This regulation would foist a considerable burden on the system, and if adopted, its cost would almost certainly be rolled over onto the public because of the banks' market power.

An example of legal risk is a bank's vulnerability to class-action suits and the like. Protection in this case requires the bank to seek suitable legal advice in properly drafting the bank's contracts and documents. Goodwill risk is an act of commission or omission by a bank that may harm its good name, such as inappropriate advertising or unseemly conduct by its employees that the bank may counter by, say, sponsoring nonprofit community activities to restore its goodwill asset.

Summary

Intelligent banking management is the ability to maximize expected profits while dealing with the industry's heterogeneous mosaic of risks. The Banking Supervision Department, for its part, has to deal with two main issues associated with banking risks: how to improve and optimize the tools and methods of measuring those risks and how to integrate all risks in order to evaluate the stability of a bank. The Department's research unit makes a contribution in both issues and the Institutional Assessment Unit is responsible for the overall assessment of the stability of each bank (see the "Means of Supervision" section).

THE NEED FOR BANKING SUPERVISION AND ITS LINK TO MONETARY POLICY

The Need for Supervision

Probability of Bankruptcy and Possible Harm to the Public

To understand the need for banking supervision, one may use the analogy of an automobile driver. Driving a car involves two types of risk: the risk that drivers take upon themselves and the risk that they impose on other users of the road. We may assume that each of these risks increases as the drivers increase their speed. Rational, risk-averse drivers adjust their speed to the degree of risk that they are willing to take (a calculated risk). Presumably, too, such drivers will slow down somewhat on account of the risk that they impose on others. This kind of consideration for others is not necessarily altruistic. "Repeated games" and "social consideration" thinking may be at work, that is, the drivers may believe that if they treat others considerately, others will reciprocate and keep them out of danger. The weight that these drivers assign to the second type of risk may be assumed, ultimately, to be less than is socially desirable. This is exactly why "top-down" intervention is justified and regulations—traffic laws—impose speed limits and invoke methods of enforcement such as laser cameras and fines.

In other words, speeding on the road has negative externalities that endanger others and that are not taken sufficiently into consideration by drivers. A bank, like the drivers in our example, manages risks and may collapse if it behaves in too risky a fashion. This kind of collapse has negative externalities that increase the risk that other banks will collapse as well. Depositors who fear for their money will withdraw their deposits when they hear about the collapse of another bank, generating a run on the banks, a domino effect that may topple additional banks if not the entire banking system. In such a case, not even a lender of last resort can halt the chain reaction. History demonstrates this; the run on banks in the early 1930s, for example, induced global trauma. It was then that the crucial need for banking supervision and regulation was acknowledged, especially when the reasonable assumption that the banks do not pay sufficient regard to the risks they impose upon others—the negative externalities—was confirmed.[41] This is why the theoretical and practical infrastructure—regulation, supervision, and means of control and enforcement—was installed in order to keep the banking system stable. Thus, banking supervisors may be likened to traffic police. Today, in the globalization era, it has become necessary to consolidate the rules. Thus, an international body, the Bank of International Settlement (BIS), has been established to draft rules and recommend that countries follow them, as most industrialized countries, including Israel, indeed do.

Deposit Insurance and Market Discipline

To blunt the severity of negative externalities, many countries have introduced de jure deposit insurance and others are following their lead.[42] Insured depositors place their trust in the government or a body that acts on their behalf to ensure that their money will be returned no matter what. Thus, the failure of one bank does not lead to a stampede of depositors against other banks. Wherever deposit insurance exists and attenuates the negative externalities, there would seem to be less need for banking supervision. The remedy of deposit insurance, however, has negative by-products. Where it exists, market discipline abates and the likelihood of bankruptcy rises. If we assume that the purpose of supervision is to reduce the expected cost to the public from the collapse of a bank, deposit insurance attains the goal of reducing the cost but increases the probability that the cost will be realized, leaving the expected value just about where it was. If so, what have we gained? Furthermore, deposit insurance forces prudent banks to pay for the imprudence of others. To elucidate this point, we return to our analogy of the driver. A driver who carries collision and accident insurance will tend to take a greater risk by driving faster.

Two steps are taken against negative by-products. First, deposit insurance is not all-inclusive. It does not cover large borrowers whose deposits exceed a certain amount; these borrowers will continue to exercise market discipline and, due to their size, one may trust that they will do so effectively. Second, the risk premium is usually graded by the level of risk. The riskier the bank is believed to be, the more it will pay to insure its depositors.[43]

In Israel, the Office of the Examiner of Banks and its successor, the Banking Supervision Department, have been debating the idea of introducing deposit insurance for more than thirty years. The issue finds its way to the agenda whenever a bank collapses and then disappears due to the opposition of the remaining banks, the most recent example being the collapse of Trade Bank in 2002.

Banking Supervision and Its Link to Monetary Policy

Should the Bank of Israel Be in Charge of Banking Supervision?

It is widely believed that the main role of a central bank is to preserve the value of the currency. Thus, the central bank is responsible for the implementation of monetary policy. Other functions, such as supervision and regulation of the banking system, are debatable. The opinion taking shape today is that these functions should be completely or partly separate. Indeed, fewer and fewer industrialized countries task the same entity with both monetary-policy management and banking supervision.[44] By presenting some of the reasons for and against this tendency, we may judge the situation in Israel. Those in favor of central-bank patronage for banking supervision contend that since the central bank and the banking supervision entity ultimately have the same goal—stability of the currency and the system of payments—they should cooperate and share the information that each gathers in the other's field. Indeed, they argue, the traditional role of a central bank as the lender of last resort necessitates such sharing.[45] Another reason is that the supervisor's status vis-a-vis the banks is stronger when backed by the governor of the central bank—a reason that appears to carry weight mainly in developing countries. Indeed, almost all developing countries place banking supervision under the umbrella of the central bank. Finally, the independence of the central bank may also serve as a shield against political pressure.

Those in favor of full or partial separation contend that in an era of globalization and high-speed electronic communication, the economy is more acutely exposed to financial crises. This, they say, necessitates a different kind of deployment by supervisory agencies: first, close cooperation among the three bodies that, in the Israeli case, supervise the money and capital markets—the Banking Supervision Department, the Commissioner of the Capital Market, and the Chair of the Securities Authority, who supervises the stock exchange. Such cooperation may be more successful if orchestrated by a single authority operating outside the confines of the central bank, due to possible conflicts of interest between the object of supervision and the monetary policy.[46] Notably, too, the central bank must also consider aspects of financial stability when it implements monetary policy. Research has illuminated distinct differences in the behavior of the banking system (pricing and performance) and the effectiveness of monetary policy (inflation rate) in countries where banking supervision is separate from the central bank as against countries where there is no such separation.[47] In other words, the location of the banking supervision authority is a matter of significance that may have important implications.

It is worth adding that recently, after the financial crises in southern Asia, central banks have started to take on the role of sentinel against financial instability. This function has more objects than the stability of the banking system and may have implications for monetary policy. The Bank of Israel recently appointed a panel alongside the Banking Supervision Department and tasked it with the monitoring of financial stability.

Governor-Supervisor Relations

The 1954 Bank of Israel Law defines the functions of the central bank: "To manage, regulate, and direct the currency system and to regulate and direct the bank credit system in Israel." Banking Ordinance No. 26, enacted in 1941 by the pre-independence British Mandate government, states: "The Governor may appoint an examiner of banks who, having been appointed, will be responsible for the general supervision and control of every banking corporation. . . . The Governor may take upon himself any power vested in the Examiner." Thus, in Israel it is the governor of the Bank of Israel who bears overarching responsibility for banking supervision. Could there be a contradiction between monetary policy and supervisory policy? One may point to many instances of monetary-policy decisions that adversely affect the stability of banks and stabilizing measures that have consequences for monetary policy. For example, raising the key rate (or, sometimes, not lowering it) may be adverse to the stability of the banking system if it degrades credit quality by destabilizing the banks' customers, that is, business firms. In another example, capital adequacy regulation may reduce liquidity in the nonfinancial sector.[48]

These possibilities of contradiction or conflict of interests may be solved in one of two ways: internalization or separation. Internalization entails the presence of the supervisor in the forum that makes monetary-policy decisions, so that she or he can explain the implications of policy proposals for stability and give them greater policymaking weight than otherwise. Separation denotes the formulation of monetary policy on the basis of macroeconomic considerations only and irrespective of stability considerations. During the SD period, when fiscal policy was dominant and the banking system was subjugated to this policy, the Bank of Israel chose internalization; in the RD period, when monetary policy is dominant, it has chosen separation. For the past fifteen years, the principle has been that the Supervisor of Banks does not take part in the monetary policy decision-making forum and takes measures in his or her domain within the given framework of monetary policy. During the 2002–3 recession, for example, monetary policy led to a lowering of the key rate in small increments while the supervisor of banks, independently, ordered the banks to increase their general loan-loss provisions in order to reduce risks. This dealt the nonfinancial sector a double blow: a credit crunch and a liquidity shortage. It may have been due to this dual-edged policy that the inflation target was undershot. The governor of the Bank of Israel also wears another hat in Israel, since the Bank of Israel Law tasks him or her with being the government's economic adviser. This creates yet another opportunity for possible conflict of interests with the supervisory policy. A controversy of this kind came to light in the kibbutz-credit crisis, which still reverberates in differences of opinion between the state comptroller and the Bank of Israel (see the section on "Instability").

Relations between the governor and the supervisor also depend, of course, on the personalities and background of the two officials and the extent of the governor's personal interest in the topic of banking. In times of crisis, the supervisor needs public support from the governor and, therefore, tends to share stability problems with him or her. For this very reason, however, we may assume that some governors tended not to get involved in supervision issues unless such involvement was unavoidable. Needless to say, certain areas of supervision are discussed in wider forums such as the Bank of Israel Advisory Committee, its subcommittee for banking affairs, and committees that deal with licensing issues.

Perhaps the recently bruited idea of a council of governors would be a suitable setting for the resolution of possible controversies and conflicts of interest between the supervisor and monetary policy in respect to the stability of the banking industry.

INSTABILITY

This section describes five episodes that rocked the Israeli banking system: two bank failures, the bankruptcy of an entire sector that almost led to the bankruptcy of a group of banks, and two capital-market crises that triggered a crisis in the banking industry. What these events have in common is their magnitude, which establishes them as the most noteworthy occurrences that have affected the banking system and banking supervision during the past fifty years.

Bank Failures and Their Lessons

The overarching goal of every supervisor of banks has been to keep the banking system stable. Part of this generality is the concern that no bank should collapse. This goal has largely been achieved; significant bank collapses have occurred about once per decade.

Below we focus on two bank failures only, for three reasons: (1) the banks at issue were relatively large and their collapse involved extensive losses; (2) in both cases, commissions were appointed to investigate the performance of the Banking Supervision Department and their conclusions laid at least part of the blame squarely at the department's door; and (3) most importantly, following these two cases the department improved its means of supervision.

The Israel-Britain Bank Episode

Embezzlement, losses on speculative transactions in the commodities and metals markets, and liquidity problems drove the Israel-Britain Bank to insolvency. The acts of fraud and concealment began in 1967 and were still going on in 1973. On July 4, 1974, the CEO of the bank notified the Office of the Examiner of Banks (as this office was known then) that he could no longer meet his obligations. On July 9, the bank was taken over.

On July 12, 1974, the government resolved to appoint a panel under the attorney general to investigate the circumstances of the collapse and recommend a course of action that would prevent recurrence. In its report, submitted in May 1975, the panel assigned direct responsibility for the collapse of the bank to the ownership and the CEO, who had camouflaged fraud and illegalities and had deceived the regulators, that is, the examiner of banks and the controller of foreign exchange. The panel's criticism of the actions of the Bank of Israel in regard to the bank (mainly from the middle of 1973) may be summed up as follows: "The actions of the Bank of Israel . . . were incomplete, indecisive . . . and belated. . . . Exhaustive, decisive, and aggressive measures should have been taken at an earlier stage."

In the wake of this event, a Bank of Israel committee submitted a proposal for the restructuring of banking supervision in a manner that the panel would find acceptable.[49] Apart from recommendations of specialization of supervision staff, standardization of auditing procedures, and the preparation of an annual work plan, the main thrust of the proposal was a recommendation to establish an institutional assessment unit, separate from the body that performed on-site audits, that would monitor the banks regularly. The committee also recommended the imposition of a single-borrower limit. All these recommendations were approved and implemented.

North America Bank

North America Bank collapsed on August 15, 1985, following shareholder embezzlement involving forged documents, a blatant policy of concealment of facts from the Bank of Israel, and mismanagement. The governor of the Bank of Israel appointed a committee of one—an individual independent of the Bank—to examine the bank-licensing procedures and investigate whether the office of the examiner could have uncovered earlier the events that led to the collapse of the bank. The investigator found flaws in the licensing procedure and determined that the office of the examiner had identified most of the improprieties of the bank's managers and shareholders before the bank failed. The investigator included a list of recommendations in his report.

After the North America Bank affair, the examiner established a joint team from the Research Unit and the Institutional Assessment Unit, which met over a period of about one year and developed ways and means to identify warning signals of a bank's collapse. Most of the team's recommendations were eventually formalized in Proper Conduct of Banking Business Directives.

Other Crises

The Share-Manipulation Crisis

In 1972, a number of banks, including the largest ones, began to manipulate the prices of their shares on the Tel Aviv Stock Exchange. Their meddling gradually increased over the next decade until it erupted into crisis in October 1983.

These banks considered share-price manipulation a way of raising money from the public even when the capital market was foundering. During the 1974 recession, for example, more than 90% of all issues on the Stock Exchange were of bank shares. The phenomenon recurred on a similar scale in 1983. The manipulation released the banks from dependence on the state in the capital market. At that time, the government manipulated the prices of its bonds for fiscal-policy purposes and regulated the exchange rate. This was its way of financing its budget amid galloping inflation.

In 1977, the banks began to compete with the government in raising capital by fostering the illusion among buyers that the yield on bank shares was as assured as that on government bonds. The investors fell for the promise of a "guaranteed" real return on their investment. The high inflation provided a convenient background for the manipulation and explains the public's great enthusiasm for an instrument that would protect its money and would even yield a nice return. Over time, the manipulation technique was fine-tuned and the volume of issues increased. In 1977, when the capital market fell into a slump, the banks had to step up their marketing efforts to keep the share manipulation going. Now they encouraged their customers to take loans to finance the purchase, using the shares themselves as collateral.

The examiner of banks fought the phenomenon, in vain. The banks resorted to indirect marketing techniques and circuitous ways to give the public the credit it needed to buy shares. The resulting bubble—the gap between the price of the shares and the real value of the underlying asset—grew steadily. The banks continued manipulating with great determination in order to improve their capital adequacy and meet their commitment to the public, in the misguided belief that the process could go on forever. For all intents and purposes, they were mimicking the government: if the government could continue raising capital from the public by regulating its bonds, then they could compete with the government by doing the same, no less successfully, with their shares.

The public, in turn, benefited from the illusion of wealth and believed in the banks' authority and their ability to keep their promise about the safety of the capital gain on the shares. The public swapped other financial assets and even real estate for bank shares. The proportion of the bank shares in total assets of the public swelled steadily. The Ministry of Finance, the Bank of Israel, and the Securities Authority all saw something "problematic" about the share-price manipulation. Some Members of Knesset also spoke out on the subject.

In the early 1980s, the minister of finance, the governor of the Bank of Israel, the chairman of the Securities Authority, and the examiner of banks were all replaced with new appointees, each of whom inherited the "problem" and saw no reason to accept blame or responsibility for it. Consequently, none of these officials was inclined to confront the determination of the banks and take courageous and unpopular action to bring the matter to a halt. Indeed, each tried to pass the "problem" onto the others. Notably, with the share-manipulation process rolling along, a fundamental solution would have required the cooperation of all the relevant bodies.

Early in 1983, the banks started to finance the manipulation by taking in loans in foreign exchange. It was a time of considerable real appreciation of the IS (the "old" sheqel), rising demand for imports and foreign currency, deterioration in the balance of payments, and soaring external debt. The public, expecting a large currency devaluation, started to dump its bank shares in favor of foreign currency and imported goods. The banks, continuing their manipulation, bought up shares from the public to quench its need for more and more foreign currency. As the spate of sales gathered strength, however, the banks could not keep up and became helpless. This is where the bubble burst and the robustness of the entire banking system was in question. The minister of finance had to shut down the Stock Exchange to save the capital market and the banking system from collapse. The exchange remained closed until an "arrangement" was worked out. The Bank of Israel was not a party to the formulation of the principles of the arrangement.

The arrangement was predicated on a commitment by the government to guarantee the value of the shares to their holders at their price on the day the Stock Exchange was closed—October 6, 1983. The bank shares, without voting rights, were transferred to the government. Management and de facto control of the banks remained in the hands of the existing controlling interests. The banks undertook to refrain from manipulating their shares in the future. The value of the government's undertaking was the IS equivalent of $6.9 billion. This was the gross cost to the taxpayer of lifting the threat from the banking system, safeguarding its international status, and keeping the capital market stable. To arrive at the net cost, one should subtract the discounted value of the assets acquired by the government, that is, the value of the nationalized banks. Notably, from the standpoint of the public at large, the arrangement solution did not, in itself, impose a high direct real cost on the economy. It amounted to a large benefit for the banks' shareholders at the taxpayer's expense. There may have been an effect of income redistribution in the direction of greater inequality, but one cannot assume that even this influence was significant, since after all the weakest strata neither paid the additional progressive tax nor held bank shares that earned the benefit. The most significant real damage to the economy from the manipulation was an increase in the cost of raising capital, as it took the Tel Aviv Stock Exchange almost a decade to recover from the share crisis.

The state comptroller's report of December 31, 1984 investigated the arrangement, and on January 17, 1985, a panel (the Bejski Commission, named for its chair, Supreme Court Justice Moshe Bejski) was appointed to look into the whole affair.[50] The report of the panel listed the factors that led to the manipulation, explained how the manipulation was financed and marketed, and described in detail how the banks, the Office of the Examiner, and the other relevant authorities had behaved before the crisis. An important conclusion arising from the report is that securities activities must be separated from banking activities in order to avert possible conflicts of interests. In the Israeli discourse, this matter was referred to as the need to erect "Chinese walls."

The Chinese walls that the Bejski Commission recommended were either not erected or were built in a way that made them easy to scale. Within ten years, the banks had indeed hurdled the separation of securities consulting services from the issue of credit. This gave rise to a new crisis, much smaller than the share-manipulation affair but with many similarities, particularly in regard to conflict of interests between banks and their customers.

The Mutual-Fund Crisis

The Tel Aviv Stock Exchange soared in the second half of 1993. Fueling the bull market were the banks, which steered large amounts of credit to the public for purchases of the mutual funds they managed. In early 1994, however, the bears moved in and the share index plummeted, leaving many customers badly stranded. Some lost all their savings; many others found their accounts over-drawn. As the banks demanded payment of their debts, the value of the assets that the customers had acquired eroded badly. The public outcry reverberated in the corridors of the Knesset and Banking Supervision Department was inundated with complaints. The department's immediate reaction was spine-less; it sided with the banks.[51] Notably, many of the affected customers had regarded bank clerks and investment consultants as unquestioned authorities who were acting on their behalf; they were unaware of the conflict of interest between them and the bank. Under pressure from the Knesset Finance Committee and following the wave of complaints, the department, whose job it is to ensure the stability and trustworthiness of the system, adopted a more effective approach. It doubled the size of its Public Enquiries Unit to allow it to investigate complaints more thoroughly and found 40% of the complaints to be justified. It was clear that investment consultants had acted unethically and against customers' interests. The department ordered the banks to compensate justified complainants partly or fully and to withdraw many of the lawsuits they had filed against customers for the payback of loans.

The supervisor of banks summed up the affair in his 1994 survey: "The banks' eagerness to sell mutual funds motivated some of them to grant credit without properly checking the customers' repayment ability and, at times, with-out taking care to provide customers with appropriate information about the risks of their investment. . . . The findings of the Department's investigations of the matter indicate again that Israel's banks work [only] for themselves, possibly to the detriment of customers' welfare."[52]

Legislation enacted in 1995 introduced compulsory licensing of investment consultants and portfolio managers. Only candidates who pass an examination on professional knowledge and ethics may be licensed. Although the law is almost certainly an improvement, one doubts whether it has changed the conflict-of-interest situation in any fundamental way.

The Kibbutz-Loan Crisis

Between 1982 and 1985, the banks granted generous loans to kibbutzim and moshavim (collective and cooperative settlements, respectively), especially kibbutzim affiliated with the United Kibbutz and the Ha-kibbutz ha-Artsi movements. Bank Hapoalim, long associated with the kibbutz movements, was the leader in the volume of credit issued. The settlements' debts were allowed to balloon due to the mutual guarantee that the kibbutz movements provided and the banks' understanding that the state was responsible for this agricultural sector and, therefore, would back the debt. This responsibility was seen as a kind of "covert contract" between the government and the kibbutzim. Due to this overt or covert government backing, neither the banking system nor the

Banking Supervision Department changed its conduct even when the debt started to swell rapidly and then exceeded the debtors' annual output. After 1985, it was not the principal that grew but only the interest, including the arrears penalty.

The banks found themselves on the horns of the well-known banking dilemma concerning a large borrower with payback problems: whether to recycle the debt, and if so, on what terms, or to stop.[53] They carried on until October 1988, when the size of the debt verged on NIS 7 billion (more than $4.5 billion). The banks, realizing that there was no alternative but to write off much of the debt, stopped recycling. The stoppage of credit endangered the kibbutz movements, the creditor banks, the banking system, and, in fact, Israel's whole agricultural sector. The government was called upon to resolve the crisis. After protracted talks among the Ministry of Finance, the commercial banks, and the kibbutzim, a framework agreement was signed in December 1989. In its main provisions, the banks would write off NIS 1 billion of debt, the government would finance an additional write-off of NIS 650 million, and the Finance Ministry would create special bank deposits from which short-term debt would be recycled at relatively high interest and NIS 3.3 billion in debt spread over twenty-five years at relatively low interest. In essence, the agreement entailed a huge payment from the public to cover the losses of the banks and the kibbutzim. In May 1990, the state comptroller issued an unusually harsh report about the conduct of the supervisor of banks in the affair,[54] the main allegation being that had the flow of credit been stopped earlier, the crisis might not have been prevented but the loss would have been smaller by far.

The lesson that the banks learned from this crisis was that when deliberating whether to grant credit, greater weight should be given to the customer's ability to repay and less to the collateral. The lesson learned by the Banking Supervision Department was to include in the lending restrictions not only single borrowers but also borrower groups.

Conclusion

In all the crises described above, the Bank of Israel and its banking supervision authority were accused of indecisiveness and hesitancy in taking preventive or damage-control actions even though they had sufficient information. It should be borne in mind that in at least in cases of bank failures, the supervisory authority faces a difficult dilemma that has characteristics similar to those faced by the holder of a call option who is considering exercise, where the exercise price may be high if he acts too soon.[55]

The Chapter 11 instrument, which allows a bankrupt manufacturing firm to continue operations, does not exist in Israel and in any event would not be effective in the case of a bank. This tool, in the hands of an official receiver, is useful in protecting shareholders, but the job of a supervisor of banks is to protect not shareholders but the public, which may be harmed by the negative externalities.

Deciding on the exact timing of the seizure of a troubled bank constitutes the very peak of the skills, the ability, and perhaps even the art of banking supervision.

MEANS OF SUPERVISION

Banking supervision tools may be sorted into two categories: ex post tools, mainly auditing, and ex ante tools, mainly regulation. The second category was almost void in the SD period but has quickly filled up during the RD period while tools in the first category also became more sophisticated and numerous. Importantly, while auditing is the crux of the supervisor's work, regulation has a twofold advantage: it contributes to the efficiency of the banking corporation by imposing clearly defined do's and don'ts and it makes the supervisory work more transparent.

The change in the quantity and characteristics of the means of supervision took place mainly due to several simultaneous processes and nonrecurrent events: (1) economic growth and the expansion of the banking industry in quantity, complexity, and range of activity (see "The Israeli Banking System" subsection); (2) the upturn in risk due to globalization processes and sweeping changes in banking technology (see the "Risks in Banking Management" subsection); (3) government policy—liberalization and the increased weight given to monetary policy relative to fiscal policy (see the "Historical Perspective on Banking Supervision in Israel" section); and (4) the capital-market and bankruptcy crises and the lessons learned from them (see the "Instability" section). A small part of this development is described in previous sections; here we describe briefly the tools used by the Banking Supervision Department today. First, however, we describe the legal infrastructure on which the supervisory activity is based.

Legal Infrastructure

The Bank of Israel and the supervisor of banks derive their authority vis-à-vis banking corporations from four laws: Banking Ordinance No. 26 of 1941, the Bank of Israel Law, 5714-1954, the Banking (Licensing) Law, 5741-1981, and the Banking (Customer Service), Law, 5741-1981.

The Banking Ordinance establishes the function of the central bank as a lender of last resort and empowers the supervisor to determine "bad debts," to maintain the stability of banking corporations, and to seize them if necessary. The ordinance also requires banks to report to the supervisor and to the public.

The Bank of Israel Law allows the supervisor to limit the credit that a banking corporation may extend relative to its capital and authorizes him or her to establish reporting requirements. The Banking (Licensing) Law establishes the requirement of a banking corporation to operate under a license, determines under what the license may be granted—"the license price"—and defines the authority of the governor or his or her deputy, the supervisor, to revoke the license. The law also demarcates the banks' operational boundaries and limits the controlling interest of a bank in a nonbanking corporation. The Banking (Customer Service) Law defines the duties of a banking corporation in providing banking services for the public. It forbids the bank to make one service contingent upon another and establishes the requirement of proper disclosure.

Ex Ante Supervision
Licensing

The license and the process for obtaining it are the entry barrier to the Israeli banking industry and an important factor in the lack of competition (see "The Israeli Banking System" subsection). Under the licensing law, a permit from the governor of the Bank of Israel is required for a controlling stake of more than 10% in a bank. Applicants must fill out a detailed questionnaire relating to their financial robustness, clean record, absence of conflict of interest, and professional experience. They must also enclose a business plan for the banking corporation.

To make sure that the applicant can inject capital "in times of need" and to preclude his or her complete financial dependence on the bank, he or she must prove that the ratio of his or her capital to his or her investment in the bank is at least 2:1. The law also limits the transfer of means of control in a bank and restricts the other businesses of the controlling party.

Until recently, as a condition for licensing, the Bank of Israel demanded the existence of "core controlling equity"—25% for a large bank and 50% for a small bank—and a minimum period of five years in which this equity must be held. The government also established this condition for prospective purchasers of the bank equity that it held after the share-manipulation crisis. In July 2003, the licensing law was amended (Amendment No. 13) to rescind the need for core controlling equity. However, the amendment added other restrictions and requirements in regard to holdings in capital-market corporations, cross-ownership of banks, reporting duties, and the appointment of directors. Although the supervisor of banks does not appoint directors, the law allows him or her to oppose the appointment of an officer in a banking corporation.

It should be emphasized that the law establishes entry barriers and allows the governor and the supervisor to regulate their height by giving these officials discretion in awarding licenses and naming the officers in banking corporations.

Regulation

Regulation, the establishment of standard rules for the activities of the banks and the supervisory authority, is a field that has been developing greatly and rapidly since the 1980s for the four reasons listed at the beginning of this section. At the center of the regulatory rules are capital and other requirements that restrict the volume of credit extended by the banking corporation in the short term when the bank is unable to increase its capital. Israel's risk-adjusted capital ratio is currently 9%, in keeping with the Basel 1 rules. There are also limits on single borrowers and groups of borrowers—15% and 30% of the bank's capital, respectively. Even though in the long term the bank can increase its capital by earnings and by issuing additional shares, controlling shareholders may not favor these methods because they may dilute their dividends and control. Thus, the capital restrictions are effective in limiting the volume of credit not only in the short term but also in the long term, especially among the large banks, which suffer from a shortage of capital. The rules not only restrain the volume of credit that a banking corporation can extend but prevent concentration of credit by borrowers, by forcing them to divide their sources of finance among several banks.

Sectoral concentration is limited by the requirement of a capital provision if the bank lends more than 20% of total credit to one industry. This limitation has proven extremely effective in certain years with regard to the construction industry. Other rules concern transactions with related persons as the law defines them, the duties and modus operandi of the board of directors and the internal auditor, risk management, treatment of and general and special provisions for problem loans, bank-customer relations, and the format for due-diligence financial reporting to the public and for increasing market discipline.

For years, the rules were issued to the banking corporations as in the form of circulars and directives from the Office of the Examiner of Banks (later renamed the Banking Supervision Department). In August 1991, these documents were collated into a volume called "Proper Conduct of Banking Business." This collection, which currently runs to some 250 pages is the codex that reflects the position of the supervisor of banks on the norms that proper banking management entails. Whenever the supervisor and a banking corporation disagree about a given directive or provision, the Proper Conduct of Banking Business folder helps the supervisor to exercise his or her authority.

Ex Post Supervision

The purpose of ex post supervision is to identify management issues in need of correction and to warn about loopholes that expose the bank to risks that may undermine its stability. Central to the level of supervision is the periodic audit at the bank's offices, which includes a review of its books and a report that warns about flaws discovered and describes actions taken to correct flaws previously discovered.

The regular reports that banks are required to submit to the supervisor, in addition to the quarterly and annual financial statements that the bank is required to publish for the public, are also closely monitored.

Structure of the Banking Supervision Department

The Banking Supervision Department is structured so that each area of activity is overseen by a specific unit. The main areas of activity and the corresponding units are Auditing, Institutional Assessment, Information and Reporting, Bank-Customer Relations, and Research.

During the SD period, banking supervision took place almost entirely at the audit level. Auditing remains the mainstay and infrastructure of supervisory activity, since there is no substitute for sending auditors to a bank to examine its activities on site. Thus, the Auditing Unit employs about two-thirds of the department staff. Its methods have become more sophisticated over the years and incorporate the lessons learned from past failures. A systematic annual working plan allocates teams to audit every bank in the system and defines the teams' tasks in accordance with the subject of the audit. The selection of subjects depends on the importance of the risks that prevail at that time and on the past conduct of the audited bank. The auditing team culminates its work with an audit report.

The Institutional Assessment Unit was established in 1975 after the collapse of the Israel-Britain Bank (see the "Instability" section) to gather information on matters that were reviewed in the audit reports and to amass information between audits. The staff of the Auditing Unit specializes in auditing matters; the Institutional Assessment Unit specializes in banks. The staff member responsible for a particular bank integrates the information that she or he has personally gathered about the bank (for which reason the unit is also called the "Integration Unit") with information from the Information and Reporting Unit and information culled from the audit reports. The resulting complete picture of the bank is submitted to the supervisor at least once a year. The same staff member is expected to keep abreast of the supervised bank at all times. The unit also serves the supervisor in a staff capacity for special duties.

The Information and Reporting Unit constantly collects quantitative information and statistics on the banking system and processes in accordance with cross-sections that institutional assessment staff, in particular, requests. The unit is in charge of the department's databases and publishes information about the banking system for the public in various ways, including the Bank of Israel Web site. Importantly, in certain regards the very demand to hand over information is itself a supervisory tool.

The Bank-Customer Relations Unit handles complaints from the public. Some supervisors of banks have believed that this unit should not have been placed in the department, arguing that it is a time-consuming function that diverts attention from the main task of keeping the banking system stable. However, since clearly it is also the supervisor's task to ensure the public's trust in the banking and the payment systems, this is a material part of his or her job. The unit also supplies the supervisor, albeit indirectly, with important information about the nature and quality of management at each bank. A bank that generates numerous complaints, especially if many of them prove justified, would appear to be poorly managed and in need of the supervisor's attention. This unit has more than doubled in size since the mutual-fund crisis, when the number of complaints also doubled (see the "Instability" section).

The Research Unit was established in the early 1970s to write the annual report of the department. For almost twenty years, supervisors used this unit for purposes not always directly related to supervision, that is, as a think tank and a forum for discussion of long-term issues such as capital adequacy, the desired market structure, the influence of various factors on the banks' spreads, the development of tools and methods for risk measurement, deposit insurance, international comparisons, and econometric models of the banking system.[56] The research papers, published in Hebrew and English, are a "public good" that the Bank of Israel makes available to international bodies, financial institutions, and private institutions in Israel and abroad, and to lecturers and students interested in banking. The Banking Supervision Department is the only viable setting for empirical research on Israeli banking because its Research Unit has access to the confidential information culled by department staff, who have signed nondisclosure commitments. In recent years, due to a change in the department's priorities, the Research Unit has declined in terms of the number of researchers and in its research output.

During the RD period, the department has created special posts to deal with matters such as international relations, modern banking technology, and money laundering.

In sum, the mechanisms of banking supervision, especially those of ex ante nature, add up to a set of guidelines that dictate the conduct of banking corporations. One of the characteristics of a public company is the separation of ownership and management. The banking supervision function in Israel crimps the controlling interests' freedom of management so severely that Israeli banks resemble public corporations even through they are privately controlled. This is undoubtedly an impediment to the privatization of banks that are still in government hands. Although the repeal of the "core controlling equity" requirement opened the way to privatization, the supervisory restrictions will lower the market price at which the government will be able to sell the bank equity that it still holds.

APPENDIX: SUPERVISION MODEL

This appendix presents a stylized model that describes the negative externalities of the collapse of a bank, the resulting need for banking supervision, and the difficulty in implementing supervision. The model provides an explanation of the deliberations that precede the selection of regulatory rules. Since the main purpose of the presentation is methodological, the assumptions are strong in order to simplify the presentation without affecting the generality of the results. The formulation is based mainly on Paroush (1988).

The model assumes an economy in which there are n identical banks. If one of the banks collapses, the entire system collapses due to the negative externalities. This domino-effect assumption is strong indeed, but again, its purpose is to simplify and does not limit the generality of the discussion. We also assume, for the sake of simplicity, that each bank has fixed share equity R.

Each bank has two monotonically rising activity functions: expected profit, $E(x)$, and probability of bankruptcy, $p(x)$. Argument x denotes a vector of activities, but let us assume initially that the vector of activities has a single dimension related to the bank's single action. Due to the substitutability of profit and risk, almost all banking activity may be represented by x—for example, credit granted to a single borrower or to a particular industry, off-balance-sheet activity, or even aggregate credit extended.

Let us assume that the bank's goal is to maximize its expected profit with respect to x at a minimal level of bankruptcy risk, say a threshold, p^*, that the bank sets for itself. Thus:

$$\text{Max } E(x) \text{ S.T. } p(x) \leq p^* \qquad (1)$$

Since profit and risk are monotonic increasing functions, the solution to this problem is the value of x, denoted x^*, that satisfies the equation: $p(x^*) = p^*$. Therefore, x^* is a monotonic increasing function of p^*. For this reason, any restriction on activity x will also restrain risk p^*. Let us assume that g is the maximum desirable risk threshold, from the aspect of the economy, of collapse of the banking system. This means that the probability of at least one bank failure among n banks will not exceed g. Obviously, this level is greater than zero; otherwise, the banking system would be paralyzed. Thus, the maximum desirable level of risk, from the aspect of the economy, of the collapse of a single bank, to be determined as its risk threshold, is the value p', which solves the equation:

$$1 - (1 - p)^n = g \qquad (2)$$

On the left-hand side of this equation is the probability that the banking system will collapse. According to the domino-effect premise, this value is equal to the probability that at least one bank out of n will collapse.

It is now clear that when a single bank determines a maximum value of p, p^*, so that $p^* > p'$, a difference is generated between the actual behavior of the individual bank and the behavior that the public expects of it. This indicates that the bank is not taking into sufficient consideration the negative externalities that may cause the system to collapse. The relative quantity of the negative externality that is taken into consideration by the bank may be expressed thus:

$$h = 1 - [(1 - p')^n - (1 - p^*)^n / [(1 - p^*) - (1 - p^*)^n] \qquad (3)$$

The numerical value of h is bounded between 0 and 1. Where there is full consideration of the externalities, $p^* = p'$ and $h = 1$. Where there is no such consideration at all, $p^* = 1 - (1 - p')^n = g$ and $h = 0$.

At any value of h, which expresses the partial social consideration that the bank takes upon itself, we determine the risk, $p^*(h)$, that the bank sets and that is actually the solution to the equation:

$$p + (1 - p) [1 - (1 - p)^{n-1}] h = g \qquad (4)$$

Note that for $h = 1$, $p^* = p'$, since (4) equals (2) in this case.

Equation (4) may also be written in a way that better elucidates the meaning of h:

$$h (1 - p)^n + (1 - h)(1 - p) = 1 - g$$

The expression on the right is the socially desired threshold probability of a stable system, presented here as a weighted average of the probability that an individual bank will not collapse and the probability that the entire system will not collapse. The greater the value of h, the greater the weight given by the individual bank to the risk to the system and the less weight it gives to the risk to itself. We propose to use the differential $e(h) = p^*(h) - p'$ to define the extent to which banking supervision is essential. According to the definition, $e(h)$ is never negative and is a descending function of h. When h is at its maximum level ($h = 1$), the individual bank integrates in its risk considerations the full negative externality that its failure would generate. In this case, the extent of need for supervision disappears and $e = 0$. The necessity of supervision may also be written thus: $e(h, g, n) = p^*(h, g, n) - p^*(1, g, n)$.

The effect of h on e is clear but the effects of g and n on e is ambiguous. To understand the ambiguity, we may liken the system to a highway. When there is heavy traffic due to the number of vehicles (a large n) or poor visibility (a large g), drivers will slow down, thereby making speed-limit signs redundant. The necessary conditions for a supervision to increase with the number of banks in the system and with society's demand for a stable system are developed and formulated in Paroush (1988).

Supervision becomes most problematic when x is not a unidimensional variable but a vector of activities. Without forfeiting generality, we now assume that the bank engages in two different activities, x and y. The bank's problem is now:

$$\text{Max } E(x, y) \text{ S.T. } p(x, y) \leq p^* \tag{5}$$

Let us assume that expected profit E is a monotonic increasing function of x and of y with diminishing rates of change, and that the probability of collapse of the bank, p, is also a monotonic increasing function of x and of y but with rising rates of change. These conditions may be written with the aid of partial derivatives:

$$E_1 > 0, E_2 > 0, p_1 > 0, p_2 > 0; E_{11} < 0, E_{22} < 0, p_{11} > 0, p_{22} > 0$$

The indices 1 and 2 denote the derivatives with respect to x or y, correspondingly.

Let us also assume that the signs of the cross-derivatives fulfill the conditions $E_{12} \geq 0, p_{12} \leq 0$. These conditions ensure the semi-concavity and semi-convexity of the functions E and p, respectively. Thus:

$$E_1^2 E_{22} + E_2^2 E_{11} - 2E_{12} E_1 E_2 < 0; p_1^2 p_{22} + p_2^2 p_{11} - 2p_{12} p_1 p_2 > 0$$

These properties assure a regular internal solution for (5), which we will denote (x^*, y^*).

The values (x^*, y^*) are actually obtained as the solution of a two-equation system:

the bank's expansion path: $E_1/E_2 = p_1/p_2$,

and

the risk threshold: $p(x, y) = p^*$

When the need for supervision, $e = p^* - p'$, is positive and the supervisor selects x as the only tool for limiting the risk p^*—for example, by imposing the restriction $x \leq x'$ where x' is selected, so that $x' < x^*$— the bank will look for a second-best solution (x', y'') for the problem:

$$\text{Max } E(x', y) \text{ S.T. } p(x', y) \leq p^* \tag{6}$$

where $p(x', y'') = p^*$, then clearly also $y'' \geq y^*$.

It is easy to see that in this solution the risk remains at its original level; the only change is that the bank has been diverted from its expansion path and is no longer as efficient as it was. Here, the supervision has inflicted damage on the bank with no benefit to the economy. This situation is quite realistic and is typical of several supervision directives. In many cases, the supervisor lacks the knowledge and/or the ability to limit all activities of the bank. If one channel remains open and unrestricted, the bank can direct its activities to that channel and increase the risk to its heart's content. The criticism of certain means of supervision is based precisely on this argument. See, for example, Koehn and Santomero (1980). In this context, Bill Seidman, president of the Federal Deposit Insurance Corporation (FDIC), one of the American supervisory institutions, remarked, "Bankers who want to take risks have ample means of doing so in today's marketplace. There is almost no end to the ways in which the determined risk-seeking banker can gamble with the FDIC's funds or his customers' deposits."[57]

The model presented here makes it easier for us to understand two important issues. The first is why supervisory authorities encourage banks to narrow their activities and not expand into nonbanking business such as insurance, despite the argument that diversification decreases risk and increases stability. The Glass-Steagall Act, for example, forbade American commercial banks to engage in investments. The universal activity of Israeli banks definitely makes the work of the supervisor of banks difficult and also explains several past events that threatened stability (see the "Instability" section). Second, even if a supervisor controls all activities of a bank and blocks activities at a certain level of risk, thereby reducing the risk, there is no certainty that the combination of restrictions will dovetail with the efficiency path of expansion. In this case, stability is attained at the price of inefficiency. Instead of blocking each activity of every bank at the appropriate level—an impossible task—Israel introduced a minimum capital requirement fifteen years ago, following the international recommendations of Basel 1. In our model, the minimum capital requirement may be expressed as $\alpha x + \beta y \leq R/\gamma$, where γ is the minimal capital requirement, for example, 9%. The coefficients α, β are the risk coefficients determined according to the provisions of the Basel 1 regulations, and R is the fixed capital according to our assumption. The problem of the bank can now be presented thus:

$$\text{Max } E(x \,.\, y) \text{ S.T. } \alpha x + \beta y \leq R/\gamma \qquad (7)$$

The risk coefficients determined by Basel 1 for a bank's assets for the purpose of computing a minimum capital restriction are applicable for small and large banks alike, with α and β independent of the magnitude of R.

The formulation of the bank's problem (7) will be the same as the original formulation (5) if two assumptions are met:

(1)   Throughout the banking system, h and, therefore, p^* have the same value. In addition, $p^* = R/\gamma$. Since this is a strong assumption, it is clear why the value of γ is carefully proposed at the beginning and changed several times, an indication of the deliberation associated with this assumption.

(2)   The functions of expected profit and risk, $E(x, y)$ and $p(x, y)$, are homothetic. Thus, the expansion path is a straight ray from the origin and the combination of restrictions is a point on the bank's expansion. This means that the slope of the ray is α/β.

Assumption (2) is also strong; it allows us to explain why the categories of assets defined in Basel 1 are so broad and so few. Any greater specificity of the risk categories could severely harm assumption (2), divert the bank from its expansion path, and affect its efficiency.

Notably, the possibility of increasing the number of risk categories is being considered (Basel 2) in conjunction with allowing each bank to determine the α and β coefficients for itself by associating estimates of the probability of default (PD) with categories of assets on the basis of an internal model and a standard formula—the internal-ratings-based approach (IRB). Giving such freedom to every bank will limit the harm to efficiency and lessen the dependence on the homotheticity assumption.[58] If the intended result is attained, system stability will improve with no detriment to efficiency. The IRB approach, however, is suitable only for large banks that can shoulder the burden of implementing an internal model and generate enough cases to elicit reliable PD estimates. For small banks, Basel 2 will apparently recommend the traditional standard approach.

We now expand the model by introducing two additional cost functions:

The function of cost to the bank due to the supervision-engendered diversion from its efficiency path is $L(x, y; p') = E(x', y'; p') - E(x, y; p')$, and the direct cost function of the supervision, including auditing the banks, collecting information, enforcing rules, etc., is $l(x, y; p')$.

Thus, the total cost to the economy as a result of banking supervision is the sum of two components: direct cost and indirect cost: $l + nL$. The closer point (x, y) is to point (x', y'), the greater the direct cost and the smaller the indirect cost. The interchange of these two types of costs creates the following problem of optimization for the supervisor:

$$\text{Min } [l + nL] \text{ S.T. } p(x, y) = p' \tag{8}$$

We denote by $B(p')$ the minimum value of the total cost of supervision obtained as a solution to problem (8). We will assume that this is a decreasing function as p' ascends and approaches p^*.

Additionally, there is the cost to the economy from the collapse of the banking system, which we will denote F. The expectation of this cost is $Fe(p^*)$, where $e(p') = p^* - p'$ is the necessity of supervision as defined.

We can now express the general problem of the banking supervision authority if it indeed faithfully represents the interest of the public:

$$\text{Min } \{B(p' + z) + F[e(p') + z]\} \tag{9}$$

The optimal value of (9), z^*, represents the added risk of the domino effect, Fz^*, intended to save on the cost of supervision. Clearly, if $z^* \geq e = p^* - p'$, then, as paradoxical as it sounds, banking supervision is superfluous even if it is essential, that is, even though $e > 0$.

If we take efficiency considerations into account, the desired risk threshold from society's standpoint, which the bank should determine for all of its activities, is $p' + z^*$. This risk is a function of g and of n, which are arguments of p' and also a function of l, nL, F, the costs that determine the value of z^*. To avoid paradoxes, we may now go back and define the necessity of banking supervision more accurately as a size: $e^* = p^* - (p' + z^*)$. Supervision is warranted only if $e^* > 0$, of course.

Conclusion

This appendix presented a stylized model of banking supervision. As part of the theory, we defined the domino effect and determined the necessity of supervision as a natural result. We also developed a synthetic measure for the necessity of supervision when the effect of various factors on it can be examined. The factors include the extent of financial stability that society desires, the size of the banking system, the extent to which banks take their negative externalities into consideration, the direct and indirect costs of supervision, and the social cost of the domino effect. The model also takes account of supervisory difficulties by limiting the activities of the bank, especially when it engages in a range of activities. It deserves emphasis that the existence of de jure deposit insurance, while mitigating the domino effect, raises the risk threshold that the banks set for their activities. Thus, even in this case the need for supervision would exist and would be similarly defined. Now, however, we must take two additional factors into account: the level of the insurance premium and the extent of the banks' tendency to be "free riders" (the moral-hazard problem).

If we add the public's demand for credit to the model, we will obtain a model of sectoral equilibrium with an optimal size of the banking sector, as well as the interest equilibrium determined in the money market with negative externalities and with banking supervision. This article, however, is not the place for this supplementary presentation.

Notes

To prepare this survey, I interviewed former supervisors of the banks (or, as known until the late 1980s, examiners of banks): Meir Heth, Galia Maor, Amnon Goldschmidt, Ze'ev Abeles, Yitzhak Tal, and Yoav Lehman. I am indebted to them for their cooperation. Of course, they bear no responsibility for the contents of this survey. I owe special thanks to Nissan Liviatan, the coeditor of this book, who suggested that I elaborate on a few subjects and discuss certain important questions.

Riki Elias, Ami Barnea, Yoram Landskroner, Meir Sokoler, Sara Paroush, Miriam Krausz, and David Ruthenberg read part or all of the chapter and gave me helpful comments about the contents, structure, and quality of the presentation. My thanks to all of them. Obviously, any errors that have been overlooked are my sole responsibility.

1. For details of the restrictions in each of the eight segments, see Haim, Swary, and Paroush (1988).

2. At the end of 1986, for example, unrestricted activity accounted for 6% of total activity but yielded 60% of income.

3. The credit to kibbutzim was extended with the blessing and backing of the government. For discussion of the division of liability between the Bank of Israel and the Treasury in the matter of regulation, see the report of the Bank Share Manipulation Commission, Jerusalem, 1986 (the "Bejski Report"). See the "Instability" section for further details.

4. See Ben-Bassat (2002).

5. The liquidity ratio was lowered from 40% in 1987 to only 8% in 1991. Today it is almost zero.

6. The number of representations of Israeli banks abroad has remained more or less unchanged since then—between 90 and 120. It seems that the banks need these operations for risk diversification. See Ber and Orgeller (2002).

7. A committee based in Basel, Switzerland, operates under the Bank of International Settlement and since 1988 has published "Proper Conduct of Banking Business Directives" (Basel 1) that all developed countries have adopted. Since 1999, the Basel Committee formulated new directives, which were published last year (Basel 2).

8. In the late 1980s, the examiner appointed a panel from the Research Unit to answer two questions: does Israel need a capital-ratio restriction as is customary in other countries, and when is the appropriate time to impose it? The bottom line of the panel's position paper was: "As long as the system is so severely restrained by restrictions that burden the segments of operation, the additional restriction of a minimum capital ratio should not be imposed, particularly when the capital adequacy of the Israeli system is not inferior to that of other similar countries."

9. The worldwide trend developed after globalization made it necessary to formulate standard supervisory rules in order to reduce the possibility of financial crises spreading from one country to another. Modern telecommunication facilitates such "contagion"; standard supervisory rules that are merely regulation rules make it more difficult.

10. For the measurement of competitiveness in the banking sector and the change that has occurred in the "market power" of each of the large banks and the system at large, see Paroush and Ruthenberg (2003a).

11. On the link between the extent of competition and the financial spread in the unindexed local-currency sector, see Elias and Samet (1998). For an attempt to analyze the components of credit interest—risk-free basic interest, risk premium, and additional interest in respect of "market power"—see Paroush and Ruthenberg (2003b).

12. For example, the "coverage ratio," the share of operating expenses covered by fee and commission income, is high in Israel by international standards. In the late 1980s, the examiner of banks deregulated many fees and charges in the incorrect belief that competition among the banks would cause them to decline. The exact opposite happened: the fees and charges increased and the coverage ratio in Israeli banking became one of the highest among banking systems with similar characteristics. See table A-8 in *The Israeli Banking System, Annual Review 1998*. An increase in regulation of bank fees and charges and the reduction of their number are once again being considered.

13. For discussion of the optimal structure of the banking sector, see Paroush and Ruthenberg (1994) and Barnea, Paroush, and Conforti (2001). The first of these references discusses the interchange between stability and competition; the second attempts to estimate the loss of welfare as a result of the oligopolistic structure.

14. See Paroush and Ruthenberg (2003a).
15. Notably, that has not always been the case. In the early 1990s, for example, banks issued credit almost without limit.
16. Within any conceptual framework of risk management in banking, the most important element as a cushion to absorb losses is shareholders' equity. This is why capital adequacy serves as a measure of a bank's strength. This cornerstone of the stability of the individual banking corporation is also applicable to the banking system as a whole.
17. For a comprehensive description of the banking system in Israel and its development, see Heth (1994). For the development of the financial mediation sector, see Ruthenberg (2002). These sources also discuss the historical development of concentration in Israeli banking. Notably, in the years 2002–4 the system has lost six small banks and now numbers seventeen. One bank (Trade Bank) collapsed; one (Industrial Development) went into receivership due to liquidity risks that were realized, three (Shipping, Polska, and Continental) have merged with or been acquired by other banks, and the license of the sixth (Olami) was revoked.
18. Short (1977, p. 14) found a significant positive correlation of 0.88 between the market size of various countries and the inverse of the Herfindhal index of concentration.
19. For example, from 1980 to 2002 the number of bank employees increased by 3%, the number of offices decreased by 10%, but the average office area increased by about 50%. Concurrently, the population grew by 70% and employment increased by 80%. The total credit/GNP ratio rose from was less than 0.5 in the 1960s to 0.6 in the 1980s, 0.8 in the 1990s, and more than 1.0 in the first years of the twenty-first century.
20. See *The Banking System in Israel, Annual Review 2002*, p. 204, table F–4.
21. See Ruthenberg (1983).
22. Israel's sports industry is similarly segmented. The Maccabi, Hapoel, Betar, and Elitzur Associations have political affiliations.
23. See Kim, Kleiger, and Wall (2000). This paper estimates the average time that elapses between bank-switching in Israel at about thirteen years, one of the longest durations in the world.
24. For the banks' involvement in the capital market in 1978–83, see Brenner and Ruthenberg (1987) and Geva (1987).
25. See Ber, Yafeh, and Yosha (2001).
26. On the influence of banks' nonfinancial holdings on firms' performance, see Ber (1999).
27. The Brodet Commission report enjoined a bank against "controlling" a nonfinancial corporation and limited a bank's holdings in a single nonfinancial corporation (to a 20% controlling stake), and the total holdings of a bank in nonfinancial corporations (15% of capital). See "Report of the Commission for Examination of Aspects of Bank Holdings in Nonfinancial Corporations," Jerusalem, 1995.
28. See Kleinman (1984) and Marom (1987). These papers express the cost of inflation in terms of "superfluous" banking product. Marom quantifies the significant positive correspondence between the share of banking in national product and fluctuations in the inflation rate and stock-exchange activity in 1955–82.
29. See Bank of Israel, *The Banking System in Israel,* for each of the years 1998–2001.
30. Credit, product, and volume of trade were taken at fixed 2003 prices and divided by the total permanent population at the end of the year to obtain per capita variables. To provide a consistent series for thirty years, we culled a proxy variable for the volume of stock-exchange trading—the volume of trading in securities of banking corporations—from a publication of the examiner/supervisor of banks, *Annual*

Information on the Banking Corporations. The dummy variable related the value 0 to the SD period and the value 1 to the RD period. The thirty years were divided into six five-year periods, where the base (the regression constant) is the first five-year period, 1974–78. Note that all coefficients are significant at 5% except stock exchange which is significant in Version 1 only at 10%, and the dummy variable is significant in Version 2 only at 15%.

31. See Zaken and Paroush (1997), p. 108.
32. On banking management of assets, liabilities, and risks in Israel, see Ruthenberg (2002).
33. See Wiener, Zaken, and Schreiber (2001).
34. See Sinkey (1989). Problems in measuring credit risk and its components are discussed by Paroush (1992) and Zaken and Paroush (1997).
35. This theory is based on a well known article by Stiglitz and Weiss (1981) that explains, among other things, why the interest rate is not a price that successfully clears the market even under conditions of perfect competition; therefore, the rationing phenomenon is preserved in the credit market. Geva and Goldschmidt (1984) apply this theory to the interest rate in Israel.
36. Hicks (1939) was the first to point out the identity between the average life of any flow and elasticity of the present value of that flow with respect to change in the interest rate. Macaulay (1938) proposed using the duration gap between assets and liabilities as a measure for interest risks; subsequently, this tool widely applied. On calculating the duration index and its use for hedging against interest risks, see Ben-Yehoshua (1988) and Ruthenberg (1989). On the influence of the change in term structure of interest rates on average life, see Zaken (1997).
37. The United States has a secondary mortgage market, i.e., one in which mortgages are traded, and Israel has given thought to establishing one. It would help to improve the money market and contribute to the development of a way to hedge against interest risks. It would make banks less willing to engage in insurance and insurance companies less willing to engage in banking.
38. See Paroush and Ruthenberg (1996). For the relationship between market risks and capital adequacy, see Zaken, Landskroner, and Ruthenberg (1997).
39. See Goldschmidt (1975), Barnea and Geva (1994), and note 5 in this chapter.
40. Interestingly in this context, the fall of the Israel-Britain Bank occurred for reasons including intensive activity in metals and commodities futures—an area far from financial intermediation (see the "Bank Failures and Their Lessons" subsection). A more familiar example was the collapse of the giant Barings Bank in UK several years ago due to futures activity at the bank's Hong Kong branch. This marked the realization of a management risk occasioned by a combination of geographical distance and occupational distance.
41. There is a rich literature on the sensitivity of banking systems to economic crises and analysis of historical events, especially the global crisis in early 1930s. See, for example, the seminal book by Friedman and Schwartz (1993) and a recent article by Calomiris and Mason (2003). The appendix of this chapter presents a theoretical framework within which the relationship between the negative externalities of bank failures and the need for, and the difficulties of, banking supervision is modeled.
42. In 1955, fifty-one countries had deposit insurance and four (including the United States) charged risk-adjusted premiums. The corresponding figures in 2002 were seventy-two countries and twenty-four countries, respectively.
43. For discussion of the optimal risk premium, see Landskorner and Paroush (1994). The considerations for introducing deposit insurance in Israel are debated in Elias

and Schreiber (1997). For a test of the existence of market discipline in Israel, see Elias and Schreiber (2003).

44. See Haubrich (1996).

45. Notably, the supervisor of banks, the chair of the Israel Securities Authority, and the commissioner of the capital market meet regularly to discuss common issues and coordinate decisions. They do so voluntarily. Such meetings, not required by law, have several advantages, but the absence of legal basis could be a shortcoming in certain cases.

46. See, for example, Barnea and Geva (1994). See also Volcker (1984), Kaufman (2000, p. 219) and Pauli (2000, p. 25). For further examples, see Goodhart and Schonmaker (1995) and Goodhart (2002).

47. Di Noia and Di Giorgio (1999), for example, found that countries where the central bank supervises the banking system have significantly higher inflation rates. Goodhart and Schonmaker (1995) found that bank failures are less frequent in such countries.

48. See Paroush and Ruthenberg (1986), who demonstrates how technological changes in banking affect demand for money.

49. See Final Report of the Panel for Investigation of Israel-Britain Bank, Ltd., Jerusalem, May 1975.

50. See Israel State Comptroller, December 1984, *Report on the October 1983 Bank-Share Crisis,* and Report of the Commission of Investigation on the Bank-Share Manipulation (the "Bejski Report"), April 1986 (Hebrew).

51. The arguments expressed resembled those made at the time of the share crisis: "The public has to be mature enough to know what to do with the credit it receives," or "Money is money," i.e., "A bank cannot distinguish in household finance between loans for consumption purposes and loans for acquisition of financial assets."

52. As evidence of the conflict of interest in bank securities-consulting services, one may note that over the years, both before and after the consulting law took effect, more than 90% of mutual funds sold by each bank have been those managed by the bank itself. It is not clear how the consultancy law can change this situation. For discussion of conflict of interest in securities consulting services, see Paroush and Krausz (2002).

53. See Geva (1989), Landskroner and Paroush (1994), and Paroush and Landskroner (1990).

54. Israel State Comptroller, "The Financial and Economic Crisis of the United Kibbutz Movement and Ha-kibbutz ha-Artsi Kibbutzim," *Annual Report 40* for 1989, May 1990. The kibbutz bankruptcy crisis also had far-reaching sociological consquences. The classic structure of the kibbutz, the crowning achievement of the Zionist movement, collapsed. The kibbutzim underwent a process of privatization, some more and some less. The structure of the kibbutz today, after the crisis, bears no resemblance to what it had been.

55. See Allen (1994).

56. See Barnea, Landskorner, Paroush and Ruthenberg (1999).

57. Dale (1986), pp. 71–82.

58. See *The New Basel Capital Accord—Third Consultative Paper* 29 (April 2003).

References

Allen, L. "Deposit Insurance and Closing Bank Policy." *Issues in Banking* 12 (November 1994): 5–26 (Hebrew).

Barnea, E., and D. Geva. "Determining Business Liquidity in a Commercial Bank—A Model Including Emergency Loan." *Issues in Banking* 12 (November 1994): 81–97 (Hebrew).

Barnea, E., Y. Landskroner, J. Paroush, and D. Ruthenberg. "An Econometric Model of the Banking System in Israel." *Issues in Banking* 14 (August 1999): 5–38 (Hebrew).

Barnea, E., J. Paroush, and H. Conforti. "The Question of the Optimal Structure of the Banking System in Israel." *Issues in Banking* 15 (June 2001): 5–28 (Hebrew).

Ben-Bassat, A., ed. *The Israeli Economy, 1985–1998: From Government Intervention to Market Economics.* Cambridge, MA: MIT Press, 2002.

Ben-Yehoshua, M. "Average Life as an Estimate for the Interest Risk and Its Application in the CPI-linked Sector." *Issues in Banking* 8 (March 1988): 41–53 (Hebrew).

Ber, H., "The Impact of Banks' Real Holdings on the Firms' Performance." *Issues in Banking* 14 (August 1999) 35–38 (Hebrew).

Ber, H., and Y. Orgeller. "The Viability of Investing Abroad: The Case of the Israeli Banking Groups." *Economic Quarterly* (September 2002) (Hebrew).

Ber, H., Y. Yafeh, and O. Yosha "Conflict of Interest in Universal Banking: Bank Lending, Stock Underwriting and Fund Management." *Journal of Monetary Economics* 47, no. 1 (2001): 189–218.

Brenner, M., and D. Ruthenberg. "The Involvement of the Banks in the Capital Market from 1978 to 1983." *Issues in Banking* 6 (April 1987): 40–52 (Hebrew).

Calomiris, C. W., and J. R. Mason. "Fundamentals, Panics and Bank Distress during the Depression." *American Economic Review* 93, no. 5 (December 2003): 1615–47.

Dale, R., ed. *Financial Deregulation.* Cambridge: Woodhead Faulkner, 1986.

Di Noia, C., and G. Di Giorgio. "Should Banking Supervision and Monetary Policy Tasks Be Given to Different Agencies?" *International Finance* 2, no. 3 (1999): 361–78.

Elias, R., and Z. Samet. "The Structure of the Israeli Banking System, the Level of Competition and the Influence of the Financial Margin in the Unlinked Shekel Sector." *Issues in Banking* 12 (November 1994): 27–48 (Hebrew).

Elias, R., and B. Schreiber "The 'Contagion Effect,' Deposit Insurance and its Possible Application in Israel." *Issues in Banking* (December 1997): 27–59 (Hebrew).

———. "Examination of the Upholding of Market Discipline in the Israeli Banking System." *Issues in Banking* 17 (March 2003): 21–51 (Hebrew).

Friedman, M., and A. J. Schwartz. *A Monetary History of the United States, 1867–1960.* Princeton, NJ: Princeton University Press, 1993.

Geva, D. "Response to Papers of Brenner and Ruthenberg." *Issues in Banking* 6 (April 1987): 53–62 (Hebrew).

———. "The Dynamic of Rebuilding Debts." *Issues in Banking* 9 (November 1989): 37–48 (Hebrew).

Geva, D. and A. Goldschmidt. "The Role of Credit Rationing in Determining the Interest Rates." *Issues in Banking* 5 (May 1975) 27–40 (Hebrew).

Goldschmidt, A. "The Business Liquidity of Banking Institutions in Israel, 1968–1969." Bank of Israel, Office of the Examiner of Banks, 74, Jerusalem, 1975 (Hebrew).

Goodhart, C. A. E. "The Organizational Structure of Banking Supervision." *Economic Notes* [Banca Monte dei Paschi di Siena SpA] 31 (2002): 1–32.

Goodhart, C., and D. Schoenmaker. "Should the Functions of Monetary Policy and Banking Supervision Be Separated?" *Oxford Economic Papers* (1995): 539–60.

Haim, Y., Y. Swary, and J. Paroush. "The Problem of Restrictions on the Financial Mediation System." *Issues in Banking* 7 (March 1988): 23–38 (Hebrew).

Haubrich, G. J. "Combining Bank Supervision and Monetary Policy." *Economic Commentary* [Federal Reserve Bank of Cleveland] (November 1996).

Heth, M. *Banking in Israel.* Jerusalem: Jerusalem Institute for Israel Studies, 1994 (Hebrew).

Hicks, J. R. *Value and Capital: An Inquiry into Some Fundamental Principles of Economic Theory.* Oxford: Oxford University Press, 1939.

Kaufman, H. *On Money and Markets.* New York: McGraw-Hill, 2000.

Kim, M., D. Klieger, and B. Wahl. "Estimated Transition Expenses and Oligopolistic Behavior." Unpublished discussion paper, 2000 (Hebrew).

Kleiman, A. "The Cost of Inflation." *Economic Quarterly* 119 (1984): 859–64 (Hebrew).

Koehn, M., and A. Satomero. "Regulation of Bank Capital and Portfolio." *Journal of Finance* 39 (1980): 759–72.

Landskroner, Y., and J. Paroush. "Deposit Insurance Pricing and Social Welfare." *Journal of Banking and Finance* 18, no. 3 (1994).

Macaulay, F. R. *Some Theoretical Problems Suggested by the Movements of Interest Rates, Bond Yields and Stock Prices in the United States since 1856.* New York: National Bureau of Economic Research, 1938.

Marom, A. "The Contribution of Inflation to the Growth of the Banking Sector in Israel." *Bank of Israel Review* 62 (June 1987) (Hebrew).

Orgeller, Y., et al. "Shareholders' Equity in Banking Institutions in Israel." Bank of Israel, Office of the Examiner of Banks, March 1976 (Hebrew).

Paroush, J. "The Domino Effect and the Supervision of the Banking System." *Journal of Finance* 43, no. 5 (1988): 1207–18.

———. "Credit Risk Measurement." *International Review of Economics and Finance* 1, no. 1 (1992): 33–41.

———. "The Effect of Merger and Acquisition Activity on the Safety and Soundness of a Banking System." *Review of Industrial Organization* 10 (1995): 53–67.

Paroush, J., and M. Krausz. "Financial Advising in the Presence of Conflict of Interests." *Journal of Economics and Business* 54 (2002).

Paroush, J., and Y. Landskroner. "The Economics of Debt Relief." *Atlantic Economic Journal* (June 1990).

Paroush, J., and D. Ruthenberg. "Automated Teller Machines and the Share of Demand Deposits in the Money Supply: The Israeli Experience." *European Economic Review* 30 (1986): 1207–15.

———. "The Optimal Structure of a Banking System: The Case of Israel." *Issues in Banking* 4 (1994) (Hebrew).

———. "The Impact of Inflation on Interest Rate Risk in Banking." *Bank of Israel, Banking Review* 5 (1996).

———. "Measuring Competitiveness in the Banking Sector in Israel—Business Customers and Households." *Issues in Banking* 16 (March 2003a): 5–19 (Hebrew).

———. "The Risk Premium and Market Power in Israeli Banking." *Issues in Banking* 16 (March 2003b): 97–110 (Hebrew).

Pauli, R. "Payments Remain Fundamental for Banks and Central Banks." Discussion Paper 6. Bank of Finland, 2000.

Ruthenberg, D. "The Function of the Production Expenses of the Banking Institutions in Israel." *Issues in Banking* 4 (May 1983): 59–73 (Hebrew).

———. "Application of Models for Estimating Interest Risks and the Securitization Process in Israeli Banking." *Issues in Banking* 9 (November 1989): 27–36 (Hebrew).

———. *Banking Management in Israel—Asset Management, Liabilities and Risks.* Jerusalem: Keter, 2002 (Hebrew).

Short, B. K. "An International Comparison of Bank Concentration and Performance." IMF Document MD/77/65. International Monetary Fund, July 1977.

Sinkey, J. F. "Credit Risk in Commercial Banks: A Survey of Theory, Practice and Empirical Evidence." *Bank of Israel, Banking Review* 2 (1989): 12–35.

Stiglitz, J., and A. Weiss. "Credit Rationing in Markets with Imperfect Information." *American Economic Review* 71, no. 3 (1981): 393–409.

Volcker, P. "The Federal Reserve Position on Restructuring of Financial Regulation Responsibilities." *Federal Reserve Bulletin* 70 (July 1984): 547–57.

Wiener, Z., D. Zaken, and B. Schreiber. "Estimating Market Risks Using the Given Value for the Risk—Application to the Banking System in Israel." *Issues in Banking* 15 (June 2001): 93–125 (Hebrew).

Zaken, D. "The Influence of Changes in the Time Structure of the Interest Rates on Estimating Exposure to the Interest Risk of the Financial Institutions in Israel." *Issues in Banking* 13 (December 1997): 61–88 (Hebrew).

Zaken, D., Y. Landskroner, and D. Ruthenberg. "The Market Risks and Capital Adequacy of Financial Institutions." *Issues in Banking* 13 (December 1997): 5–26 (Hebrew).

Zaken, D., and J. Paroush. "Credit Risks in Israeli Banks—Measuring Methods and Findings, 1992–1995." *Issues in Banking* 13 (December 1997): 97–117 (Hebrew).

6

The Israeli Banking System from a Historical Perspective: Diversification versus Competition

Oved Yosha, Sharon Blei, and Yishay Yafeh

The State of Israel inherited a relatively competitive banking system from the British Mandate. In 1948, the country had ninety-three providers of banking services—twenty-three independent commercial banks and seventy credit unions—and the share of the three largest banks in total assets amounted to 50%. By 1954, the number of credit unions had risen to ninety-five, while the number of commercial banks and the share of the three largest banks in total assets remained unchanged (see Heth, 1994; Shuv, 1998). In 1954, a gradual consolidation began, as small banks foundered and the credit-union sector contracted. Most entities of these types merged with large banks; some banks were taken over by banking groups but continued to function as separate legal entities, and several bank mergers took place. As the process continued during the subsequent decades, the industry became increasingly concentrated. By 1975, the share of the three largest banks in total assets amounted to 92%. Five years later, only two credit unions remained in operation. By 1996, the number of independent commercial banks—those not affiliated with a group headed by one of the five hegemonic banks—had fallen to twelve. Most assets were concentrated in the hands of five large groups; the remaining seven banks commanded only a tiny fraction of the market. Finally, unlike their American and British counterparts, banks in Israel gradually became truly universal, managing mutual and retirement provident funds and controlling subsidiaries that specialize in underwriting, brokerage, and mortgage origination, with considerable market power in many of these market segments. The banking groups became veritable financial conglomerates with tremendous influence on financial markets and the economy.

There are several possible and not mutually exclusive explanations for the consolidation of Israel's banking industry. The smallness of the Israeli economy in its early years and various forms of government intervention and regulation must have played a role in this process. Economies of scale and scope in the banking industry, and perhaps even the desire of bank executives to build

This chapter was written prior to the dramatic reform in Israel's financial markets following the Bachar Committee of 2005.

"empires," may have been important factors as well. This article, however, is limited in scope and does not seek to evaluate (theoretically or empirically) the relative importance of these factors. Our focus is solely on the role of the Bank of Israel (BOI) in the consolidation of the banking industry, and, in particular, on one possible economic rationale for the central bank's apparent support of this trend.

Anecdotal historical evidence suggests that the Bank of Israel was well aware of the increasing concentration in the banking sector. However, not only did the BOI neither oppose consolidation nor take any measures to halt it, it seems to have encouraged the trend deliberately. This may have been due to the BOI's wish to improve its control over one of two parameters: liquidity in the economy or credit allocation (e.g., through "directed credit" programs that allocated capital according to the government's preferences; see Yafeh and Yosha, 1998). These considerations are not explored in this chapter. Instead, we focus only on the possibility that the BOI favored consolidation in the banking industry in order to make the system more stable, albeit at the expense of competition among financial intermediaries.

The tradeoff between competition and stability (diversification) has been discussed at length in the literature.[1] Using a simple model, we show that, insofar as fostering stability in the banking system was a deliberate policy of the Bank of Israel, it may well have been a reasonable one. In a small economy that is relatively closed to international capital flows, a large number of small financial intermediaries may be highly risky (not diversified enough in their activities). Therefore, a move to a smaller number of more diversified (less risky) large banks may enhance social welfare even if it makes the banking industry less competitive. We also provide historical evidence suggesting that the Bank of England and the Bank of Japan adopted similar policies to reduce competition and increase stability in their banking systems (the United Kingdom in the late nineteenth century and Japan in the interwar period). Somewhat similar policies were adopted in the United States in the 1980s. However, the Israeli economy is far more developed and open today than it was in the 1950s. The concentrated market structure that may have been ideal for the banking industry in the 1950s is no longer optimal. We argue that even if more competition is introduced, today's financial intermediaries will still be diversified enough to ensure the stability of the banking system.

This chapter proceeds as follows: The next section briefly discusses the consolidation processes of the British, Japanese, and American banking industries and presents some empirical evidence on the tradeoff between competition and stability in banking systems around the world. The following section presents a simple model, close in spirit to Yosha (1997), which describes the tradeoff between diversification and competition in the banking industry and evaluates the welfare implications of the BOI's policy. The final section concludes the chapter by evaluating the reform in Israel's financial system that began in the mid-1980s and its impact on the degree of competition in this system. This section also contains some suggestions for desirable directions for future banking policy.

COMPETITION AND DIVERSIFICATION IN
ISRAEL AND AROUND THE WORLD

International Perspectives

The tradeoff between competition and stability in banking systems, a well-recognized phenomenon in the theoretical literature, is supported by several recent empirical studies. Using data on banking systems in seventy-nine countries between 1980 and 1997, Beck, Demiguc-Kunt, and Levine (2003) provide evidence that (controlling for other factors) concentrated banking systems are less crisis-prone. They argue that this is not necessarily due to higher profits (reduced competition) but possibly due to improved supervision or better diversification.[2]

Allen and Gale (2000, 2004) present country comparisons suggesting that more concentrated banking sectors are less prone to financial crises. For example, the United States, which is characterized by a large number of small banks, has a history of substantially greater financial instability than the United Kingdom and Canada, where the banking industry is dominated by a small number of large banks.

Grossman (1999), studying the dramatic consolidation of the British banking industry between 1870 and 1914, argues that the consolidation process was mostly market driven without much government intervention. Controlling for the demand for banking services, he finds a positive relation among banking concentration, profitability of banks, and banking-system stability, which is consistent with the tradeoff between competition and diversification.

Saunders and Wilson (1999), documenting long-term consolidation trends in the British and Canadian banking industries starting in the late nineteenth century, claim that, at least in the case of the United Kingdom after World War I, consolidation was encouraged by the central bank. They also show that the interwar consolidation wave coincided with a substantial decline in bank failure rates.

In their extensive review of the literature on the consolidation of financial institutions in the United States, Berger, Demsetz, and Strahan (1999) report that the FDIC provided financial assistance with which sound banks were able to acquire more than a thousand insolvent banks between the years 1984 and 1991. The motivation for this policy was the view that larger, more diversified institutions would be less vulnerable to crises and more efficient in allocating scarce financial capital. Therefore, the authorities perceived consolidation as an efficient alternative to bankruptcy.

Okazaki and Sawada (2003) describe the consolidation of the Japanese banking industry in the interwar period and note that the Bank of Japan encouraged this process in response to numerous bank runs and an acute crisis in the banking system in 1927 that drove hundreds of small banks into bankruptcy. Of more than two thousand banks in existence in Japan around the turn of the century, only sixty-five financial institutions remained in 1945. Okazaki and Sawada view this consolidation policy as a substitute for the formal deposit-insurance scheme that Japan refrained from introducing until much later. An important benefit of consolidation, they argue, is the reduction in "related lending," in which banks lend to companies with which they maintain ties of various forms, sometimes not on the basis of strictly economic criteria.[3] Nevertheless, in Japan of the 1930s, as well as in Israel of the 1950s, it is hard to distinguish between the central bank's wish to ensure bank stability and the wish to control the main channels of credit allocation for political purposes.

Banking Consolidation in Israel

As noted earlier, Israel's banking system also underwent dramatic consolidation starting in the early 1950s. To some extent, market forces played a role in this process: some financial institutions were driven out of business because their clientele, concentrated in particular economic activities or geographical areas, experienced economic decline. Yet the consolidation process seems to have been at least tacitly encouraged by the Bank of Israel. There is no doubt that the BOI was well aware of the ongoing consolidation of the banking system and apparently regarded it as a favorable trend that should be encouraged. As noted, one plausible reason for the Bank's proconsolidation policy was the desire to improve control over the allocation and price of credit by routing credit through a small number of powerful banks. A second likely rationale was the need to make the banks safer and sounder, albeit at the expense of less competition in the banking sector.

Evidence of the Bank of Israel's attitude toward the consolidation of the banking sector is, however, sporadic. Heth (1994) describes BOI policy in the 1960s and 1970s as one that clearly favored considerations of business stability and sound management over considerations related to the competitive structure of the banking system. Almost immediately after its establishment, the bank adopted a policy of restricted entry into the banking industry by limiting the number of banking licenses granted. Even before mandatory BOI approval of all bank mergers was enshrined in law (1969), the central bank appears to have viewed bank mergers with favor and even actively encouraged them after 1967. The guiding principle was that large banks were inherently sounder than small financial institutions (see, for example, Heth, 1994, part 2, p. 21). Indeed, in almost all cases when small banks were in distress, the Bank of Israel encouraged larger and sounder financial institutions to acquire them (p. 31). This policy was particularly evident in the 1960s, when many small banks faced financial difficulties.[4]

Shuv (1998, p. 8, relying on Heth, 1994) argues that several bank mergers took place with explicit assistance and mediation of the Bank of Israel. These include the merger of United Mizrahi Bank with Hapoel Hamizrahi Bank; the merger of Export Bank and Israel Industry Bank with Foreign Trade Bank; and the merger of Zerubavel Bank and Israel Savings and Loan Bank with Bank Hapoalim. BOI also helped Bank Hapoalim to acquire control of Yefet Bank (subsequently renamed American Israeli Bank). Ruthenberg (2002, p. 352) argues that the central bank's intention in this policy was to assure the stability of the banking system even if this entailed less competition. He, too, traces the policy to several failures of small banks and credit cooperatives during the 1960s recession.

Mergers of relatively weak banks that face likely collapse do not necessarily reduce competition in all cases. Nevertheless, our overall (subjective) impression is that the Bank of Israel seemed to favor a relatively concentrated system with a small number of financially sound intermediaries, even if these intermediaries wielded considerable market power.

Before concluding this section, we should note that, beyond direct encouragement of mergers and consolidation, the Bank of Israel had an indirect impact on the industrial organization of the banking system. For example, regulated interest rates combined with high liquidity requirements weakened the competitive position of small banks in the 1950s and 1960s (see Heth, 1994, part 1, pp. 49–52). The inflationary pressures of the early 1970s also favored large banking groups because they were better equipped than smaller ones to handle these risks.

THE WELFARE IMPLICATIONS OF BANKING CONSOLIDATION IN ISRAEL

Was the Bank of Israel's proconsolidation policy reasonable? How can one evaluate the welfare implications of the tradeoff between competition and risk (diversification) in the banking industry? How does economic development affect the tradeoff?

In this section we attempt to answer these questions using a simple two-period general equilibrium model with a single good and no storage.[5] Consumers save by purchasing securities from financial intermediaries that invest the proceeds in risky technologies. We assume that each intermediary has access to a subset of the risky technologies in the economy and that the intermediaries are Cournot competitors.[6]

The role of financial intermediaries as providers of risk-sharing services is well recognized. Implicit in the assertion that intermediaries provide such a service is the assumption that insurance markets are incomplete; if they were perfect, the risk-sharing services of financial intermediaries would be redundant. A second implicit assumption is that intermediaries can sell securities whose return structure cannot be mimicked by a portfolio of publicly traded securities, either because not all firms are traded or because not all state-contingent consumption plans can be spanned by the available portfolios.

For risk sharing through financial intermediaries to be effective, the intermediaries must be large. Otherwise, each intermediary would be able to invest in only a small number of risky assets and would be perceived by investors as risky. Investors would then have to diversify by purchasing securities from several intermediaries—an activity that we assume is prohibitively costly. Although large intermediaries may diversify more easily, they may behave as imperfect competitors, selling securities at a price exceeding marginal cost.

Thus, in a small economy (with no international capital flows), there is tension between the wish to have large, amply diversified intermediaries and the desire to have a competitive financial sector. The model below examines what happens to this tension as the economy becomes more developed.

Consider a two-period economy with a single non-storable good. There is a (continuous) measure I of identical consumers with a first-period endowment of w, which is saved, so that consumption can take place in period 2. In particular, consumers maximize $E[-e^{-\rho c}]$, where c is consumption in period 2 and ρ is the discount factor.

Consumers have access to one risk-free technology that yields an output of 1 in period 2. Additionally, there are K risky constant returns to scale technologies, $k = 1, \ldots, K$ of the form $(-C, X_k)$, where the C is invested in period 1 and X_k is obtained in period 2.

There are G intermediaries, denoted by $g = 1, \ldots, G$ selling securities in period 1 (there is no stock exchange). Every intermediary may invest in $N \leq K$ risky technologies and each technology may be used by exactly one intermediary, that is, $K = N * G$. Units are normalized, so that one security is a claim to the output generated by an investment of C.

Each intermediary invests equally in N technologies. Each security generates a return of $\xi = 1/N \sum_{k \in N} X_k$, the expected value of which is denoted by μ. All securities are identical ex ante and are sold for price P, which is paid to an intermediary in period 1. As noted, we assume that every consumer buys securities from *exactly one* intermediary.

Demand for Securities

Consumers choose α to maximize $E[-e^{-\rho\alpha\xi + (w - P\alpha)}]$, where α is the "quantity" of securities purchased and ξ is the return on each security. Thus, the first term in the utility function is period 2 consumption generated by investment in risky securities, and the second term is consumption generated by the part of the endowment that is used to purchase the risk-free asset. The consumers' maximization problem may be rewritten as:

$$\text{Max}_\alpha \{(\mu - P)\, \alpha - 1/2\, \rho\alpha^2 \,\text{var}\,(\xi)\}. \tag{1}$$

The quantity of risky securities purchased, derived from the first-order condition generated by equation (1), is:

$$\alpha = (\mu - P)\, / \,[\rho \,\text{var}\,(\xi)]. \tag{2}$$

We now derive the aggregate demand for securities. Summing up for all I consumers
$Q = I\,\alpha = I\,(\mu - P)\, / \,[\rho \,\text{var}\,(\xi)]$, from which the inverse (aggregate) demand can be derived:

$$P = \mu - (1/\,I)\, \rho \,\text{var}\,(\xi)\, Q. \tag{3}$$

Supply of Securities

Intermediaries compete in quantities à la Cournot and choose the quantity of securities that they offer in order to maximize their profits:

$$\text{Max}_{qg} \left[\mu - (1/\,I)\, \rho \, \text{var}\, (\xi)(q_g + \Sigma_{j \neq g}\, q_j) - C \right] q_g, \tag{4}$$

where $q_g + \Sigma_{j \neq g}\, q_j = Q$ is the aggregate quantity and the price is described by equation (3).

In the (symmetric) solution to this maximization problem, each intermediary offers:

$$q = I(\mu - C) / \left[(G+1)\, \rho\, \text{var}\, (\xi) \right]. \tag{5}$$

Market Clearing

The aggregate demand for risky securities, $I\alpha$, has to equal the aggregate supply, Gq. Using equations (2) and (5), we may express the condition for market clearing by:

$$\alpha = G(\mu - C) / \left[(G+1)\, \rho\, \text{var}\, (\xi) \right]. \tag{6}$$

The utility function described in equation (1) may now be rewritten using the equilibrium levels of α (the quantity of securities purchased by each consumer) and market price P. Denoting consumer welfare (utility) by CW, this equals:

$$CW = \tfrac{1}{2} \left[G^2 / (G+1)^2 \right] (\mu - C)^2 \left[1/\, \rho\, \text{var}\, (\xi) \right]. \tag{7}$$

We now turn to the optimal number of intermediaries, G, that will maximize consumer welfare (7). In general, this number depends on the size of the economy (the number of available technologies, K) through the impact of K on the last term in equation (7), the variance of returns on the risky security. Note that the analysis is based on the premise that entry into the banking sector is regulated, so that the number of intermediaries is a choice variable of a welfare-maximizing social planner.[7]

As noted above, all securities are identical ex ante with an expected return of μ. The variance of the return consists of two parts. The first is aggregate or macroeconomic risk, which affects all technologies (investments) equally and is denoted by σ^2_{agg}. The second component is an idiosyncratic, investment-specific variance, denoted by σ^2. Since every security is allocated among the N technologies available to the intermediary, the variance of return ξ may be written as:

$$\text{var}\, (\xi) = \text{var}\, \left[1/N\, (X_1 + X_2 \ldots X_N) \right] = \sigma^2_{agg} + \sigma^2/N. \tag{8}$$

Equation (8) suggests that diversification by intermediaries can lower the idiosyncratic technology (or project) risk whereas the aggregate risk is, of course, unaffected by diversification. Bear in mind that the extent of possible diversification by any intermediary is determined by the number of intermediaries, G, and the number of available technologies (or the size of the economy), K: $K = N * G$. Therefore, equation (8) may be rewritten as

$$\text{var } (\xi) = \text{var } [1/N (X_1 + X_2 + \ldots X_N)] = \sigma^2_{agg} + \sigma^2 G/K. \qquad (8)$$

Thus, the higher the number of intermediaries and the smaller and less developed the economy, the riskier the security that the intermediaries offer is.

Returning to equation (7), the effect of the number of intermediaries on consumer welfare consists of two parts, representing the classic tradeoff between competition and diversification or banking-system stability. First, since the intermediaries are Cournot competitors, the more intermediaries, G, there are, the more competitive the market becomes and the aggregate quantity of securities offered increases (even though each intermediary offers a smaller quantity). As a result, the prices of securities fall. However, as the number of intermediaries increases, each intermediary becomes smaller and less diversified; consequently, the risky asset becomes even riskier (equation [8]).

Using equation (8) and solving for the number of intermediaries that maximizes CW (equation [7]), we obtain G^*:

$$G^*(G^* - 1) = 2K(\sigma_{agg}/\sigma)^2. \qquad (9)$$

In the special case where there is no aggregate risk ($\sigma^2_{agg} = 0$), returns on each technology are independent of each other. Here, social welfare is maximized by a monopoly, regardless of the number of tasks in the economy, K. This is because the increase in risk when the investments are i.i.d is too high for the reduction in price (due to increased competition) to compensate consumers. In the more general case where $\sigma^2_{agg} > 0$, however, the larger the value of K, the larger the optimal number of intermediaries will be. This is because in a developed economy, relatively small intermediaries may be sufficiently diversified. Note also that the greater the aggregate risk relative to the idiosyncratic risk, the higher the optimal number of intermediaries will be.[8]

The analysis in this section suggests that in a small, underdeveloped economy that is closed to international capital flows and offers few domestically available investment technologies, a concentrated banking system with a small number of relatively large intermediaries is beneficial to consumers. In this sense, the Bank of Israel's policy of encouraging consolidation in Israel's financial system may have had a positive effect on social welfare in the 1950s and 1960s. As the economy develops and new investment opportunities become available, however, the same small number of intermediaries that may have been optimal in the early days is no longer the desired market structure. A larger number of intermediaries, even if smaller in size, will be able to offer securities that are not prohibitively risky, at a low price.

Evidence from around the world (table 6.1 and figure 6.1) suggests that this prediction of the model is generally borne out in the data and that more developed economies tend to have more competitive banking systems

Table 6.1. Economic Development and Competition in the Banking System

Country	Per Capita GDP(1995)	Concentration*	Net Interest Margins**
Burundi	148.3912	1	10.74
Malawi	152.9812	0.98	N/A
Nepal	215.3934	0.77	5.41
Rwanda	219.3682	1	5.74
Nigeria	253.6188	0.62	8.94
Bangladesh	338.663	0.7	2.05
Kenya	339.1736	0.57	7.46
Ghana	393.4352	0.79	11.61
India	414.1506	0.37	3.48
Moldova	666.4434	0.83	10.03
China	676.757	0.88	N/A
Honduras	707.5186	0.42	8.82
Sri Lanka	771.86	0.9	4.48
Bolivia	938.5472	0.61	5.62
Indonesia	1044.543	0.51	5.62
Egypt, Arab Rep.	1107.538	0.58	2.42
Philippines	1124.696	0.4	4.56
Macedonia	1295.016	0.87	9.57
Morocco	1341.06	0.77	5.01
Romania	1364.908	0.78	8.45
Guatemala	1503.248	0.26	7.53
Jordan	1609.71	0.89	3.47
Jamaica	1747.602	0.92	9.43
Lithuania	1906.576	0.94	8.43
Namibia	2086.378	0.83	6.64
Latvia	2189.351	0.53	6.92
Russia	2214.142	0.43	5.99
Belarus	2234.906	0.84	10.68
Peru	2334.94	0.64	7.92
Thailand	2835.27	0.66	2.30
Lebanon	2878.09	0.32	4.18
Turkey	3006.744	0.55	N/A
Panama	3123.946	0.24	2.86
Poland	3216.036	0.57	6.81
Mexico	3392.84	0.64	5.70
Botswana	3546.1	0.92	7.03
Estonia	3663.85	1	6.15
Croatia	3845.528	0.62	5.40
Mauritius	3851.668	0.93	3.91
South Africa	3919.812	0.78	6.22
Brazil	4489.084	0.45	N/A
Trinidad	4526.282	0.8	4.68
Malaysia	4536.222	0.45	N/A
Hungary	4705.654	0.53	4.86

Continued

Table 6.1. Continued

Country	Per Capita GDP(1995)	Concentration*	Net Interest Margins**
Chile	4992.066	0.48	5.02
Czech Republic	5163.394	0.72	2.88
Oman	5668.36	0.7	N/A
Seychelles	7047.698	1	N/A
Argentina	8000.604	0.36	N/A
Malta	9243.91	0.94	2.28
Bahrain	9403.15	0.92	2.45
Slovenia	10226.36	0.64	4.00
Korea (ROK)	11474.96	0.37	N/A
Portugal	11582.1	0.46	N/A
Greece	11901.26	0.71	3.50
Cyprus	12516.82	0.82	2.53
Taiwan	13759.12	0.31	2.42
Kuwait	14872.86	0.68	1.87
Spain	15858.02	0.54	3.40
Israel	16299.06	0.76	3.22
New Zealand	16695.46	0.7	3.03
Italy	19645.96	0.3	3.67
United Kingdom	20186.58	0.47	2.98
Canada	20548.96	0.56	2.03
Ireland	21600.2	0.68	3.49
Australia	22132.68	0.63	3.12
Singapore	25373.76	0.85	2.86
France	27719.92	0.33	2.86
Finland	27794.34	0.75	1.99
Sweden	28258.28	0.78	2.39
Belgium	28327.18	0.75	2.38
Netherlands	28445.08	0.81	1.97
Iceland	28490.72	0.87	4.15
United States	29252.96	0.2	4.34
Austria	30344.2	0.44	2.16
Germany	30794.02	0.32	2.66
Denmark	35965.52	0.71	5.28
Norway	35971.65	0.61	2.68
Japan	42390.98	0.27	2.07
Switzerland	44382.78	0.77	1.75
Luxembourg	47988.24	0.21	1.19

*A measure of the extent of concentration in the banking industry, calculated as the fraction of assets held by the three largest commercial banks in each country, averaged over the 1995–99 period.
Source: Fitch IBCA Bankscope Database.
**Interest income less interest expenses divided by interest-bearing assets during the 1995–99 period (percent).
Source: Demirguc-Kunt, Laeven, and Levine (2004).

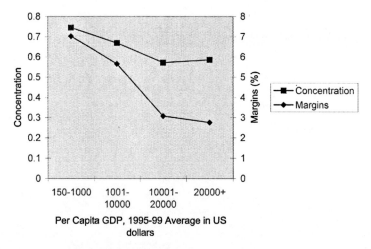

Figure 6.1. Banking Competition by Income Group.
Sources: See table 6.1. "Concentration" is the fraction of assets held by the three largest commercial banks.

(less concentration and smaller interest margins). The relation between financial development and banking competition is not very strong, however, perhaps because regulators are sometimes "captives" of the strong banking system and may therefore be reluctant to introduce very intense competition. Moving to a more systematic empirical analysis, Demirguc-Kunt, Laeven, and Levine (2004) analyze data on more than fourteen hundred banks in seventy-two countries. They document a negative correlation between net interest margins (interest income less interest expense divided by interest-bearing assets over the 1995–99 period) and per capita GDP. The simple correlation between the two variables is –0.45 (significant at the 5% level; see their table 3, panel B). Moreover, in multiple regressions that explain net interest margins controlling for various other factors (e.g., their table 7), the per capita GDP coefficient is negative (and statistically significant at the 1% level). The interpretation of these findings by Demirguc-Kunt, Laeven, and Levine, however, is related neither to banking diversification nor to the stability of the banking system but rather to more competition and better institutions in more developed economies. Thus, the next section discusses measures taken from the 1980s to encourage more competition in the Israeli banking sector.

MEASURES TO INCREASE COMPETITION IN THE BANKING SYSTEM

Evaluation of the Past and Reflections on the Future

Much has been written about competition in the Israeli banking system.[9] While the simple model in the previous section focuses on one parameter only, the number of intermediaries (an adequate measure of competition in a symmetric Cournot world), the reality is of course much more complex. Banks are multi-product firms and competition may be more intense in one sector (e.g., retail banking) than in others (lending or underwriting). Furthermore, unlike the hypothetical intermediaries in our stylized model, the Israeli banking system is far from symmetric and the intensity of competitive pressure may vary not only with the number of intermediaries but also with their distribution in size and types of products offered.[10] Banks may also take deliberate measures to restrict entry and competition in the banking sector (Yafeh and Yosha, 2001), and their universality may, under certain circumstances, facilitate collusion (Ber, Yafeh, and Yosha, 2001). This section evaluates the general trends and measures taken toward making Israel's banking system less concentrated and generally more competitive.

Until the reforms of the 1980s, the government played a central role in the Israeli financial system. Until 1990, most credit to firms was "directed credit," government-subsidized and distributed via the banking system. Following the stock-market crash in 1983,[11] the government also became the owner of most of the country's banking system. The financial-system reform that began in the mid-1980s involved a variety of measures designed to modify, to some extent, the status quo in the banking system. Despite some notable successes, these measures have not been able to substantially change the equilibrium, in which a small number of powerful large banks dominate the economy.

As part of the reform, firms were allowed to issue corporate bonds without explicit approval of the Ministry of Finance and regulation of share prices in IPOs was abolished in 1993. Other measures eased restrictions on investments in shares and bonds by banks and provident funds and relaxed reserve requirements for various types of bank deposits. Many restrictions on transactions in foreign exchange were lifted and since the early 1990s firms have been allowed to raise capital on overseas stock exchanges. Finally, limited reforms in the market structure of the banking sector were undertaken: Two small banks (Otsar Hahayal and Union) were spun off from two large banks and sold. Mercantile Discount Bank was spun off from Israel Discount Bank and designated banks (for specific industries, export-import, etc.) were allowed to operate as ordinary banks, although these banks were typically small.[12]

Notwithstanding some reformers' hopes, however, nothing fundamental has changed in the Israeli financial system. The market for corporate bonds has remained small, relatively inactive, and wholly unable to challenge the dominance of a small number of large banks as sources of capital. The Tel Aviv Stock Exchange has been dormant, with very few new issues between 1994 and 2003.[13] Due to the universality of Israel's banks, it is not clear whether the stock market, even when active, offers a truly independent alternative to bank finance. Provident funds have not yet become independent financial intermediaries; they do not compete with the large banks and seem to be rather poorly managed. Financial liberalization has had some competitive effects, as documented by Ribon and Yosha (1999), but overseas competition, at least in the form of raising capital on foreign exchanges, seems to be an especially viable alternative for a relatively small number of high-tech companies (Ber, Lokomet, and Nachmany, 2002; Blass and Yafeh, 2001). Even among these firms, the phenomenon of a large number of firms raising equity finance on New York's NASDAQ has become far less common since the sharp decline in technology stock prices in 2000.

None of these changes has so far resulted in the emergence of any intermediary that is in a position to challenge the supremacy of the major banks. After more than a decade of reforms, the Israeli financial system still revolves around three large (and universal) banks. The banking system remains highly concentrated; the two largest banks (Hapoalim and Leumi) hold almost three-quarters of total bank assets. The Herfindahl index of concentration for the banking sector has slipped a bit from its 0.3 level in the early 1990s, partly due to certain changes in the size distribution of intermediaries within the banking sector. The spinning off of several small banks has hardly affected the competitive conditions in the banking sector and there has been no significant entry of new intermediaries, domestic or external, even though some formal entry barriers have been removed.[14]

The model in "The Welfare Implications of Banking Consolidation in Israel" section suggests that this state of affairs may no longer be optimal. The promotion of banking-system stability by means of consolidation and the formation of large banks may have been desirable in Israel's early decades but is no longer so. In the developed and diversified economy that has evolved in Israel, the welfare loss occasioned by the absence of banking competition has become substantial. There is little doubt that a larger number of banks could be diversified enough to offer consumers a more competitive environment without substantial risk of system collapse. Furthermore, globalization and increased activities overseas can make even relatively small banks well diversified. In the coming fifty years, one hopes that the policies of the Bank of Israel will be able to foster more competition in this sector, possibly through measures that will convert the bank-controlled provident funds into truly independent quasi-banking financial intermediaries.

Notes

Oved Yosha died in August 2003; this article was written on the basis of his outline and notes by Sharon Blei and Yishay Yafeh. We thank Galit Dayan and Tomer Yafeh for superb research assistance, Eugene Kandel for an extremely helpful contribution to the formulation of the model, and Hedva Ber, Nissan Liviatan, Jacob Paroush, David Ruthenberg, and an anonymous referee for many helpful comments and suggestions.

1. See Yosha (1997) and Berger, Demsetz, and Strahan (1999) for reviews of the literature, and Paroush and Ruthenberg (1994) in regard to the Israeli economy. Allen and Gale (2004) revisit the theoretical foundations of this tradeoff.
2. These conclusions are based on several specifications of LOGIT regressions, where the dependent variable is the occurrence of a crisis in a given year and variables on the right-hand side include controls for macroeconomic environment, banking regulation, and other institutional factors.

3. On the risk associated with related lending, see also La Porta, Lopez de Silanes, and Zmarippa (2003).
4. This is reminiscent of the Japanese "convoy system," in which weak banks were often merged into stronger ones until the 1990s. See Hoshi and Kashyap (2001).
5. Based on Yosha (1997).
6. Consumers own the intermediaries and receive their profits in the form of dividends.
7. This is natural not only because the banking industry is regulated but also because free entry in a state of Cournot competition will result in too much entry (relative to the number of players that maximize social welfare) because of the "business stealing" effect. See Mankiw and Whinston (1986).
8. If there is only aggregate risk, the optimal number of intermediaries is infinite, i.e., perfect competition will maximize social welfare. The reason is that in this case large intermediaries will be no less risky than small ones and competition among many small banks will result in optimally low security prices.
9. Examples are Ribon and Yosha (1999), and Paroush and Ruthenberg (2003).
10. For further discussion of these points, see, for example, Yosha (1995), Ribon and Yosha (1999), Barnea, Paroush, and Konforti (2001), and Paroush and Ruthenberg (2003).
11. See also the chapter by Paroush in this volume.
12. See Yafeh and Yosha (1998) and Blass and Yosha (2002) for more detailed discussions of these reforms.
13. Recent data suggest, however, that stock offerings and the number of corporate bond issues increased substantially in 2003 and 2004.
14. The model in Yafeh and Yosha (2001) suggests that the banks responded to the removal of some formal entry barriers by strengthening relations with their corporate clients, thereby creating a formidable (albeit informal) entry barrier.

References

Allen, F., and D. Gale. *Comparing Financial Systems.* Cambridge, MA: MIT Press, 2000.
———. "Competition and Financial Stability." *Journal of Money, Credit and Banking* 36 (2004): 453–81.
Barnea, A., J. Paroush, and H. Konforti. "The Optimal Structure of Israel's Banking System." *Issues in Banking* 15 (2001): 5–27. (Hebrew).
Beck, T., A. Demiguc-Kunt, and R. Levine. "Bank Concentration and Crises." NBER Working Paper 9921. NBER, 2003, forthcoming, *Journal of Banking and Finance.*
Ber, H., R. Lokomet, and E. Nachmany. "The Entrance of Foreign Investment Banks into Israel and its Effect on the Competitive Equilibrium in the Underwriting Market." *Economic Quarterly* 49 (2002): 773–805 (Hebrew).
Ber, H., Y. Yafeh, and O. Yosha. "Conflict of Interest in Universal Banking: Bank Lending, Stock Underwriting and Fund Management." *Journal of Monetary Economics* 47 (2001): 189–218.
Berger, A, R. Demsetz, and P. Strahan. "The Consolidation of the Financial Services Industry: Causes, Consequences, and Implications for the Future." *Journal of Banking and Finance* 23 (1999): 135–94.
Blass, A., and Y. Yafeh. "Vagabond Shoes Longing to Stray: Why Foreign Firms List in the United States." *Journal of Banking and Finance* 25 (2001): 555–72.

Blass, A., and O. Yosha. "The Reform in the Israeli Financial System and the Flow of Funds of Publicly Traded Manufacturing Firms." In *The Israeli Economy, 1985–1998: From Government Intervention to Market Economics*, ed. A. Ben-Bassat. Cambridge, MA: MIT Press, 2002.

Demirguc-Kunt, A., L. Laeven, and R. Levine. "Regulations, Market Structure, Institutions, and the Cost of Financial Intermediation." *Journal of Money, Credit and Banking* 36 (2004): 593–622.

Grossman, R. "Rearranging Deck Chairs on the Titanic: English Banking Concentration and Efficiency, 1870–1914." *European Review of Economic History* 3 (1999): 323–49.

Heth, M. *Banking in Israel.* Jerusalem: Jerusalem Institute for Israel Studies, 1994 (Hebrew).

Hoshi, T., and A. Kashyap. *Corporate Financing and Governance in Japan.* Cambridge, MA: MIT Press, 2001.

La Porta, R., F. Lopez de Silanes, and G. Zamarippa. "Related Lending." *Quarterly Journal of Economics* 118 (2003): 231–68.

Mankiw, G., and M. Whinston. "Free Entry and Social Inefficiency." *RAND Journal of Economics* 17 (1986): 48–58.

Okazaki, T., and M. Sawada. "Bank Merger Movement and Evolution of Financial System: Experiences of Prewar Japan." Unpublished manuscript. University of Tokyo, 2003.

Paroush, J., and D. Ruthenberg. "The Optimal Structure of a Banking System: The Case of Israel." *Bank of Israel Banking Review* 4 (1994): 1–29.

———. "Measuring Competition in the Israeli Banking Sector." *Issues in Banking* 16 (2003): 5–19 (Hebrew).

Ribon, S., and O. Yosha. "Financial Liberalization and Competition in Banking: An Empirical Investigation." Bank of Israel Research Department Discussion Paper 99.05. 1999.

Ruthenberg, D. *Bank Management in Israel.* Jerusalem: Keter Press, 2002 (Hebrew).

Saunders, A., and B. Wilson. "The Impact of Consolidation and Safety-Net Support on Canadian, US, and UK Banks: 1893–1992." *Journal of Banking and Finance* 23 (1999): 537–71.

Shuv, S. *The Israeli Banking Market.* Jerusalem: Institute for Advanced Strategic and Political Studies, 1998.

Yafeh, Y., and O. Yosha. "Financial Markets Reform, Patterns of Corporate Finance, and the Continued Dominance of Large Banks: Israel 1985–95." *Economic Systems* 22 (1998): 175–99.

———. "Industrial Organization of Financial Systems and the Strategic Use of Relationship Banking." *European Finance Review* 5 (2001): 63–78.

Yosha, O. "Privatising Multi-product Banks." *Economic Journal* 105 (1995): 1435–53.

———. "Diversification and Competition: Financial Intermediation in a Large Cournot-Walras Economy." *Journal of Economic Theory* 75 (1997): 64–88.

Index

A page number followed by the letter t or f indicates a table or figure, respectively, on that page.